The Poetry of Thom Gunn

A Critical Study

STEFANIA MICHELUCCI

Translated by Jill Franks
Foreword by Clive Wilmer

McFarland & Company, Inc., Publishers
Jefferson, North Carolina, and London

The book was originally published as *La maschera, il corpo e l'anima: Saggio sulla poesia di Thom Gunn* by Edizioni Unicopli, Milano, 2006. It is here translated from the Italian by Jill Franks.

LIBRARY OF CONGRESS CATALOGUING-IN-PUBLICATION DATA

Michelucci, Stefania.
[Maschera, il corpo e l'anima. English]
  The poetry of Thom Gunn : a critical study / Stefania Michelucci ; translated by Jill Franks ; foreword by Clive Wilmer.
    p.   cm.
  Includes bibliographical references and index.

  ISBN 978-0-7864-3687-3
  softcover : 50# alkaline paper ∞

  1. Gunn, Thom — Criticism and interpretation. I. Title.
PR6013.U65Z7513   2009
821'.914 — dc22   2008028812

British Library cataloguing data are available

©2009 Stefania Michelucci. All rights reserved

No part of this book may be reproduced or transmitted in any form or by any means, electronic or mechanical, including photocopying or recording, or by any information storage and retrieval system, without permission in writing from the publisher.

Cover photograph ©2008 Shutterstock

Manufactured in the United States of America

McFarland & Company, Inc., Publishers
  Box 611, Jefferson, North Carolina 28640
  www.mcfarlandpub.com

To my sons Jacopo and Mattias

We are tied to our bodies like an oyster to its shell
— Plato

Acknowledgments

First of all I would like to thank Thom Gunn, who in 1990 invited me to his home for an interview. This meeting provided new stimulus for my interest in his poetry.

A very special thank you to Jill Franks for her kind offer to undertake the translation of this book. I am deeply indebted to her for the sensitivity, perception and clarity she displayed throughout.

I am thankful to Giovanni Cianci who encouraged me to expand my research on Thom Gunn into a book, patiently following its course. His perceptive and sensitive comments, as well as his constant scholarly support, have been of great value to me.

I owe a special recognition to Clive Wilmer for his availability and generosity, and for the scruples and patience with which he followed this project; his valuable suggestions were a great help. I am also deeply grateful that he was kind enough to write the Foreword to this book.

I would like to thank Francesco Gozzi who, in the years of my university studies, wisely guided my research on contemporary poetry, and passed on his enthusiasm for the subject.

Thanks to Lidia De Michelis, who patiently read this book; her advice and suggestions have always been valuable.

I would also like to thank Bruno Gallo and Richard Ambrosini, who followed this project in its first phase and whose observations were a real help.

Thanks to Giuseppe Sertoli for having read parts of this book.

I am also grateful to Massimo Bacigalupo, Remo Ceserani, Martin Dodsworth, Elmar Schenkel, Peter Schwaab, Gregory Woods and John Worthen for the stimulating exchange of ideas which enriched my work.

Finally I thank Michael Bell, Bethan Jones, Mike Kitay, August Kleinzahler, Wendy Lesser, Seán and Jessica Lysaght, Ronald Packham, Alessandra Petrina, Andrea Pinotti, Neil Roberts, Stan Smith and Luisa Villa for their help in many different ways.

Contents

Acknowledgments	vii
Foreword by Clive Wilmer	1
Preface	5
Abbreviations	9
Introduction	
The Fifties	11
A Virtual "Movement"	12
Criticism and Poetry	15
The Canonization of the Movement	20
Thom Gunn and the Movement	22
I — "I'm an Anglo-American poet": Profile of Thom Gunn	
Premise	25
Artistic Development	25
II — In Search of an *Ubi Consistam*	
Boasting Concealment: The Staging of Passion in the Early Collections	43
Between Tradition and Innovation	49
The Prison of the Intellect	51
Choosing Inertia	52
Action as Existential Absolute	54
III — A Challenge to the Void	
Heroes in Motion	59
Shaping the Fog	69
IV — Surrender and Recovery	
The Phenomenology of Defeat	81
The Twilight of Heroism	87

From Senses to Sense	94
Contact	100
V — An Experiment in Artistic Collaboration	
Premise	109
Positives	110
VI — The Liberating Sixties	
Gay Pride	124
Rebirth	128
VII — The Body, Disease, and Death	
The Outsider	133
The Annihilation of Self	135
Regression to a Primal State	136
The Tortured Body	140
The Aging Body	143
The Dismembered Body	147
Thom Gunn Today	153
Appendix: Cole Street, San Francisco: A Conversation with Thom Gunn	159
Chapter Notes	175
Bibliography	199
Index	207

Foreword
by Clive Wilmer

Like many readers of my generation, I first read Thom Gunn in 1962. That was the year of two celebrated anthologies: the *Selected Poems* of Thom Gunn and Ted Hughes, and A. Alvarez's classic Penguin *The New Poetry*, in which the same two poets were prominently featured. To a boy of seventeen obsessed with poetry, this new work came across with tremendous force and the fascination of novelty. Here were two poets in their early thirties who spoke with the voices of a wholly new generation. In Gunn's case it was partly a question of subject matter: his love of the modern city and pop music and adolescent rebellion. There was also his frankness about sex, desire, violence and restlessness. Moreover, though I did not consciously register it then, I have always valued the absence from his work of an over-sensitive ego defending itself with irony. By contrast, there was something about both tone and subject matter that struck me as heroic, despite the fact that the era we were living in was said to be unheroic. What was more, the heroism coincided with real emotions, as momentous as those in Donne or Shakespeare, but belonging to a world I recognized as mine: a world overshadowed by the experience of the Second World War and the knowledge it had brought of our capacity for evil and self-destruction as well as for courage and endurance. It was eventually to be important to me that, unconventional as his morals were, Gunn was a profoundly ethical writer and that he was so in contexts that recognized the demands of our physical nature. It was also important that his engagement with irrational forces was conducted in poems of elegant and traditional formality. Gunn is one of the great masters of English poetic form, both traditional and experimental, and, as a result, his best work has the power of a bomb about to go off: one is always conscious of intense passion, but a passion contained and directed by the disciplines of language and versification. In his poem "To Yvor Winters" he praises a similarly powerful American poet for combining "Rule and Energy" in his verse. It was an aspiration he lived up to himself.

Eight years before I first read him, Gunn had moved to the United States, where, without becoming an American citizen, he was to stay for the rest of his life. This was not at first a change of much significance, but in time it was to separate him from much of his audience. He called himself "an Anglo-American poet." He began to use the odd Americanism, though he never really lost his British manner. He kept, for instance, his English love of reticence: his was the sort of poetry one associates with Wordsworth or Ben Jonson, in which the feeling and significance is often left entirely to implication. (It was this quality that, in the 1980s, made his elegies for men who had died of AIDS so very moving.) But America changed the atmosphere of his poems more than it changed their style. The tense Existentialist loneliness of his earlier work gave way to something more casual, an easy Californian hedonism, though his poems were seldom without their darknesses. When he combined this new-found optimism with free verse in the manner of William Carlos Williams—which, from the 1960s on, he did intermittently—he lost those rather many British readers who are deaf to the music of American speech and seem to relish anxiety in their poetry. As the 1960s turned into the '70s, his restraint and dislike of self-expression began to look unfashionable, so that even when, in his 1975 collection *Jack Straw's Castle*, he "came out" as a homosexual, it attracted little attention. The AIDS elegies, collected in *The Man with Night Sweats* (1992), restored something of his early fame, but it was a fame that often depended less on specific poems and their quality than on the news value of his subject and his "right on" attitudes. These were not reasons that appealed to him. Committed to gay liberation, he was glad to contribute to wider understanding of homosexuality, but he never saw such things as the point of poetry. In truth, he was not much interested in public success; when I complained once of the way his publishers treated him, he replied, "I'm famous enough." He was a modest, generous, self-deprecating man, but one who at the same time knew his worth. To write well by his own standards was what mattered to him, and it was doing this that enabled him to avoid the tribalism which has done so much harm to modern American poetry. This partly accounts for his extraordinary range: in his last book *Boss Cupid*, for instance, he was able to shift from the elegant Elizabethan stanzas of "Troubadour" to the throwaway free verse of the section he aptly called "Gossip."

His sudden death in 2004 has left his reputation still uncertain. In my judgment, he was the finest poet of an era much richer in talent than is widely acknowledged. What gives him that distinction, for me, are the Jonsonian range and variety of his work ("There are many Ben Jonsons," he once wrote, "and each of them is a considerable poet"), the profundity of his themes, his unostentatious technical accomplishment, the striking relevance of his writing to our own time despite (or perhaps because of) his deep roots in tradition. Take "Touch" for example, his first major poem in free verse. Though technically indebted to the minimalist American Robert Creeley, who made a fine art of hesitant stumbling, the poem alludes by implication to certain love poems by

John Donne. Notable among them is Donne's *aubade*, "The Good-Morrow," an awakening to ideal love with echoes of the Christian Resurrection. In "Touch," by contrast, the lovers discover their closeness and common humanity by falling asleep, drifting from the cold detachment of waking thought into shared warmth and collective unconsciousness. Where Donne develops his thought through three elaborate stanzas, Gunn follows the apparently shapeless drift of a mind falling asleep. "Touch" is as carefully constructed as "The Good-Morrow" but it exemplifies our modern avoidance of closure: it is poem-as-process.

Modern Western society is preoccupied with personality. No doubt this is due, at least in part, to mobility. Technology and the globalized economy have effaced our sense of belonging and rootedness, with the result that the individual is often removed from stable contexts. But we have become so obsessed with personality that we will surely soon begin to tire of it. Gunn is instructive here. By the time he died, he had to a large extent forsaken his English origins without really becoming an American. This is reflected in the curious rootlessness of his "Anglo-American" language, a factor which is sometimes said to have lost him his early following, but which seems to me likely to attract the world of the future, freer as that will be of national distinctions. Moreover, throughout his career, Gunn brooded on the problem of identity. Identity, not personality. Personality lacks the resonance of myth, which makes it too thin a subject for poetry. But the question of how we become what we are is unlikely to fade.

Stefania Michelucci has taken the quest for identity as the focus of this remarkable study of Gunn. She writes with admirable clarity and insight on Gunn's adoption of poses, the variety of his masks and the mysterious self—both physical and spiritual—that generates his work's integrity. There is a paradox here. Gunn disliked the notion that art should aim at universals, insisting on the contrary that artists are moved by particulars. At the same time, he eschewed the Confessional poet's obsession with mere personality. What makes Gunn, for me, the poet of the future is his capacity to make myths or masks of his own very particular self. In the later work, for instance, one sees it in his emphasis on homosexual experience. The speaker of "The Man with Night Sweats," for example, is talking about a problem that might be thought peculiar to gay men: the fear that, through sexual adventure, he may have contracted AIDS. Yet it is also a poem about something all of us share: the fear of death combined with the consciousness that a risk-free life is hardly a life at all.

This archetypal element in Gunn is something that Michelucci has captured in her book. This is, to the best of my knowledge, the first full-length monograph on Gunn in any language, including English. It looks at the work in many contexts that would not immediately occur to an English-speaking critic, and this is often immensely illuminating. At the same time, Michelucci explores the language of the poems in a manner that owes as much to Anglo-Saxon close-reading as to modern European literary theory. She sees and shows how there is something unprecedented in Gunn's vision — that his was a new way of living your life and seeing the world — and yet how the fundamental myths and patterns of our common culture inform his work from the start. That she succeeds in doing so — a heterosexual Italian woman writing about an Anglo-American gay — seems to me little short of miraculous, especially as so much of her wider meaning is strictly located in Gunn's specific words. It may seem like faint praise to say that the book is also remarkable for its factual accuracy, its readability, its knowledge of the relevant literature and its consistent illumination of the poems, but these are important matters, and Michelucci's depth quite often exposes the superficiality of other assessments. It is wonderful to read so rich an account of a great poet, recently dead, which honors his work and vision by giving them the seriousness of attention they deserve.

Cambridge, 2005

Clive Wilmer, poet and critic, teaches English Literature at the University of Cambridge. He met Thom Gunn in 1964 when he was nineteen and Gunn thirty-five. They remained friends for the next forty years. Wilmer has written extensively on Gunn's poetry, interviewed Gunn twice and edited the collection of essays, *The Occasions of Poetry* (1982). He is working on a critical edition of Gunn's poems for Faber and Faber. Wilmer has also published several collections of his own poems, including *The Falls* (2000) and *The Mystery of Things* (2006).

Preface

This book is the result of a long-lasting interest in the work of a poet whom I consider one of the more significant of the second half of the 20th century. When, in the 1980s, I was a student of modern languages and literatures at the University of Pisa, my professors suggested I write a dissertation on a contemporary poet. I went through many anthologies and texts, fell in love with some of them, and finally chose Thom Gunn. I was attracted to his intellectual honesty, to his surprising and subtle metaphors, and above all to his open-mindedness and lack of prejudice towards the new tendencies and myths of his age. I was struck, at the same time, by his firm grasp on the "great tradition" (as Leavis put it) of masters of the past, which did not prevent him from presenting with extraordinary vividness, immediacy, and originality the contradictions, problems, anxieties, and paradoxes of his own age. I therefore decided to devote all my energy to the study of his work; I spent some time in England collecting bibliographical material on him, including BBC recordings of interviews and readings. Hearing his voice was for me a moving experience.

After my graduation, I was offered a job as an Assistant Professor at Arizona State University. I was finally across the ocean, not very far from "my" poet, who had left Europe for a more congenial place, San Francisco. I sent him a copy of my dissertation and was thrilled when he granted me an interview in his home in March of 1990. What had belonged to books and to libraries was now acquiring a life of its own. My interview was a long talk on his poetry and his ideas about contemporary British and American poets. Then he invited me to listen to one of his lectures on Modern Poetry at the University of California at Berkeley where he was teaching.

When I was back in Italy, I began my Ph.D. on Modernist fiction and went on with my academic career, working on a variety of fields, but I never abandoned Gunn's poetry. I kept up with his latest collections, planning to write a book about him. This project resulted, at first, in articles I wrote for different conferences (including one for the celebration of his 70th birthday) and for literary magazines.

I was fascinated by his rejection of any label (both national and sexual) and by his describing himself as an Anglo-American poet, which heightened my esteem of him. I saw that his art aimed at overcoming national and cultural borders, although this had quite a negative effect on his popularity, because to the audience and critics he was neither one thing nor the other — too British to be American, too much influenced by the American scene to keep his Britishness intact. My aim therefore was first to restore the reputation of a poet who had been neglected, if not quite forgotten (after the first years of his career) on the Old Continent, but who, on the other hand, had never been completely accepted as part of the American canon across the Atlantic. Thom Gunn, in my opinion, has much to say to our age, tormented as we are by the plague of globalization which paradoxically goes hand in hand with medieval-flavored ethnic and religious conflicts.

Starting with theoretical premises drawn from philosophy, anthropology, and sociology, and adopting a method in some respects similar to the "close reading" of Anglo-American tradition, in my study I try to analyze Thom Gunn's entire poetic career. I start from his first collection, *Fighting Terms* (published when he was still an undergraduate — see Chapter II), when the influence of Sartre's existentialism is clearly seen in his attempt to achieve authenticity through the liberation from the prison of paralyzing self-consciousness. In Chapter III the analysis focuses on *The Sense of Movement*, completed when the poet moved to the United States, and in the following chapters on his later collections, from *My Sad Captains* to *Boss Cupid*, most of which were written after he settled in San Francisco. From *My Sad Captains* onwards it is possible to note a gradual opening to human relationships and to Nature, which coincides with the poet's expression of his own nature, of his long repressed and hidden homosexuality. These later collections are informed by an increasing vitality, which manifests itself in the celebration of the liberating experience of LSD, in appropriating the culture of the 1960s (*Moly* and *Jack Straw's Castle*), in the happiness he felt with other homosexuals (see *The Passages of Joy*), as well as in the deep compassion for friends struck by the tragedy of AIDS (*The Man with Night Sweats*). Later there emerges in his poetry a sort of dry regret for the decline of both spirit and body brought about by old age (*Boss Cupid*).

In Chapter V, I also pay attention to the collection *Positives*, which constitutes an outstanding experiment, one neglected by critics. The work was a collaboration between Thom Gunn and his brother Ander, a photographer, during a year (1964) spent in London. The book offers an interesting image of London covering the entire arc of human life, combining Ander's photographs and Gunn's captions.

Characterized by a rigorous intellectual honesty and sincerity that give Gunn's voice its unmistakable timbre, his poetry constitutes a unique artistic experience in that it seeks to mediate between opposite poles: old Europe and contemporary America, traditional meter and free verse, the language of the present (including American slang) and the lessons of the great writers of the past, in particular the Metaphysical Poets.

Some friends of mine, to whom I am very grateful, encouraged me in this project of writing a monograph on Thom Gunn. The poets and writers Clive Wilmer, Gregory Woods and Elmar Schenkel helped me while I was completing the Italian version of the book, which was published in 2006. The book has been warmly received by both readers and critics and has been positively reviewed in Italian literary journals. It has also been adopted in some university courses on contemporary poetry and on the culture of the Sixties. Some scholars suggested to me that an English-language edition of the book would fill a major welcomed gap in the literature. Jill Franks (an American scholar of D.H. Lawrence and other modernists and a dear friend of mine to whom I am very grateful) has translated the book from the Italian into English. Some sections have been revised and updated and some parts specifically focused on Italian criticism were omitted.

I hope this work will help make Gunn's poetry better known and more popular and will give new and long-deserved life to an important artist of the 20th century.

Abbreviations

BC	Thom Gunn, *Boss Cupid* (London: Faber, 2000).
CP	Thom Gunn, *Collected Poems* (London: Faber, 1993).
OP	Thom Gunn, *The Occasions of Poetry*, edited by Clive Wilmer (London: Faber, 1982).
Positives	Thom Gunn, *Positives* (verses by Thom Gunn, photographs by Ander Gunn) (London: Faber, 1966).
SL	Thom Gunn, *Shelf Life: Essays, Memoirs and an Interview* (London: Faber, 1994).

Introduction

THE FIFTIES

In the years after World War II, the scope of British poetry was varied and heterogeneous. Unlike what was occurring in theater and fiction, poetry lacked, at least in the beginning, a prevailing tendency; there was no leader that could give a definitive imprint to the period and a reference point for contemporaries.

As Thom Gunn said in an interview,

> After Pound's generation, the next generation died off rather early, like Robert Lowell and Robert Duncan; they didn't live quite to an advanced age. I compare it in my mind to what happened at the beginning of the 19th century in England, and there you get Wordsworth and Coleridge and Keats and Shelley and that group of people. They are so big and so impressive, that even though many of them died quite early, the rest of the century spent the rest of the time trying to deal with them, and they actually did not get free of them until the beginning of the next century, when we started off with these big people again, another generation, almost exactly a hundred years later, and you know, round about 1910 into the 1920s, and we are still trying to deal with them too.[1]

After Modernism, the age of experimentation was over, and the heroes of the first decades of the century—Yeats, Pound, Eliot, Dylan Thomas—if not physically dead (like Yeats), had exhausted their creative cycle. However, they continued to exercise an influence, together with Robert Graves, Edwin Muir, W.H. Auden, and the so-called "Thirties Poets." After the war this group (especially Auden, who, in moving to the United States and taking U.S. citizenship, made the opposite choice to T.S. Eliot), developed a poetry that was no longer intellectually and ideologically committed, as it had been in the years preceding World War II. This compound inheritance undoubtedly hindered the birth of a new and powerful movement or school with precise goals and projects of its own.

A strong sense of English literary tradition contributed to the scant propensity for technical and formal experimentation of the emerging group of middle-class, university trained poets. This tradition included Thomas Hardy and William Empson, but had its roots in Augustan poetry, in the "early, bland, eighteenth-century English Rationalism, in the expressive clarity of Alexander Pope."[2] Their respect for tradition sometimes manifested as a subordinate attitude towards the great masters of the past, and was influenced by postwar critical debates, the Cambridge School, and the charismatic F.R. Leavis.[3] This love of tradition shows in the critical essays of one of the new poets, Donald Davie, *Purity of Diction in English Verse* (1952) and *Articulate Energy: An Enquiry into the Syntax of English Poetry* (1955), which exalted the moral and social responsibilities of the Augustan poets and their expressive clarity; in the mid-fifties these essays were read as expressions of the aesthetic values of the author's generation.

Most of the new poets were molded in academic environments, in particular, Oxford and Cambridge, and had affinities to one another that inspired reciprocal promotion.[4] In this endeavor they were aided by the diffusion of new modes of publication such as university "little magazines" and mimeograph machines. As Gunn recollects,

> we promoted each other consistently. For example, the university newspaper *Varsity* featured a profile of a local celebrity each week, and it seems to me that we all wrote each other's profiles, thus creating and perpetuating each other's celebrity.... Cambridge is a place of privilege, and things are usually made easier for those who have been there. My first books were reviewed more kindly than they deserved largely, I think, because London expected good poets to emerge from Oxford and Cambridge and here I was, somebody new with all the fashionable influences and coming from Cambridge [*OP* 165–67].

Although they lacked a true leader, these poets found in F.R. Leavis an important reference point; Leavis had a dominant influence on the critical and literary debates of those years. It was especially his idea of the English "Great Tradition," only temporarily interrupted by the distinctly cosmopolitan movement of Modernism, that influenced the new writers to curtail and "domesticate" the literary and linguistic experiments of the avant-garde. Despite their intrinsic diversity and individuality, the new poets have a common denominator in their choice of a clearly organized and comprehensible language, even when the subject matter is the elusive one of sensations and emotions.

A Virtual "Movement"

The absence of a leader (the role played by Auden for the 1930s poets and by Dylan Thomas for the Apocalyptics) and of their own school seems incongruous with the tendency of certain critics and some of the poets to group the works of the fifties under the label "the Movement," which was not, in the strictest sense, a movement, because it lacked a manifesto, or explicit aesthetic program, shared by all of the poets.⁵ Despite its canonization in literary history, the critical foundations of the Movement remain problematic today. Although the publication of anthologies dedicated to the Movement seems to confirm and legitimize its existence, it is denied by some of the poets recognized as belonging to the group.

The term "Movement" made its first appearance in an anonymous article in the *Spectator* (1 October 1954), later attributed to the editor J.D. Scott, which proclaimed in its title, "In the Movement," the presence of a dominant trend in English poetry in the post–World War II years. The term referred to emerging figures in the university milieu, later known as the "New University Wits."⁶

William Van O'Connor introduces them thus:

> most of them either are or have been university lecturers (two are university librarians) and as a consequence have also been called the "New University Wits."... University Wits seems the preferable term, since it does not carry the connotation, as Movement does, of "band-wagon" or "mutual admiration society." But Movement is the term that has been more widely used.⁷

The *Spectator* article signaled, in a tone not lacking in irony or polemics, profound changes in English postwar society along with new cultural attitudes and tastes:

> Genuflections towards Dr. Leavis and Professor Empson, admiration for people whom the Thirties by-passed, Orwell above all (and, for another example, Mr. Robert Graves) are indeed signs by which you might recognize the Movement. It is bored by the despair of the Forties, not much interested in suffering, and extremely impatient of poetic sensibility, especially poetic sensibility about "the writer and society." So it's goodbye to all those rather sad little discussions about "how the writer ought to live," and it's goodbye to the Little Magazine and "experimental writing." The Movement, as well as being anti-phoney, is anti-wet; sceptical, robust, ironic, prepared to be as comfortable as possible in a wicked, commercial, threatened world which doesn't look, anyway, as if it's going to be changed much by a couple of handfuls of young English writers.⁸

The concluding words of the passage delineate an important cultural phenomenon connected to the inception of the welfare state, by which the writer and the poet now assume the function of cultural workers, making themselves spokespersons of a professionalism negotiated from inside of, and sometimes against, institutions. They renounce *a priori* the desire of the Thirties Poets to intervene in society, as well as the Modernists' alienation.⁹

The *Spectator* article maintained that in 1954, the Movement was still in an embryonic stage, but affirmed its importance as "part of that tide which is putting us through the Fifties and towards the Sixties."¹⁰ Only two poets, Thom Gunn and Donald Davie, were named in the article, and Davie was the only one to recognize the existence of the Movement, though minimizing its importance in a 1959 essay called "Remembering the Movement." He insisted that the Movement was the result of a process of publicity, promotion, and commercialization:¹¹

> All of us in the Movement had read the articles in *Scrutiny* about how the reputations of Auden and Spender and Day Lewis were made by skilful promotion and publicity and it was to placate *Scrutiny* readers that we pretended (and sometimes deceived ourselves as well as others) that the Movement was not being "sold" to the public in the same way: that John Wain on the BBC and later Bob Conquest with his anthology *New Lines* weren't just touching the pitch with which we others wouldn't be defiled. Again, I limit myself to my own case, I remember nothing so distastefully as the maidenly shudders with which I wished to know nothing of the machinery of publicity even as I liked publicity and profited from it.[12]

The *Spectator* article was repeatedly reprimanded for having created a nonexistent Movement (the generic nature of its name did not help), and there were attacks on the new-generation writers, who were accused of having used it as a propaganda instrument to publish their works and capture the public's attention. As Ian Hamilton said,

> in the weeks following the *Spectator*'s P.R. job, there were some sardonic rejoinders from, as it were, the battle-front: Alan Brownjohn and Anthony Thwaite (both at the time editing Oxford poetry magazines in which some of the supposed Movementeers were often to be found) wrote deflating letters, with Thwaite ironically acknowledging that the article had the importance of a white paper in a field where previous remarks merely had the nature of, say, interdepartmental memoranda.[13]

Such criticisms—which perhaps adumbrated petty professional jealousies—did not stop the success of the *Spectator* article and the tarnishing effect it had on the intellectual debates of the Fifties. They actually had some foundation, if not otherwise than in the way in which they stressed the importance of the media in the promotional campaign organized around the Movement. Already in this period, poetry and literary texts were capturing public and critical attention, especially by the new means of communication; poetry revealed itself as subject to the same market logic that governs the promotion of bestsellers.

While the activities of the *Group* were widespread in the Sixties, thanks to the intervention and publicity of the BBC, the press played a fundamental role in launching the Movement, unifying quite different poets in fairly arbitrary ways.

Although the *Spectator* named only two poets of the new generation, the names of other possible members of the Movement appeared in two anthologies of 1955 and 1956. The first, *Poets of the Fifties*, edited by D.J. Enright, includes poetry by himself, Kingsley Amis, Robert Conquest, Donald Davie, John Holloway, Elizabeth Jennings, Philip Larkin, and John Wain. The second, *New Lines*, edited by Robert Conquest, added another name—Thom Gunn.

In 1956 the term *Movement* was used mostly in reference to these new poets, and the anthology *New Lines* (followed by *New Lines II* in 1963) became its official text. The editor's intention was simply to unite, in one volume, poets who came on the English literary scene in the Fifties and who showed affinities of taste, aesthetic orientation, and language, without being bound to a well-defined aesthetic program:

> If one had briefly to distinguish this poetry of the Fifties from its predecessors, I believe the most important general point would be that it submits to no great systems of theoretical constructs nor agglomerations of unconscious commands. It is free from both mystical and logical compulsions and — like modern philosophy — is empirical in its attitude to all that comes.... It will be seen at once that these poets do not have as much in common as they would if they were a group of doctrine-saddled writers forming a definite school complete with programme and rules.[14]

CRITICISM AND POETRY

D.J. Enright echoes Robert Conquest's position of extraneousness to the publicizing of the Movement, in the introduction to the anthology he edited:

> This anthology should be considered as an interim report — not as the presentation of a "movement" but as the presentation of selected poems by individual writers, some of whom share common attitudes.[15]

Teaching in the Far East, and therefore far from the critical and theoretical debates erupting in England, Enright's intention was to present certain emerging poets whose voices revealed alternatives to T.S. Eliot's experimentation, on the one hand, and Dylan Thomas's apocalyptic language, on the other, poets "who neither flog the dead horse of 'Wastelanditis' nor fly to its sentimental opposite in a vain attempt to achieve a new romanticism."[16] Enright's words present a rather similar image to that found in the *Spectator*. Between the two poles of Eliot and Thomas's experimentation is a type of poetry characterized by formal discipline and self-control, in a language that is clear and immediately recognizable, free of the neologisms, verbal assembly, and multi-linguistic virtuosity of both the modernist avant-garde and Dylan Thomas's poetry.

Even if we accept the idea, as did most of the poets involved, that it was the *Spectator* that created the Movement, given that in these years they did not know each other personally nor elaborate a common artistic agenda, several critics tend to emphasize the fact that their similar backgrounds might have contributed to the creation of affinities and occasional similarities which the poets only later realized.[17]

Despite his distaste for being inserted into any group, and his proclaimed differences from Philip Larkin, Ted Hughes, and other Fifties poets, Thom Gunn recognizes their shared attitude of refusing any masters or father figures, a refusal that permits the new generation of poets to voice their own creativity without being overpowered by what Harold Bloom, in his seminal 1973 text, called the "anxiety of influence"[18]:

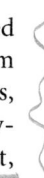

That is what my generation was doing: we were disregarding the leading figures. It is not opposing, it is just not taking any notice, and that is what Larkin and I had in common and Ted Hughes too, the three of us, though we were not writing at all similarly.[19]

In the Sixties, Gunn emphasized his sense of not belonging to the Movement:

> I'm very sceptical about the existence of the Movement, which strikes me as a very journalistic grouping together of certain poets who all amassed at the same time, and who don't really have that much in common. At the time when I was associated with them in the minds of journalists, I had met only one of them, and had read very, very little by any of them. I had not heard of some of them when I first heard about the Movement, and I think this is probably true of some of the others.[20]

Elizabeth Jennings is the only female voice in the Fifties anthologies. She describes the literary climate of the Fifties and the Movement:

> In 1956 and 1957 the words most commonly used about the current poetry were "consolidation," "clarity," "intellectual honesty," and "formal perfection." Indeed a number of poets (vaguely called the Movement), who were supposed by some critics to exemplify these qualities, were hustled into a group often very much against the will of the poets themselves.[21]
>
> They may have common aims—but this is something very different from that deliberate practice and promulgation of shared views which a true literary movement implies.[22]

One cannot help but notice the difference between Jennings' tone and the detached positions of Thom Gunn and Philip Larkin, who accused the press of having given life to a virtual group which was effectively nonexistent, created only through publicity. Jennings' words evince a certain irritation at having been classified as part of a group to which she feels no sense of belonging. Hers is also the minority voice—female—which sees itself manipulated by processes of institutionalization and conformity.

Beyond the polemics regarding the existence of the Movement, there is the problem of establishing the artistic value and importance of its poetic output. The most in-depth study of the subject is the monograph by Blake Morrison called *The Movement* (1980). Although conscious of the arguments regarding the Movement and of the refusal of the poets to recognize it, Morrison maintains, from the perspective gained by several decades, that the Movement was not a "promotional" phenomenon, nor was it limited to the Fifties, but was an important moment in English poetic history, with deep roots in the past and with repercussions far beyond its own decade. Recognizing that it is not a true movement limited to a precise historic period, the critic nevertheless delineates common traits among the poets in Conquest and Enright's anthologies. In particular, they are revisiting a native English tradition which, in containing qualities of "rationalism, realism, and empiricism," is rooted in Alexander Pope's "purity of diction" and eighteenth-century Realism:

> The identity of the Movement has, it seems, transcended both the group and the decade, coming to stand for certain characteristics in English writings—rationalism, realism, empiricism — which continue to exert their influence today. It is even possible to talk of a Movement "ideology"— an identifiable "line" on sex, religion, politics and other non-literary matters.[23]

To demonstrate his thesis, the author reconstructs the various phases of the process of aggregation among the emerging poets, showing the importance of their social class, their education, and their relations with the public. The Englishness of the Movement stems from definite sociocultural characteristics: a background that produces certain commonalities of attitude and intention.

Particularly interesting is Blake Morrison's description of a type of provincialism which links the writers of the new generation to each other, and connects them to the sociocultural transformations produced by the welfare state. In Morrison's view, these transformations contribute to a phenomenon, the re–Anglicization of English literature, which is quite different from the literary cosmopolitanism of the early decades of the 20th century.[24]

> By the middle of the 1950s the image of the typical Movement writer as a provincial, lower-middle-class, scholarship-winning, Oxbridge-educated university lecturer was firmly established, though it was apparent even then that there were certain incompatibilities between this image and the kind of work which the Movement produced.... The identification of the Movement with a wider class-struggle was one reason why the group established itself so quickly in the years 1953–5: it gave them the advantage of seeming to represent a newly empowered class, and it helped them to define themselves in opposition to the "haut-bourgeois" 1930s generation.... The philistinism and little Englandism which alarmed and angered many older readers also bear a relation to the Movement's "provincialism."[25]

Morrison frames the new poets in the dynamic of the class struggle typical of Anglo-Saxon culture. Besides attention to the quotidian rituals of the middle class, they stress the importance, in their works, of belonging to a specific place, a regional island inside of Great Britain (itself an island), which is increasingly out of touch with the world, in part because of the fall of the empire and the process of decolonization. It is no coincidence that, in speaking of Philip Larkin, Morrison notes his "post-imperial *tristesse*." Ties to their land of origin are particularly evident in certain poets. In Ted Hughes the spirit of place in the moors of Yorkshire, those wild places of Brontë novels, become a "mindscape" dominated by primordial instincts. Philip Larkin evokes the urban provincialism of a dark, grey town in northern England. However, attention to the land of origin, the place of belonging, indicated by provincial aspects absent from the cosmopolitan cities of Modernism, does not necessarily signify provincialism. In Ted Hughes's poetry, for example, the search for the primordial, for deep roots in Nature, invokes Celtic and Mediterranean myths that form the substratum of many cultures whose borders lie far outside English national territory.

Even though the provincial attitude is more attenuated in a poet like Thom Gunn (probably because of his move to the United States), in his work the sense of place has an important role that manifests in strong references to the environment, whether the most hidden aspects of the London metropolis (*Positives*), or the open, sun-filled places of the California coast (*My Sad Captains, Moly, Jack Straw's Castle*), and the streets of New York and San Francisco, pulsing with life and homeless people (*The Passages of Joy, The Man with Night Sweats*).

Closely connected to their profound respect for tradition, and their tendency to recover traditional metrical forms and expressive clarity, is the Movement poets' intolerance of the Romantics' lack of order and control, their effusiveness and self-reference. These basic characteristics provided points of agreement for the new poets of the Fifties, attracting sometimes ferocious criticism from those who saw in them a phenomenon of regression (especially with regard to Modernism) or who otherwise minimized their importance.

For example, A. Alvarez speaks condescendingly of them in the introductory essay to his anthology, *The New Poetry*, significantly titled "The New Poetry or Beyond the Gentility Principle." Advocate of Modernism and particularly of its cosmopolitanism and openness to radical artistic experimentation, Alvarez discerns a regressive and abstruse tendency in English poetry, caused by what he finds one of the most restrictive and emasculating aspects of English culture: "The disease so often found in English culture: gentility."[26] According to Alvarez, after the openness of Modernism there occurred a process of closure that Thomas Hardy, as early as the 1920s, had foreseen in the future of English poetry. Hardy wrote to Robert Graves (in response to American cultural influences), that "*vers libre* could come to nothing in England. All we can do is to write on the old themes in the old styles, but try to do a little better than those who went before us." "Since about 1930," writes Alvarez, "the machinery of modern English poetry seems to have been controlled by a series of negative feed-backs designed to produce precisely the effect Hardy wanted."[27]

According to Alvarez the process of regression, identified in three distinct stages ("feed-backs"), began in the late thirties, when "experimental verse was out and traditional forms, in a chic contemporary guise, were back in."[28] The reaction to Auden "took the form of anti-intellectualism."[29] In the forties, which constituted the "second negative feed-back,"[30] especially among the followers of Dylan Thomas, "all that mattered was that the verse should sound impressive."[31] The third and final phase of this regression was the emergence of the Movement, whose exponents, even though he praises some of them, he judged as a group of unpretentious dilettantes:

> The third stage was yet another reaction: against wild, loose emotion. The name of the reaction was the Movement, and its anthology was Robert Conquest's *New Lines*. Of the nine poets to appear in this, six, at the time, were university teachers, two librarians, and one a Civil Servant. It was, in short, academic-adminis-

trative verse, polite, knowledgeable, efficient, polished, and, in its quiet way, even intelligent. What it had to offer positively was more difficult to describe.[32]

Alvarez vehemently criticizes all of English poetry after Modernism. His anthology, the success of which is evidenced by its numerous republications (almost one every year, from 1962 to 1982), includes, in accordance with his declared cosmopolitanism, both British and American poets. The volume bears a predominantly male imprint. The section of American poetry includes four poets, two of whom are women — John Berryman and Robert Lowell (whom he calls the best), Anne Sexton and Sylvia Plath — but the much larger English section leaves out female voices altogether. Among the various poets (Norman MacCaig, D.J. Enright, Donald Davie, Philip Larkin, Kingsley Amis, David Holbrook, Michael Hamburger, John Wain, Arthur Boyars, Christopher Middleton, Charles Tomlinson, Ian Crichton Smith, Thom Gunn, Peter Porter, Ted Hughes, Jon Silkin, Geoffrey Hill, George Macbeth, Peter Redgrove, Ted Walker, David Wevill, John Fuller, Ian Hamilton) not even one female, such as Elizabeth Jennings, finds a spot.[33] It is not clear why she (and others) were ignored, while much space was given to figures like David Wevill, of Canadian origin, and Ian Crichton Smith, a Scots poet who writes primarily in Gaelic.

Even more critical towards the new Fifties poets is Ian Hamilton. While on the one hand insisting on the minimal value of Movement poetry (calling the Movement a momentary trend), on the other hand, he reluctantly admits its importance, recognizing the magnitude of the influence it exerted:

> Almost every young university poet had become a Movementeer; the Oxford and Cambridge magazines, the Fantasy Press pamphlets, the column-ends of many of the weeklies, were brimming over with neatly tailored ironies, with feeble new–Augustan posturings, and effortful Empsonian pastiche. The talentless had been given a verse-recipe only slightly more difficult to follow than that handed out by Tambimuttu fifteen years earlier.[34]

Also strongly disapproving was the judgment of an authoritative critic, Bernard Bergonzi, although his words suggest an intention to redeem the Movement from bitter, excessive criticism like Hamilton's:

> The Movement poets, however, were eminently rational in their approach to writing verse; their poems may not have been very passionate — as hostile critics were quick to point out — but they did write in the syntax of ordinary discourse, and their meanings were, for the most part, readily apparent.... The Movement did not lead to any great poems. But it did produce in a short time a sizeable body of extremely decent verse, amid much that was obsessively minor.[35]

In reality these judgments, appearing mostly in the early Sixties, overstress what is controlled, educated, and comprehensible in the poetry of these years (i.e., the element identified by Alvarez as "gentility" and by Bergonzi as "decency"). They fail to recognize the notable emotional intensity and thematic complexity present in the major exponents of the style.

The position of recent criticism is quite different. As seen already in Blake

Morrison's monograph, recent criticism tends towards a more objective and deeper analysis, which tries to emphasize, beyond occasional similarities among the exponents of the Movement, their intrinsic diversity and their "personal timbre." Florence Elon's essay "The Movement Against Itself: British Poetry of the 1950s" provides an example. Citing copiously from the anthologies that promoted the Movement, Elon evidences the presence, in certain poets such as Donald Davie and Philip Larkin, of an attraction to the irrational and the imaginary, an almost wild yearning for escape from the quotidian which also appears in Thom Gunn's work, with a strong vein of instinct. This vein, in D.J. Enright, is a frank openness to the unconscious and to mystery. This irrationalist tendency among Movement poets finds expression in a style that is, however, controlled by traditional meter, rhyme, and a type of language justified by the need to find a balance between form and content. Elon's conclusion emphasizes a new aspect that redeems these poets from the discredit heaped upon them by sixties and seventies criticism:

> What they have in common is not the assertion of the power of reason, wit, order and civilization over chaos, destruction and instinctual life but rather an unflagging interest in the question itself.... The poets differ: some have chosen one path, some another; some write in the language of aesthetic controversy, some in symbolic terms.... yet the connection among them — the sense of a group of poets grappling with a subject of common concern — finally seems at least as significant as their divergences.[36]

THE CANONIZATION OF THE MOVEMENT

Stephen Regan's essay "The Movement," written for the volume *A Companion to 20th Century Poetry* (2001), carefully analyzes the Movement's history and the various pro and con positions regarding its existence. Regan argues that the Movement reflects the reaction of the young poets to the postwar cultural climate and the "restrictive conditions of the Cold War,"[37] and concludes by insisting on the time-sensitive nature of the Movement's poetry: "By 1962, however, any sense of a coherent Movement project had largely dissolved and the writers who were briefly identified with it had already gone their separate ways."[38]

In the chapter "In and Out of the Movement: The Generation of the 1950s in England" (*A History of Modern Poetry: Modernism and After*), David Perkins recognizes the importance of the journalistic promotion of the Movement, which helped the new voices of English poetry to be heard, and limits the Movement to the years just after World War II ("by the early 1960s the Movement was under strong attack").[39]

> The 1950s were the heyday of the so-called Movement.... The effort to characterize the poetry of the Movement gave the poets involved a clearer sense of their

own values and aims, the more so since many of them were also critics and provided the characterizations. For these reasons literary history cannot ignore the Movement. But as with many other such events in the arts, the grouping was half accidental.[40]

After describing certain essential traits of Fifties poetry — those commonly attributed to the Movement — Perkins analyzes some of its poets, including Roy Fuller, C.H. Sisson, R.S. Thomas, and "Larkin and his contemporaries," showing their diversity and individuality of style. In the next chapter, "English Poetry in the 1960s and 1970s," Perkins introduces the work of four poets, Charles Tomlinson, Ted Hughes, Geoffrey Hill, and Thom Gunn, presenting it as a break from the tone of the Fifties, and even as approaching the Modernist experimentation of European and American poetry:

> Their work is formed in tension between the strong, persisting appeal of native English styles, on the one hand, and on the other hand, the Modernist and Postmodernist styles of the United States and of Europe. The interaction of opposed values shows itself not only in particular volumes and poems but in a poet's reversals of directions over the years.[41]

Emphasis of differences rather than similarities also characterizes the work of Neil Corcoran, author of *English Poetry Since 1940* (1993) in the *Longman Literature in English Series*. Corcoran subdivides the poetic voices of the Fifties into three distinct groups, starting with Philip Larkin (in a section appropriately called "A Movement Pursued"), whom he describes as "undoubtedly the most Movement of Movement poets in the sense that in him the true spirit of postwar English dispiritedness quickly reached, and subsequently maintained, its most quintessential form."[42] The second group includes Donald Davie, Charles Tomlinson and Thom Gunn, and is significantly titled "Movements," a term in line with the critical tendency to emphasize the variety instead of uniformity of literary and artistic movements.[43] The third and last chapter of the section on the Fifties is dedicated to voices such as Ted Hughes' and Geoffrey Hill's and is called "Negotiations."

Corcoran's choices are matched in Italian studies of English literature. The section dedicated to poetry of the second half of the twentieth century in *Storia della Letteratura inglese* (History of English Literature) edited by Paolo Bertinetti (2000) begins with a paragraph on Larkin and the Movement, followed by others dedicated to single poets. In the chapter "La poesia del dopoguerra" (Poetry after the War) in *Storia della civiltà letteraria inglese* (History of English Literary Civilization), edited by Franco Marenco (1996), Renzo S. Crivelli dedicates a paragraph to the Movement, in which he focuses on the critical debate related to it ("the war of the anthologies" which characterizes nearly a decade), before moving on to the analysis of single poets.

Thom Gunn and the Movement

As mentioned in the previous paragraphs, most of the poets in Conquest's anthology showed a more or less pronounced resistance to being included in the Movement. This is also true for Thom Gunn; beyond simply denying his involvement, Gunn refused on several occasions to acknowledge its existence. In many interviews the poet stated his complete separation from that "journalistic promotion" which in his eyes had only the effect (partly positive) of publicizing new talents. For him, the term Movement had the value of an epoch marker:

> When I started publishing I found myself identified with some people who eventually became classed as the Movement. However, my contention is that the Movement didn't really exist: what we had in common was a period style. I'm pretty sure I'm right because people not included in the Movement wrote in the same style [SL 219].
>
> About six months ago, somebody introduced me before a reading, saying that I had been a member of the Movement. Well, it wasn't anything that one was a member of. I never met Philip Larkin, and I'd met very few of the others by the time the Movement is supposed to have started. People love to classify: a group of new poets came up all at once, so all of us—except Ted Hughes, who turned up a little bit later—were classed as a movement. But I'm glad to see that most people who mention me as associated with the Movement say that I'm rather different from the rest of them.[44]

The fact that his poetry—even from the Fifties—is distinguishable in both tone and subject from that of the other poets included in Conquest's anthology is recognized by most critics, including Italians.[45] For example, in his introductory essay to the first Italian edition of a selection of poetry by Gunn (*I miei tristi capitani e altre poesie*, 1968), entitled "Thom Gunn e il Nuovo Movimento" (Thom Gunn and the New Movement), Agostino Lombardo says:

> although sharing, and clearly demonstrating, the mood of the New Movement ... he moves ... on more open and risky (but for that reason more fertile) ground, than most of his contemporaries.[46]

Also Giorgio Melchiori ("Il Nuovo Movimento e i giovani arrabbiati" [The New Movement and The Angry Young Men]), describing the Fifties anthologies and the grouping of the new young poets, stresses Gunn's marked differences from them:

> Alongside them [Kingsley Amis, Robert Conquest, Donald Davie, D.J. Enright, John Holloway, Elizabeth Jennings, Philip Larkin, John Wain] it was customary to name another younger ... and more famous poet, Thom Gunn; but a widespread impression holds that his inclusion among these is somewhat arbitrary; the new movement derived, in a certain sense, from him.[47]

Alberto Arbasino confirms this opinion of Gunn's difference from other Movement poets. The title of his article, "Thom in Frisco," accentuates Gunn's cosmopolitanism and choice to settle in the American environment (note the use of the colloquial "Frisco" for San Francisco). In Arbasino's view, "inside the dutiful gloom of the Movement in the postwar anthologies, its moans, its howls, its deaths," Gunn distinguishes himself as "leader ... of the most intense and seductive poetry in the current production of English literary creation."[48]

In the Sixties, especially after the publication of *Selected Poems by Thom Gunn and Ted Hughes* (1962), Gunn is often associated with Ted Hughes, who occupies a decidedly anomalous position in the Movement. His poems are not found in Conquest's *New Lines* or Enright's *Poets of the Fifties*, but appear in the anthology edited by A. Alvarez, *The New Poetry* (where an extremely negative judgment of the Movement is given) and the book edited by Philip Hobsbaum (*A Group Anthology*, 1963). Hobsbaum forms a new association of poets (among them Hughes, Martin Bell, Alan Brownjohn, Julian and Catherine Cooper, Edward Lucie-Smith, George MacBeth, Peter Porter, and Peter Redgrove), revolving around the literary workshops he founded in the late Fifties, whose principal common denominator was their openness to the problem of violence.

Among Gunn's poems in Conquest's anthology, *New Lines* ("Lerici," "On the Move," "Human Condition," "Merlin in the Cave: He Speculates Without a Book," "Autumn Chapter in a Novel," "A Plan of Self-Subjection," "Puss in the Boots to the Giant," "Inherited Estate") only one, "Lerici"—though not very English in attitude—is chosen from Gunn's first collection. The others come from the second, *The Sense of Movement* (1957), completed and published after his move to the United States. As we will see in a later chapter, *The Sense of Movement*, despite being English in feeling and form, begins to reveal, especially in the subject matter, the influence of his new American world. It is not surprising, therefore, that most critics considered his poems "eccentric" in respect to the other poets in the anthology.

Gunn's association with the Movement, besides being arbitrary in his view, is of very short duration because of his gradual estrangement from the English literary scene and his insertion into the American one. His encounter with this new world, the teachings of American poet/critic Yvor Winters, his exposure to a tradition completely different from that which he inherited in England, were all destined to play fundamental roles in his artistic evolution and leave an indelible imprint on his style. As he matured, Gunn was more disposed to respond to diverse influences and stimuli, and to express them in verses that were increasingly varied in theme and form.

Choosing to live overseas and leaving the European scene ("I am so far away from it — and I am certainly not part of the European scene")[49] also changed his attitude to the English poetry of his contemporaries, the poets with whom he had been associated in the years of the Movement's promotion. In an interview with Ian Hamilton, Gunn insisted on the greater richness of American poetry, than English poetry, whose range, excepting some talents like Donald Davie, Ted Hughes, and Philip Larkin, seemed rather discouraging.⁵⁰ Gunn's position on Larkin is interesting: "a wonderful poet, but a bad influence" on the English poetry of future generations ("there is no daring left in the people who learned from Larkin")⁵¹:

> He [Larkin] made people less romantic, less ready to dare, more timid. He writes so delightfully of the suburban, and of failure, and things like that, that they feel that's enough.⁵²

Even in Larkin's poems from the 1950s, some of which are included in Conquest's anthology, Gunn admires the "least Larkinesque" aspects, those essentially outside of the major traits of the Movement (self-control, formal discipline, provincialism, etc.), of which Larkin is commonly considered one of the major exponents:

> Philip Larkin was an extraordinary revelation when I first read him in 1954.... there was a poem I really admired tremendously, called "Wedding Wind." It's a very Lawrentian poem, not a Larkinesque Larkin poem, and it's very good, too. The poems I like best by Larkin are those that are least like Larkin ... a bit like Lawrence, perhaps, rather than what one thinks of as Larkin — Larkin the irritable, Larkin the suburban. He's dealing much more with passions and the unironic in such poems, and I think he did it splendidly.⁵³

This passage confirms Gunn's sense of being outside of the Movement (whatever that term might mean). Following his move to America, his timbre and style are open to new stimuli and experimentation. He liked to call himself "an Anglo-American poet."

In the final analysis, connecting Gunn to the Movement is legitimate, since the Movement was the point of departure for his artistic journey. He shared tastes, sensibility, and language — whether or not deliberately — with other English poets who appeared on the literary scene at the same time. He also shared a similar cultural climate, one that influenced his early work, in which we detect formal choices that are quite typical of English poetry in the Fifties.

CHAPTER I

"I'm an Anglo-American poet":
Profile of Thom Gunn

Premise

In the last decades of the twentieth century there emerges, in the Anglo-American arena, a sudden development of the biographical genre, and especially biographies of artists written with the intention of popularizing them — in which the subject becomes the hero of a more or less hagiographic story — and other times, with appropriately critical intentions.[1] Biographies of living artists are less frequent because of their inevitable incompleteness, the fact that the human and artistic trajectory of their protagonist has not been completed, rendering a full picture impossible. The pitfalls and limitations of biography are clearly pinpointed by Thom Gunn in his essay "My Life up to Now":

> The danger of biography, and equally of autobiography, is that it can muddy poetry by confusing it with its source. James's word for the source of a work, its "germ," is wonderfully suggestive because the source bears the same relation to the finished work as the seed does to the tree — nothing is the same, all has developed, the historical truth of the germ is superseded by the derived but completely different artistic truth of the fiction [*OP* 187].

Acknowledging this invitation to look in the life of the author for nothing more than the germ of his work, we will attempt to trace it in this poet, seeking only those experiences most essential to his artistic development. Other than the above-cited autobiographical essay, the primary source is interviews, among which is the one granted to James Campbell, and published in the series *Between the Lines* in 2000.[2]

Artistic Development

Thomson William Gunn was born August 29, 1929, at Gravesend, a small city in Kent, to journalist Herbert Smith Gunn and Ann Charlotte Thomson.

His mother committed suicide when the poet was fourteen, causing a traumatic experience that he evoked in his poem, "The Gas Poker," published in *Boss Cupid*.[3] Both parents were of Scottish origin. Unlike his mother, to whom the poet was deeply attached, his father was immersed in his own work, and never established any intimacy with his son. The situation got worse after the parents' divorce, when Gunn was nine years old:

> He [my father] and my mother were divorced when I was eight or nine, and I never found myself close to him. Neither of us ever invited each other into any intimacy: from my mid-teens onward we were jealous and suspicious of each other, content merely to do our duty and no more [*OP* 169].

Unlike the father, who was detached and distant, the mother figure and her family (Baptists "on the way to becoming Methodists..., pacifists, Keir Hardie socialists, and anti-royalists" *OP* 170) had a daydream aura that fascinated Gunn from an early age: "I was close to my mother and, while I never heard much about my father's family, the history of my mother's formed a kind of basic mythology for me" (*OP* 169).[4] Despite his mother's religious background, Gunn did not grow up in a churchy climate; instead, to cite his own words, "my brother and I were brought up in no religion at all" (*OP* 170). He never professed any faith and always considered himself an "atheist humanist."[5]

When Gunn was eight, his family moved permanently to Hampstead, where he spent a typically middle-class, peaceful childhood, finding plenty of inspiration for poetry in his home. Books were always an important part of his life, due to his mother's influence:

> And the house was full of books. When she was pregnant with me she read the whole of Gibbon's *History*. From her I got the complete implicit idea, from as far back as I can remember, of books as not just a commentary on life but part of its continuing activity [*OP* 170].

His artistic nature showed early; at a young age he wrote novels, plays and poetry, all of which he promptly destroyed. His first serious literary effort, encouraged by his mother, was a novel called *The Flirt*, written when he was twelve years old; it is about a colonel who resembled his father. In this period, and for the duration of his adolescence, the most important influences were not novelists, however, but poets: "In my teens I became concerned with grandiloquence, under the influence first of Marlowe and Keats, then of Milton, then of Victorians like Tennyson and Meredith" (*OP* 172). Meredith was the only one of these who also wrote fiction, but Gunn appreciated his poetry more than his prose, finding it richer in that "grandiloquence" he sought in his reading of the period.

After attending University College School of London for ten years, Gunn served in the military for two years, a highly influential experience because, as he said, it gave him greater contact with life and developed his interest in the "soldier type" found in some of his poetry:

> My imagination retreated too easily into the world before my mother's death, a world that in practice excluded most of the 20th century. I read an enormous number of 19th century novels in my teens. It was the present that I couldn't deal with in my imagination or in fact. The army, surprisingly, had been of some help, by forcing me into what were for me extreme situations with which it was necessary to cope for the sake of survival. But by twenty-one I was strangely immature, a good deal more so than any of my friends [*OP* 173].[6]

The soldiers in the first collections (from *Fighting Terms* to *My Sad Captains*) are characterized by their passivity in the face of violence, and obtuse insensitivity to pain. Paradoxically, this passivity and insensitivity become a form of innocence, as in the poem called "Innocence" (*My Sad Captains*) in which the German soldier "Could watch the fat burn with a violet flame / And feel disgusted only at the smell" (*CP* 100, ll. 21–22). The years of military service, evoked in "Clean Clothes: A Soldier's Song,"[7] put him in touch with some of the harder facts of life, hitherto unknown by him. He also remembers the discomfort, tedium, and depression of these years:

> I don't think of it [National Service] as a happy experience. I think of it as an experience of prolonged boredom. But I did find out something about my limits. I was a spoilt middle-class boy, and it was good for me in basic training to have to sleep between blankets. It was also good for me to have to accept that ignorant people were in power over me and to have to deal with that as intelligently as I could. I learned a lot of negative things that it was about time I learned. I don't regret anything that's happened to me, and I don't regret National Service, but it did contain a lot of wasted time, boredom, drudgery.[8]

Although it brought him into contact with what the poet called "extreme situations," military service also provided, thanks to many hours of enforced idleness, occasion to read Proust's *Recherche*, which made him wish to imitate the French novelist and go to Paris. Once there, he quickly abandoned this project, realizing that "he was losing himself in a mass of psychological insights and complicated syntax."[9] This sentence is interesting because it shows Gunn's first clear perception of himself. During adolescence and early adulthood, Gunn oscillated between opposite temptations: one, towards literature that was boundless, various and complex (like *Recherche*) and the other, towards that which was short and concise; and also, between abundance and measure, eloquence and reserve.

Baudelaire's poetry exerted a heavy influence:

> Baudelaire has always been a tremendous influence on me. I've always loved his poetry. I was attracted first of all by his desire to be shocking, which doesn't interest me at all now. What I have come to love are the later poems, like "Le Cygne" or ["Les Sept Vieillards"].... They are wonderful, so complicatedly put together.[10]

Gunn's artistic development passed through many phases before he recognized himself as a poet:

> In my teens I wanted to be a novelist. I read so many Victorian novels that later when I did my undergraduate work I didn't need to read any more to answer the

novel questions on the exams. I wanted to be a novelist very much in the Victorian sense [*SL* 222].

Other than his failed attempt to imitate Proust, Gunn's choice of poetry also arose from his awareness of the difficulty of writing dialogue: "When I was about 20, ... I found out that I wasn't cut out to be a novelist. I just couldn't write dialogue."[11] However, an aspiration to diversification continued when he had chosen poetry, as he wanted at all costs to avoid specialization and to write all kinds of poetry:

> After a while, you find you're better at one form than at others, or you like one form better than others, and so you tend to, after you've been writing poetry for ten years or so, your thoughts, your ideas come to you very much in terms of poems.... at some stage or other I realized I wanted to be in at least one respect like an Elizabethan like Ben Jonson, and I — Ben Jonson and pretty well all of his contemporaries thought that one should be able to write in every possible different style — songs for plays here, plays of different sorts there, maybe philosophical poems, epistles so there wasn't the same kind of specialization of style that we consider appropriate nowadays — and <u>I wanted to be a various poet</u>.[12]

He realized these aspirations primarily through mediating between different poetic traditions (English and American), between meter and free verse, and between past and present.

The apprenticeship that served to clarify his idea of himself as a poet took place at Trinity College, Cambridge (1950–53), where he studied literature and wrote poetry. He describes these years as "an escape from the drudgery of the army into the bright and tranquil life of the mind" (*OP* 157), a serene Parnassus where he discovered Chaucer and Donne's poetry. At the end of his first year of study, Gunn published a poem in the university magazine *Cambridge Today*, which featured mostly young undergraduate writers. During this phase of immersion in the world of culture he followed an equally fertile path into nature, making an intoxicating discovery. His summer vacation in the French countryside gave him a profound sense of physical and spiritual freedom, along with a spontaneous creative impulse that resulted in several poems which combined the strong influence of Shakespeare, Donne, Yeats, and Auden with the beginnings of a personal style.

In Gunn's Cambridge years, F.R. Leavis played an important role in his aesthetic development. Gunn absorbed more than Leavis's ideas; from the older man he acquired a taste for precise expression, self-control, formal discipline, objectivity, and essentialism. As he says,

> I went to the lectures of F.R. Leavis, then in his prime, whose emphasis on the "realized" in imagery and on the way in which verse movement is an essential part of the poet's exploration were all-important for me [*OP* 175].
>
> I only met F.R. Leavis once, at a party, but I was very influenced by him. The interesting thing about Leavis is that he's considered such an orthodoxy now, whereas he was considered a bad boy at that time, and was not liked by the literary journalists I had mostly read up to then. He was not, probably, a very like-

able person, but he had a very interesting view of literature, seeing it as a part of life.[13]

The effects of his teachings (related to ideas circulated thirty years earlier by Hulme and Pound and, later, T.S. Eliot) showed up in Gunn's first volume, *Fighting Terms*, published by Fantasy Press of Oxford in 1954. In later editions (New York: Hawk's Well Press, 1958; London: Faber & Faber, 1962), the poet cut and revised his poetry in ways he later criticized, convinced that he had taken away the book's personal stamp:

> And I revised the whole of my first book, *Fighting Terms*, when it came out in the U.S. in 1958. Then Faber reissued it in 1962, and I de-revised it! I kept trying to tidy up something better left alone. All I seemed to do was remove what was maybe the book's only charm, a certain rhetorical awkwardness.[14]

What Gunn defined as "a theory of pose" was taking shape in his poetry. It was influenced by Yeats's theory of the mask, by the dramatic personae of Donne and Shakespeare, and by the behavior of the heroes in Stendhal's fiction.

> The theory of pose was this: everyone plays a part, whether he knows it or not, so he might as well deliberately design a part, or a series of parts, for himself. Only a psychopath or a very good actor is in danger of becoming his part. One who is neither psychopath nor actor is left in an interesting place somewhere in between the starting point — the bare undefined and undirected self, if it ever existed — and the chosen part [*OP* 162].

The assumption of a pose, the delineation of a persona in which to objectify the self, and especially the oscillation between the poles of one's own personality and an assumed one, constitute some of the fundamental themes of Gunn's poetic reflection. Even in the poems of his last volume, *Boss Cupid*, dedicated to serial killer Jeffrey Dahmer, who ate his victims, the protagonist is a hero whose mask and behavior are the products of particular social pressures that make him hunger and lust for people he meets and loves. He hungers for possessions and affections previously denied. Gunn's says that the use of the mask and the pose in reference to the figure of the serial killer is related to one of the most famous villains in Shakespeare — Macbeth — revealing, once again, the profound sense of tradition with which Gunn continues to converse, in the style of T.S. Eliot (see Eliot's essay "Tradition and the Individual Talent," 1919)[15]:

> When I wrote these poems, I thought I was just doing the sort of thing Shakespeare did with Macbeth, another serial murderer. I've been surprised by the way people have been so shocked by them.[16]

Gunn links Jeffrey Dahmer to other past heroes who were victims of a cruel fate and a tortured and twisted personality. In the poem, "A Wood Near Athens" (*Boss Cupid*), Dahmer appears alongside history's literary heroes: "But who did get it right? Ruth and Naomi, / Tearaway Romeo and Juliet, / Alyosha, Catherine Earnshaw, Jeffrey Dahmer? / They struggled through the thickets as they could" (*BC* 106, ll. 33–36).

The Cambridge years were essential to Gunn's maturation, thanks to meeting intellectuals like Tony White, who he called "my best reader and most helpful critic" (*OP* 174). White introduced Gunn to the works of Jean-Paul Sartre and Albert Camus, who were outside the academic curricula. He also met John Coleman, Mike Kitay (destined to become his life's companion), and Karl Miller (then director of the *London Review of Books*). Miller was particularly important for helping Gunn to understand, through advice and criticism, the nature of his own poetic inspiration:

> When I wrote a new poem I would give it to him [Karl Miller] for criticism, and he would pin it to the wall above his desk for several days before he told me what he thought of it. He helped me in other and greater ways. He matured my mind amazingly, and I learned from his habit of questioning, of questioning everything. There was always something rather childish about the way I submitted to the enthusiasms of others. If I learned to argue with them a little, it was from him [*OP* 161].

But, to reach true maturity, it is necessary to leave a comfortable academic environment and confront the world. Leaving Cambridge, Gunn spent some months in Rome on a grant, an experience which he remembered with these words:

> I didn't know anybody in Rome, but I had a good time there, I was very poor, I didn't have very much money. I was given a grant, which had been founded in about the year 1910 and which was probably a lot of money in the year 1910, but by the time I was given it, that was very little money, and I couldn't afford to stay in Rome any longer than I did, I was eating those terrible *spaghetti al sugo* from a stall. You know, there is a market somewhere in Rome, where you can get *spaghetti al sugo*, the least expensive, the cheapest plate of spaghetti you can get anywhere. I was getting them and I do not think it was, er ... good nutrition. Yes that is the right expression. But I was very young then, yes, I was twenty three or four.[17]

Right after Rome, he came to America, having obtained a creative writing fellowship at Stanford University in California. The primary reason for moving to the United States was his desire to travel and be reunited with his friend, Mike Kitay. At Stanford, he worked under the direction of poet/critic Yvor Winters, who would exercise a profound effect on him.

During a conference organized by London University's Senate House on the occasion of Gunn's seventieth birthday (October 22, 1999), Karl Miller said Gunn's prime motivation for going to America was the desire to be free from Leavis's sometimes paralyzing influence. This may be true, but it is undeniable that Yvor Winters became, in Gunn's eyes, a sort of American alter ego of Leavis, one who shaped his development in a similar way (directing him to read many American modernists still unknown in England). Winters was just as paralyzing an influence on Gunn, however, which induced him to leave Stanford before Winters could "trim his wings":

> For some of his students his formulations provided a refuge, a harmonious world where everything had already been decided in accordance with certain rules.... I had seen the whole thing happen before, among the students of F.R. Leavis at Cambridge. But on the whole I find Winters' disciples a much humaner and better-tempered lot than Leavis's [SL 207].
>
> People used to say of Leavis that he never influenced poetry, but that's not true. He did influence my poetry.... Leavis and Winters were important to me, mainly because of their technical remarks.... I fought Winters a lot at first. I mean, I quarreled with him and disagreed with him. He kind of liked that.... He liked me in a grim sort of way because I opposed him. I didn't really oppose him that much. I did argue with him, though.[18]

Contact with Winters sometimes had a troubling effect on the young poet, who was used to taking a completely different approach to the traditions of American and English poetry compared to Winters' sometimes iconoclastic attitude towards the masters on whom young Gunn had been raised:

> The first course of Winters' I attended, on "the criticism of poetry," was an immediate shock to my assumptions, in that he set about the systematic demolishing of my favorite twentieth-century poetry, Yeats, in ruthless detail. After Yeats the chosen victim was to be Hopkins, not one of my favorite poets but one I certainly respected [SL 200].

Both Yeats and Hopkins, but particularly the latter, had been presented by Leavis as veritable pillars of the great English tradition (see *New Bearings in English Poetry: A Study of the Contemporary Situation*, 1932) and therefore proposed as models for imitation.

Above all, his relationship with Winters had the merit of introducing Gunn to the American poets William Carlos Williams and Wallace Stevens, who were spokesmen for a major tradition — little known by Gunn — which also encouraged him to try his hand at free verse.[19]

Winters' conception of poetry as a tool for the exploration of reality through language more exact and essential than that of prose became a fundamental principle of Gunn's. However, Gunn avoided acting as Winter's disciple, out of a spirit of self-preservation:

> He was a man of great personal warmth with a deeper love for poetry than I have ever met in anybody else.... However, taken as I was with the charm and authority of the man and with the power of his persuasiveness, it already seemed to me that his conception of a poem was too rigid.... The rigidity seemed to be the result of what I can only call an increasing distaste for the particulars of existence [OP 176].
>
> It would have seemed to him an insult to the poem that it could be used as a gymnasium for the ego. Poetry was an instrument for exploring the truth of things, as far as human beings can explore it, and it can do so with a greater verbal exactitude than prose can manage [OP 176].

That the American critic was a great teacher for Gunn is evidenced by the poet's statements ("he speaks of poetry with a peculiar intimacy and dedication for the art about which he had more to tell than anyone else I have known" *SL* 211), and by the poem dedicated "To Yvor Winters, 1955," where part of the tribute is paid by stylistic imitation. In the autobiographical essay, "On a Drying Hill, *Yvor Winters,*" Gunn focuses on the intellectual and humane qualities of his American teacher. A 2003 edition of Winters' selected poems opens with Gunn's interesting and impassioned introduction that emphasizes Winters' vexed trials of various poetic forms, which range from the imagistic fragments of the early period to the dense and archaic language of the late period, what D.H. Lawrence would have called "poetry of the past." "It is now a *closed* poetry," writes Gunn.[20]

One of the essential traits of Winters' personality and teaching method is the search for balance between opposites, for the happy medium between "wisdom and emotion" which Gunn calls "the disconcerting oppositions between the rigor of his critical presence and what I could almost call the tenderness of his private presence" (*SL* 211).

Winters exercised a profound influence when Gunn was still willing to learn, but Gunn was never so ingenuous as to let himself be carried away "by his ideas of what a poem should be — which were perhaps rather narrow."[21] Among the debts Gunn owes to Winters is learning the need for extreme concentration on poetic form and rhythm, which are not only vehicles for meaning, but which also, at the same time, modify it: "Winters was one of the few people I have ever come across who has spoken — spoken at all, let alone intelligibly — about the way meter works and about the way poetic movement (whether in metrical or in free verse) influences poetic meaning" (*SL* 203).

Taken in by American cultural influences, Gunn composed most of the poems of his second collection during his first year there. He calls *The Sense of Movement* (1957) a second work of apprenticeship:

> *The Sense of Movement*, then, was a much more sophisticated book than my first collection had been, but a much less independent one. There is a lot of Winters in it, a fair amount of Yeats, and a great deal of raw Sartre (strange bedfellows!). It was really a second work of apprenticeship. The poems make much use of the word "will." It was a favourite word of Sartre's and one that Winters appreciated, but they each meant something very different by it. What I meant by it was, ultimately, a mere Yeatsian willfulness. I was at my usual game of stealing what could be of use to me [*OP* 176–77].

As he says, the poet is still in a formative phase, in search of stimuli, models, and imitable examples that will help him realize his own potential. The influence of the American environment, with its myths and living examples, began to bear fruit, even though in this phase the distinctive imprint was definitely English. His encounter with this new reality showed especially in the themes and imagery. Instead of the elaborate metaphors of the first collection, those "great personages" of traditional literature ("I had been reading so much Shakespeare, Donne and Stendhal, and I was writing about the heroic"),[22] America supplied new themes and environments, among which stand out the images of motorcyclists inspired by Marlon Brando in *The Wild One* by Laszlo Benedek (1954). Though these themes might have been quintessentially American, Gunn's rhythms remained essentially English.[23]

The word "will" and its multiple echoes in literary tradition, especially Elizabethan, constitute the leitmotif of the collection. Despite his attentive reading of Shakespeare and the classics, the poet was completely uninformed, in the fifties, of the sexual connotations of the word "will" in Elizabethan drama and poetry.

> Well ... I didn't know, what I later learned, that "will" in Shakespeare refers to the penis, or more generally to the sexual organs of either sex. I'd got a degree from Cambridge without ever having been informed of this fact. None of the editions of the sonnets that I used told me this. I couldn't have known it, and I don't think any of my friends knew it either, though, like a lot of people at university, I learned more from my friends than I did from my teachers. I think I was unconsciously using it for that, though.... It was very much a male kind of will, a penis-like will.[24]

At the end of his scholarship year at Stanford, Gunn taught for almost a year at the University of Texas at San Antonio, where Mike Kitay was in active service in the Air Force. This first teaching assignment was neither profitable nor satisfying for Gunn:

> I was a really terrible teacher, didn't know anything about it. The football players who were in my freshman English class were very amused by me, and I was very amused by them, so we all got on well. But that was a year of considerable tedium, and dust storms, and other Texan things like that.[25]

The poet returned to Stanford to enroll in the Ph.D. program and take creative writing courses with Yvor Winters, but by now his apprenticeship was over and school work began to bore him. He left Stanford as soon as he received an offer to teach at the University of California at Berkeley in 1958.

During his year in Texas, Gunn made a brief visit to Los Angeles, where he had the opportunity to meet Christopher Isherwood, whose transparency and clarity of both style and character he admired. Isherwood could "present complexity through the elegance of simplicity, but without ever reducing it to mere simplicity" (*OP* 177). One of the qualities Gunn most admired in Isherwood's work was the colloquial immediacy of the style, elegant but discreet, not calling attention to itself, never stooping to self-reference, a style that "can handle the most banal of experiences and is also capable of eloquence" (*SL* 181). Gunn dedicates to Isherwood both the essay "Getting Things Right" (1990) and a poem called "To Isherwood Dying." By repeating with small variations the words, "It could be," the poet compares Isherwood's past and present, his unfulfilled expectations of a courtship during his Berlin sojourn (the voices and whistles of boys, unfortunately not directed at him), and the sounds of his current California residence, including the voice of death that invites him to declare his sexual preference ("come out") before dying:

> You hear a single whistle call
> *Come out*
> *Come out into the cold.*
> Courting insistent and impersonal.
> [*CP* 445, ll. 18–21][26]

Gunn feels disappointed that recent critics do not praise Isherwood's transparency of style, which he appreciates so greatly; instead, they are oriented towards ambiguity, irony, and paradox, being convinced that only a contorted style can suggest true complexity or profundity:

> The prestigious critics of today are interested in "indeterminacy" and writing that subverts itself, nor is solipsistic confusion frowned upon. Portentousness, jargon, imprecision, and mannerism are widely accepted and imitated in literary criticism now—and Isherwood's kind of transparency, since it clearly springs from a rigorous authorial control, is therefore to be considered authoritarian, thus reactionary, thus fascist [*SL* 182].

Next, Gunn stayed a few months in Berlin, where he came into contact with the reality of the war and what it meant, expressing it in the poem, "Berlin in Ruins: Anhalter Bahnhof" (*Touch*, 1967). In its signs of the tarnished present, the poem evokes the ineradicable monsters of the past, the collective hysteria which involved entire populations:

> The mind does not rest without peril
> among the tarnished blades of laurel:
>
> it may cut on them, it may fester
> —until it throbs with a revived fear
> of the dark hysteric conqueror.
> [*CP* 157, ll. 11–15]

Later he returned to America, establishing San Francisco as a permanent residence. In the city which attracted him particularly by its liberal customs and tolerant atmosphere, he found his ideal habitat:

> I went to San Francisco often. It was quite an open city. Flourishing whorehouses, a lot of gay bars. I was taken to my first gay bar, and you might say I haven't looked back since. The freedom this city offers to homosexuals was a big attraction. One day I was walking down Columbus Avenue in the fog ... and I suddenly thought that the ultimate happiness would be for me and Mike to settle in San Francisco. And here we are, still.[27]

America, with its open spaces, mixture of cultures and races, and homosexuals, especially in northern California, aroused in Gunn a sense of liberty—physical and emotional—which had a definitive role in the decision to move there:

> Certainly, you get the sense of spaciousness. When I first went back to England, I got an incredible sense of claustrophobia which was not only because the streets were narrower and things like that, but it's very difficult to tie down the potentiality, to find what it comes from.[28]

Like other homosexual artists, including W.H. Auden and Christopher Isherwood, Gunn found that the United States offered freedom of movement and space for his own life and artistic activities. However, tolerance of homosexuals and their integration into the larger American society, was limited to certain places (like San Francisco) and occurred only after the sixties. The fifties were a particularly reactionary and repressive era, not only in England, but in America as well. Gunn never revealed his homosexuality to his mentor Yvor Winters even though their relationship was close and friendly: "He [Winters] would have been *appalled* at the idea that I was queer."[29]

Even though he continued to publish his poems in England with Faber & Faber, and to maintain, at least initially, a relationship with his early environment, even so far as becoming an "Anglo-American poet," as he loved to call himself,[30] the choice of America was due in part to his need to extricate himself from the "latest fashions."

> If I'm conscious of the exact audience for which I'm writing, it pretty well dries me up, and the less conscious I am of a specific audience, the better I am ... and maybe this connects back with why I live here, because not being particularly read and not being particularly known except by very small groups here, this can be a great advantage to me — I can have my cake and eat it because I can have popularity in England but I don't need to be present on the scene of the popularity and this is enormously convenient.[31]

What Gunn calls "enormously convenient" had also, over time, some less positive effects. On the one hand, he was not entirely integrated into the American literary scene; on the other hand, his fame in England steadily decreased after his move to the United States. While lately he has reappeared on the English literary scene, especially after the publication of *The Man with Night Sweats* (1992), which contains elegies dedicated to AIDS sufferers, Gunn does not appear in most contemporary English poetry courses in British universities. With the exception of an edition of the *PN Review* and a monograph of *Agenda*, published on the occasions of his sixtieth and seventieth birthdays, respectively,[32] recent criticism pays scant attention to his work. Even his death received no significant press.[33] Not for some time has a monograph on Gunn been published, and the most recent essays (with some exceptions) are focused on particular aspects of his poetry (such as gay issues and the AIDS epidemic).[34]

Besides poetry, Gunn wrote criticism, revealing a continuing interest in the contemporary literary scene, both American and British. Between 1958 and 1964 he was reviewer at *Yale Review*, a job he later abandoned because he felt increasingly dissatisfied "with the business of making comparatively fast judgments on contemporary poets" (*OP* 178). After 1964, Gunn continued to write reviews and essays, but only "about poets I liked," and on works to which he could dedicate much time:

> I stopped regular reviewing because I felt more and more that I had to live with a book for some time before I could really find out its value for me. And I was

less ready to say unkind things about those who were practicing the same art as I was, however differently [*OP* 179].[35]

One of the fruits of this new focus was his 1968 edition of Fulke Greville's poetry, preceded by a carefully documented introduction. He followed this in 1974 with an edition of Ben Jonson's poetry, and one of Charlie Hinkle's poetry (co-edited with William McPherson in 1988). He wrote critical essays, some of which were autobiographical, and published them in *The Occasions of Poetry* (1982), edited by Clive Wilmer, and *Shelf Life: Essays, Memoirs and an Interview* (1993). He published various essays and reviews in American and British journals, and, for Faber & Faber, an edition of poetry by Ezra Pound (2000). Gunn's introduction to this work is an impassioned defense of Pound's poetry ("he is demonstrably a poet of the highest order")[36] and his moral integrity.[37] Gunn consistently published critical essays in several literary magazines, revealing his constant awareness of culture, and especially of the poetry of his time. Gunn's cultural awareness is much more open and free from preconceptions because, in both prose and poetry, he always refused any identification or simple association with a particular group or school and never adhered to any manifesto. Remember his sharp reaction to the "journalistic invention" of the Movement of the Fifties. In his studies of poets of the past as well as of the young up-and-comers, he is always attracted to individual figures, usually quite different from one another, but rarely to schools or groups ("Another poet I admire tremendously, who's extremely different from Powell is August Kleinzahler.... I have sympathies with such a broad range of poetry: I'm surprised that everybody doesn't").[38] His judgment is detached and decidedly cool towards recent American movements (apart from the Beats of the Fifties),[39] such as the Language Poets, the New Formalists, and even the Black Mountain Poets (with the exception of Robert Creeley and Robert Duncan, whom Gunn admires):

> I am not interested in movements, and so I am not interested in the New Formalists and I am not interested in the Language Poets on the other hand. Both strike me as a big bore. They don't interest me. I mean, I read them but I am bored by them.[40]

What counts most is a perfect balance between form and content, and not obedience to particular aesthetic or formal principles; theory in itself, not aimed at the refinement of practice, is beyond his interests ("Poetics is such a big word nowadays, such a fashionable word.... I'm interested in writing poetry and I'm genuinely not very interested in the theory of poetry" *SL* 227). When they do not create a real innovation, schools of poetry are sterile, useless experiments which limit new talents rather than contributing to their stimulation and development: "I don't think I'm particularly against schools as such.... But I think that they are only useful when there is a central monolithic tradition that is worth opposing. And we don't have such a central tradition now" (*SL* 227–28). Movements that create a manifesto and a well-defined poetics, whether at the thematic or formal level, are useful, according to Gunn, only when they are mouthpieces for counter-currents. Only when art is innovative and revolutionary, determined to fight and replace a tradition proven to be obsolete and limiting by its contemporaries, can such a thing as a "movement" prove helpful.[41]

In 1961 the poet publishes his third collection of poems, *My Sad Captains*, a particularly important book that signals a turning point in his work:

> The collection is divided into two parts. The first is the culmination of my old style — metrical and rational but maybe starting to get a little more humane. The second half consists of a taking up of that humane impulse in a series of poems in syllabics [*OP* 179].

These words suggest how conscious Gunn was of the lack of human warmth in the preceding collections. The first poems, characterized by violent scenes,[42] insist on the figure of the "elect," of the hero capable of challenging the void, like Nietzsche or Sartre. Images of common people, or of humanity conscious of its own limits and finitude, were almost non-existent. Opening himself to the external world, and abandoning the heroic pose, coincide with his experimentation in a new poetic form called "syllabics,"[43] which was a vehicle for gradual access to free verse:

> When I started writing in England in the late '40s and early '50s, I did what was fashionable. I thought I was being independent, but actually I was just imitating what other people were doing, which was writing in metre and rhyme. Then I came over to America and I discovered the works of the Modernists, who weren't in print in England when I left, in 1954, amazing as that is to realize.... I wanted to write free verse, but it's not that easy suddenly changing. It's very difficult getting that iambic-thump out of your ear. And so I invented a way for myself. I wrote syllabics.... using syllabics was a way of teaching myself free verse rhythms.[44]

Though never abandoning traditional meter, Gunn began, in *My Sad Captains*, to experiment with free verse. He accompanied formal experimentation with new themes:

> I have not abandoned metre, and in trying to write in both free verse and metre I think I am different from a lot of my contemporaries. Poets who started writing in the early fifties began with metre and rhyme, but most of them — especially the Americans — who switched to free verse at the end of the decade rounded on their earlier work with all the savagery of the freshly converted. I haven't done so: there are things I can do in the one form that I can't do in the other, and I wouldn't gladly relinquish either [*OP* 179].

With regard to the inherent potential of both forms, Gunn refers to an essay by D.H. Lawrence (the only English poet, in his view, who had fruitfully experimented with free verse), titled "Poetry of the Present" (1919), and to his distinction between "poetry of the past" and "poetry of the present." In Gunn's opinion, metrical verse corresponds to Lawrence's definition of "poetry of the past" (but also to "poetry of the future"), and signifies a type of poetry that treats something which has occurred, such as events, acts, and thoughts. In contrast, free verse reflects Lawrence's definition of "poetry of the present," a poetry which is concerned with the future, like a "thought in progress." "Free forms," says Gunn, "invite improvisation and are hospitable to the fragmentary details of one's life."[45]

Parallel to his interest in free verse, Gunn was exploring the new voices of American poetry, mostly unknown by the English public, which came out in 1963 in an anthology called *Five American Poets: Edgar Bowers, Howard Nemerov, Haym Plutzik, Louis Simpson, William Stafford*, which he co-edited with Ted Hughes. The previous year the poetry of Thom Gunn and Ted Hughes had come out together in a collection by Faber & Faber. From this time until the eighties, the two poets would often appear together in anthologies, and they would be closely linked in the public eye.[46]

The association between Gunn and Hughes, who are very different stylistically, thematically, and temperamentally (Hughes' romantic passion contrasting with Gunn's cold, formal rigor), is not the result of a deep affinity, but of editorial operations, the effects of which were not dissimilar to the journalistic and publicity promotions of the Movement in the Fifties:

> It was our editor Charles Monteith's idea that we should publish the joint *Selected Poems*.... We emerged at about the same time, and he thought that neither of us was sufficiently well-known to have his own *Selected Poems*. But a *Selected Poems* of the two of us would be ideal. Originally, his idea was to include Philip Larkin as well. Larkin was older than us and had started publishing earlier, but he didn't get well known until about that time.... It was a publisher's device that associated us, that and the fact that we were both considered to be violent.[47]

In 1964 Gunn returned to London where he spent "a year of great happiness" (*OP* 180). For the first time, he participated in a recording of his poems organized by the British Council, later published under the title *The Poet Speaks* (1965), together with poems by Ted Hughes, Sylvia Plath, and Peter Porter. This was a particularly interesting experience, but it was followed by later recordings which left the poet unsatisfied: "All [my records] are terrible, either because I was not reading at my best or because of the conditions of recording. *The Poet Speaks* is the only one I like" (*OP* 181).

Also in London, Gunn collaborated with his brother Ander on a volume called *Positives* (1966), in which visual and verbal elements, Ander's photographs and Thom's verses, interact:

> I had always wanted to work with pictures, and he [Ander] was taking just the kind that made a starting point for my imagination.... I was never very sure whether what I was writing opposite the photographs were poems or captions—they were somewhere between the two, I suspect [*OP* 181].

Most of the poems in this collection integrate well with the images they accompany, and show that Gunn is open to experiments and stimuli of different kinds. This is his first experiment with free verse (some parts are written in syllabics, others in free verse). The experiment of a dual-media expression (photography and poetry) was limited to this one collection, which was not greatly praised by critics.[48] Even though Gunn did not pursue further the possibility of working with photographs, the visual arts continued to play a major role in his poetry. In "Before the Carnival" (*The Sense of Movement*), "In Santa Maria del Popolo" (*My Sad Captains*), "Bravery" (*Touch*), "Expression," "Selves" (*The Passages of Joy*), "Her Pet" (*The Man with Night Sweats*), and "Painting by Vuillard" (*Boss Cupid*), certain elements were inspired by a picture or sculpture, the observation of which occasioned a particular intersection between a visual image from the past and contemporary reality, which was far more prosaic. Gunn's juxtaposition suggests an experimentation with T.S. Eliot's mythic method.

The year in London provided the occasion to finish one of his most ambitious (though perhaps less successful) projects, "Misanthropos," begun nearly two years earlier in San Francisco and conceived "at times as science fiction and at times as pastoral" (*OP* 180). Initially planned as a single poem, it become a narrative cycle composed of seventeen parts, which were then inserted in the center of the collection *Touch*[49]:

> There was one poem I was working on with which I had a different kind of problem, though it turned out simply to be a matter of scale.... My trouble with it, I began to realize, was that there was too much exposition for me to cram into a single short poem. Then somewhat later..., I fell on the notion that perhaps I could extend it into a long poem, or rather a series of poems in different forms that would add up to a narrative [*OP* 180].

The "Misanthropos" cycle concerns the survival of a man in a nuclear catastrophe, and describes, primarily through bodily sensations, the impact on the protagonist of the desolation surrounding him, the disease that gradually invades him, the slow and arduous recovery of memory, the meeting with other survivors, and the realization of the need to coexist with them because there is no other solution:

> Turn out toward others, meeting their look at full,
>   Until you have completely stared
> On all there is to see. Immeasurable,
>   The dust yet to be shared.
> [*CP* 151, 17, ll. 14–16][50]

The next year (1965), Gunn returned to San Francisco with "half thoughts of ultimately moving back to London" (*OP* 180), but the atmosphere so particular to the times held him. America in particular, and in consequence, Europe as well, was experiencing a memorable, revolutionary, historical phase, starting from the late fifties. This counter-cultural and anti-conformist phase was marked by completely new styles of behavior, which were intended to undermine the foundations of the establishment and the bourgeois respectability of the first half of the century. The legendary sixties were animated by human rights and anti-war movements, flower children, the amazing success of the Beatles, the Rolling Stones, and Bob Dylan, and especially by the artificial paradise provided by drugs such as LSD. Opening himself to this type of experience was fundamental to Gunn, both as man and poet, revealing unknown dimensions of his personality, and offering a new source of inspiration:

> I know it is no longer fashionable to say a good word for LSD, but one thing acid does is open up new possibilities. I was about thirty-five when I first took it, and that's a time when one is developing a certain complacency, you feel you know just what you think and have everything in its proper pigeon-hole. LSD shakes complacencies, it opens doors on other worlds. I learned things about my own nature that I'd concealed from myself.[51]

Drug-induced experiences were the inspiration for the collection *Moly*, published in 1971:

> It [the acid-tripping] was an important experience for me, and you should be able to write about *anything* that matters to you. Anyway, nearly all the poems in my fifth book, *Moly*, which I wrote between 1965 and 1970, have some relation to acid.[52]

Gunn always expressed a great appreciation for this experience, which helped liberate him from many inhibitions ("I was more assured as a person, and when you're surer of yourself, you're nicer to others because you're having it easier"),[53] induced him to explore unknown aspects of himself, and played an important role in the full acceptance and expression of his own homosexuality. It is worth emphasizing that the poems in which acceptance of his homosexuality is most apparent are those that are due to the acid experience[54]:

> And now that the great sweep of the acid years is over ... I can't deny the vision of what the world might be like. Everything that we glimpsed — the trust, the brotherhood, the repossession of innocence, the nakedness of spirit — is still a possibility and will continue to be so.[55]

It was also, in his view, a particular phase of his life, an epochal event, related to the atmosphere of those years, yet later regarded with a certain detachment[56]:

> Allen Ginsberg said he went through tremendous psychic change because of taking acid. We all *hoped* for that, and thought that's what we were undergoing at the time. But I'm a little more skeptical about it now.... What we used to take in the '60s was *so strong*. What I've had since then has been, oh, good for sexual play, but very mild. It used to be quite difficult getting up there, but once you got there, once you were peaking, that was great, and you'd start to come down and it was just wonderful from then on. The first stages could be quite difficult, but we never talked about that — we said it was all good.[57]

The collection *Moly* (1971) is a testimony to the discovery of communal life, of total openness to the external world and all of humanity, of a completely natural sexuality, with full reciprocity and awareness. The visionary experience is also present in his next collection *Jack Straw's Castle* (1976), but here the atmosphere is darker and the liberation occurs not in a garden (as in *Moly*) but in a castle which takes on some aspects of a prison. When this happens, the dream transforms into a nightmare:

Moly was a very happy book because taking drugs made me very happy. It's a book partly about dreams, whereas the next book, *Jack Straw's Castle*, has a nightmare sequence at its center. I lifted the furies direct from Dante.[58]

According to Clive Wilmer, *Jack Straw's Castle* is "a strikingly experimental book": "there are rhymed stanzas, heroic couplets, songs, and free verse both in the cadenced Whitmanesque long line and in the short, tense, run-over line associated with William Carlos Williams."[59]

In 1968, Gunn participated for the first time in a public reading of his poetry, an experience destined to repeat itself in coming years, and one that proved an effective means of communication:

> I learned that I should treat a poetry reading not as a recital for a bunch of devotees, which my audiences were clearly not, but more as an entertainment — and advertisement for poetry as a whole [*OP* 183].

In the late sixties, Gunn became interested in Robert Duncan's poetry, and wrote essays and poems on him, such as "Duncan," which opens the collection *Boss Cupid*. Duncan's work attracts him particularly for the importance it gives to the compositional act, conceived as a search into unknown realms and an instrument of self-knowledge, "where you find yourself using limbs and organs you didn't know you possessed" (*OP* 183). Duncan is also a poet who, much earlier than Gunn, had made peace with his homosexuality. In repressive, pre-sixties society, homosexuals were "forced into enclaves ... like ghettos" (*OP* 124), with the alienating and devastating effect of making them feel constrained to embrace stereotypical behaviors and a lifestyle generally identified with their "eccentricity":

> It is due more to Duncan than to any other single poet that modern American poetry, in all its inclusiveness, can deal with overtly homosexual material so much as a matter of course — not as something perverse or eccentric or morbid, but as evidence of the many available ways in which people live their lives, of the many available ways in which people love or fail to love [*OP* 134].

From the sixties on, Gunn lived in America, principally in San Francisco, with brief sojourns in New York, which he called "my dear old whore" (*OP* 178), and periodic visits to England: "my life insists on continuities — between America and England, between free verse and metre, between vision and everyday consciousness" (*OP* 183).

The Passages of Joy came out in 1982, six years after *Jack Straw's Castle*. As the title suggests, Gunn gives free expression to the happiest and freest aspects of life as a homosexual.[60] Ten years later, in 1992, *The Man with Night Sweats* was published, and was received more favorably, bringing him into the spotlight in England because of its elegies for victims of AIDS.

Many years pass between the publication of this collection and the next: *Boss Cupid* appears in 2000, eight years after *The Man with Night Sweats*. Central to this collection, in which Gregory Woods detects a re-evocation of many of the themes and tones of the preceding books, is the image of old age, the reflection of a poet at the threshold of death, who reviews the important stages of his past, and projects them, like Eliot, into the present.[61] Making present his past, Gunn manages to regenerate it, to somehow exorcise death, which in the twilight years begins to feel so close. Testimony to this regeneration is the triumph of Eros (for good reason the collection is called *Boss Cupid*, and the Greek god is described as "devious master of our bodies" *BC* 101), in a series of poems in which images of decay and death are more and more frequent. Eros is the engine of the universe, the vital fulcrum of myth and history (in "Arethusa Saved," "Arethusa Raped," "Arachne," "To Cupid," and the cycle called "Dancing David"), capable of regenerating, even in its most tormenting and cruel aspects, all those on the brink of death.

A bit like Virginia Woolf, who was subject to depressive spells when her works were published, Gunn suffered debilitating effects when his collections came out. The fear of these sometimes moved him to expedients to trick himself so that he would be able to continue to write:

> I finished *The Man with Night Sweats* last August and plan to have it come out in 1992. The reason I decided to wait is quite simply that after I publish a book I have trouble starting composing poetry again. After my last book it was about two years, and after the book before that it was about two and a half years. I simply got stuck and couldn't seem to write anything. So I thought I'd play a game with this and see if it worked. Since the periods not writing seem to be connected with the idea of closing off some whole area of experience in publishing a book, I thought that perhaps this time if I simply put the book in a drawer for a few years I could perhaps go on writing. And I have, indeed, gone on writing [*SL* 228-29].

In March of 2003, he made his last visit to London, where, with writer Beryl Bainbridge, he received the David Cohen British Literature Award.[62] It was the first time that the prize had been given to a poet. In an interview, Gunn said: "It is really a good surprise. I am very grateful. At 73, this is probably the last award I shall get." Evoking Yeats's reaction to the death of a rival, "this makes me the king of cats," Gunn added: "Maybe this prize makes me the prince of cats."[63]

Gunn's poetic vein was cut off unexpectedly by death, caused by a heart attack on the night of April 25, 2004. As Clive Wilmer points out in an obituary published in *The Independent*, even the preceding year when he met Gunn in London on the occasion of the David Cohen British Literature Award, he "was beginning for the first time to look like an elderly man. He was conscious of it, and one felt it made him less at ease with himself than he had been. He told me then that he had given up writing verse. He had tried to force himself but the poems never flowered. 'I've got no juice,' he said."[64]

CHAPTER II

In Search of an Ubi Consistam*

BOASTING CONCEALMENT: THE STAGING OF PASSION IN THE EARLY COLLECTIONS

Life and Poetic Form

In *Fighting Terms*, his first collection, Gunn appears to be still in his apprenticeship, still struggling to find his own style. Notwithstanding a certain youthful rhetorical awkwardness, later acknowledged by the author himself, the work immediately caught the public eye. Readers saw a promising poet full of vitality and energy, who was inserting himself in the tradition of the canonical seventeenth-century Metaphysical and Cavalier Poets, and giving them new life. This favorable reception was due in part to qualities that Gunn shared with contemporary poets, especially the "angry young men." On the other hand, it was also due to his repudiation of the Modernist heritage, and acceptance of F.R. Leavis's invitation to discipline, control of form, and the recovery of the great English tradition. One of the characteristics of this collection is in fact the dialogue between the poet and tradition, which he finds indispensable for forging his own poetic language. Rediscovery of the past includes adopting traditional meter, not merely as a stylistic exercise, but as an important tool for his formal accomplishment, though in a later phase he will temporarily abandon it, while experimenting with the influences of American poetry (Walt Whitman, William Carlos Williams, and Wallace Stevens), syllabics, and free verse.[1] Running parallel to this alternation of forms are oscillations between "rule" and "energy," thought and action, immediacy and mediation, which constitute the distinguishing characteristics of the early poetry and which create a

---

*The first section of this chapter is a revised version of the essay "Celare ostentando: la messa in scena della passione in Fighting Terms di Thom Gunn," in Le passioni tra ostensione e riserbo, ed. by Romana Rutelli and Luisa Villa (Pisa: ETS, 2000) pp. 199–207, published in English with the title "Passion and Performance in Fighting Terms," English 50, 2001, pp. 39–46.

dialectical tension at various levels, a personal conflict which *Fighting Terms* expresses in the title itself. Ultimately, such tension is expressible as the classic one between intellect and passion, two extremes between which his work seeks constantly to mediate in a variety of ways.

In the poem "Confessions of the Life Artist," Gunn indicates that the search for balance between passion and intellect is the major impetus for his creative activity:

> To give way to all passions,
> I know, is merely whoring.
> Yes, but to give way to none
> Is to be a whore-master.
> [*CP* 161, ll. 57–60]

Beneath the Bergsonian dilemma between life and form suggested by these four lines lies the great cultural archetype, the opposition between nature and culture, which leads to other binaries such as that between daring and reticence, impulse and self-control, and therefore also between passion and the expression of passion. Gunn expresses nature as movement, action, energy, and as a dynamic element that is powerfully, though in reality only potentially, liberating, inasmuch as it is always required to negotiate cultural codes that regulate, entrap, and negate it; the result is the inexpressibility of impulses, especially those most personal and profound, which are incompatible with the cultural means designated to express them — language — the agreed-upon code of social communication, with all of its rules and conventions. This code imposes an *impersonal* representation which is always "other" with respect to the impulse. From this condition arises the inevitable inauthenticity of any expression of passion, the lack of sincerity in the communication of one's most personal emotions, the necessity of assuming a mask which becomes a point of contact between the self and the world, and therefore the inevitable division of the self.[2] Individual identity, in fact, is bound to oscillate (to use the poet's words) between "the starting point — the bare undefined and undirected self, if he ever existed — and the chosen part" (*OP* 162), in concordance with what Erving Goffman said in his sociological study, *The Representation of Self in Everyday Life* (1959). There is no true identity behind the mask insofar as the self is both actor and observer, roles pertaining to representation and not to living. Since he is an actor, the individual is required to recite several different parts adapted to models which society imposes — in other words, to assume poses.[3] Goffman's idea that identity is not stable and permanent, but only an effect periodically produced and reproduced in various ritual dances of daily life, recurs in Gunn's poems, in which the self seems to exist only in service to the pose that is sometimes assumed, to the masks or personae that the speaker has decided to adopt (or that he is forced to adopt) in his interactions with the surrounding world.[4]

So ineradicable is the mask that the heroes in Gunn's poetry — particularly in the early works from *Fighting Terms* to *My Sad Captains*—manage to relate to reality, or to exist, only by virtue of the mask, or more specifically, "the uniform," which is inseparable from the self and through which the self, otherwise meaningless, expresses itself metonymically—for example, the soldier and the motorcyclists in the collection *The Sense of Movement*. But the human being does not profoundly identify with this uniform or role, and Gunn's poetry describes a process of ironic self-estrangement that splits the individual into two entities, actor and voyeur, who observe each other in the act. The theme of the impossibility of discarding the mask characterizes most of his poetry, even the later, in which there is a greater openness to the outside world, to contact with others. In "At the Barriers" (*Poems from the 1960s*), for example, in which Gunn celebrates the freeing experience of a San Francisco street party, comparing it to a seventeenth-century masque, he describes the scene: "...a show, a play, / a play of strength, a show of power put on to be disarmed / through the lingering dénouement of an improvised masque / in which aggressiveness reveals its true face as love / its body as love at play" (*CP* 400–01, ll. 46–50).[5]

The awareness that to live means to act draws the poet to literary models supplied by the erotic poetry of the seventeenth century, mostly dramatic monologues in which passion is described by a persona who varies from poem to poem. The speaker is well aware that acting means seducing one's auditor, in his case a silent interlocutor, so that acting and seduction unite in a drama in which passion must adorn itself with sumptuous rhetoric, fashion itself into captivating lies, mediate, filter, and ultimately deny its own nature in order to achieve its end. From this artifice comes the ironic, and often cynical, element of the Cavalier Poets which Gunn finds particularly congenial. He also traces to seventeenth-century poetry a related attitude towards amorous subject matter: "fighting terms," or "struggling elements," are incarnated in the figures of two lovers who experience Eros as a skirmish, or even a battle without quarter, totally lacking in illusions or ideals.[6]

Eros as Competition

In the poem "Carnal Knowledge," the first line skeptically proclaims the impossibility of taking off the mask: "Even in bed I pose..." (*CP* 15, l. 1). Gunn owes his "early fame to a reputation for plain-speaking-about-sex"[7] to this skeptical, anti-romantic tone. It should be added, however, that for him, sexuality is also an existential metaphor through which he reifies the isolation of the individual, his incapacity to communicate his own alienation from others and himself, an alienation which finds expression in the metaphor of a wound to the head in the two poems which open and close this collection, "The Wound" and "Incident on a Journey."[8]

Representative of his way of rendering the experience of Eros is "To his

Cynical Mistress," whose title echoes the famous poem by Andrew Marvell, "To His Coy Mistress." From this inter-textual referent Gunn draws the imagery, the clarity and accuracy of language, the rigorously regular structure of the stanzas, but not the theme, since in his poem the invitation to love is substituted by the chilling acknowledgment that Eros is nothing but a "pact," precarious and illusory like almost all others entered into by human beings[9]: "And love is then no more than a compromise? / An impermanent treaty..." (*CP* 5, ll. 1–2). The echoes of seventeenth-century poetry (more of the Cavalier Poets than the Metaphysicals) are present in this skeptical, poetic reasoning, which, in place of the romantic idealization of Eros, presents a love already wasted before it starts. Love is ultimately nothing more than a compromise, a truce between two people who find the essence of their relationship in the dimension of challenge and opposition. After the completion of their ritual of love, which has been emptied of significance by sheer repetition, they return to "fighting terms," ready to annihilate each other:

> Forgetting their enmity with cheers and drunken breath;
> But for them there has not been yet amalgamation:
> The leaders calmly plot assassination.
> [*CP* 5, ll. 10–12]

These lines suggest that the sexual relationship is only a momentary inebriation, a chaotic satisfaction of desire ("drunken breath") that does not bring communication and fusion ("amalgamation"), but only mutual hostility, or even mortal hatred ("plot assassination"); and that is because each partner seeks—or snatches from the other, like Marvell's "am'rous birds of prey"—his own pleasure, rather than giving pleasure or giving himself. Reducing pleasure to "drunkenness," Gunn sees it as something contemptible and degrading (he seems to have Shakespearean sonnets in mind); it arouses nausea and self-contempt, and causes him to denounce the pretentious hypocrisy of love. In the poem "Adultery" (*The Passages of Joy*), the line "(you know how bored we are, darling?)" is a brusque response to the question "(you know how I love you, darling?)" (*CP* 313–14, ll. 15, 32).

Elsewhere, love presents itself as a mere pretence, a cultural construct adopted by man to make noble that which is only mechanical, physiological behavior. For example, in the second of the two poems entitled "Modes of Pleasure" (*My Sad Captains*), the speaker first asks himself cynically:

> Why should that matter? Why pretend
> Love must accompany erection?
> [*CP* 102, ll. 17–18]

Then, again recalling Shakespeare, he denounces the vanity of an act of mere lust, which is bound to end in fatigue and post-coital lassitude:

> This is a momentary affection,
> A curiosity bound to end,

> [...]
> — Exhausted into sleep at length —
> And will not last long into day.
> [*CP* 102, ll. 19–20, 23–24][10]

The theme of failed love relationships, and therefore of the erotic encounter as a moment of communication and awareness, is expressed in its most explicit form in "Carnal Knowledge." The biblical title is used by Gunn to present oxymoronically the intrinsic contradiction between an experience which obscures and abases consciousness and the idea of discovery, of spiritual and physical enrichment. If knowledge is the experience of truth, then sexual intercourse is exactly the opposite, since it is nothing but a mutual lie between two lovers who are obliged to "perform" passion ("Even in bed I pose"). The assumption of the pose causes the individual to observe himself in the act, and the act seems a grotesque repetition of a series of movements which, viewed dispassionately, cannot appear other than ridiculous:

> Cackle you hen, and answer when I crow.
> No need to grope: I'm still playing the same
> Comical act inside the tragic game.
> [*CP* 15, ll. 13–15]

These lines verify Gunn's sense of dissociation between a body that acts and a conscious mind that observes, with the effect of negating all spontaneity and making the gratification of impulse impossible:

> 'There is a space between the breast and lips.'
> Also a space between the thighs and head,
> So great, we might as well not be in bed:
> I know you know I know you know I know.
> [*CP* 15, ll. 21–24][11]

The last line revisits the theme of carnal knowledge, declaring that the awareness acquired through the sexual act is merely mental, due to the impossibility of filling the space between "thighs and head," the dissociation between intellect and instinct, which causes the individual to define, catalogue, classify, and verbalize his emotions, and therefore prevents him from comprehending their essence.[12] In this context it is worth mentioning the poem "For a Birthday," which significantly begins with the line: "I have reached a time when words no longer help," and continues in the second stanza asserting that, because of "...the intellectual habit of our eyes,"

> ... either the experience would fade
> Or our approximations would be lies.
> [*CP* 32, ll. 1, 12–14]

Man is thus caught in the vice of a dualism at several levels, such as the contrast between reason and instinct, between signifier and signified, between an idea and realization of the idea, between the real self and the constructed self, reflected in a particular behavior. Such is the case for the protagonist of the poem "Lofty in the Palais de Danse," who roams anxiously in search of a girl who might correspond to a real but lost model, whom he knew before she died:

> Passed in the street, they seem identical
> To her original, yet understood
> Exhaustively as soon as slept with, some
> Lack this, some that, and none like her at all.
> [CP 9, ll. 21–24]

In his anguished search for an unrepeatable experience, the victim of the dissociation between an idea and its impossible realization, Lofty is a "hero" prevented from action, imprisoned and isolated, whose passion dries up in the mental trap of his own ideal. In this poem too, it is the manifestation of lust, and its consummation in the embrace ("as soon as slept with"), that exposes the emptiness of every sexual relationship.[13]

The theme of failed sexual relationships interlaces directly, in the early collections, with the war between the sexes, addressed in a way that betrays Gunn's homosexual tendencies. The individual who undergoes the relationship is usually a "male man," in a struggle with a woman who is always presented in negative terms. She is seen in the sexual act as an aggressive, dangerous, and threatening person, against whom one must defend oneself, as, for example, in "Carnal Knowledge," where the lover is called "an acute girl."[14] The adjective "acute" evokes, like the metaphor of the head wound, the double face of danger represented by woman: she can hurt physically, but also intellectually. She can penetrate the mind of a man and violate his thoughts. In the same poem she seems to ask the man to be a "competent poseur," or an actor capable of playing his part well.

In "Without a Counterpart," where Gunn takes up, in a metaphysical manner, the theme of dreaming and waking, the speaker has a distressing nightmare of losing his beloved, who turns into an enormous volcano ready to suck him into its fiery abyss. On awakening he discovers this abyss to be the mouth of his companion, his relationship with whom is characterized by constant tension, fear, and menace[15]:

> The bad hole in the ground no longer gaped —
> [...]
> It was your mouth, and all the rest your face.
> [CP 31, ll. 21, 24]

In a poem from *Jack Straw's Castle*, appropriately titled "An Amorous Debate: Leather Kid and Fleshly," the woman, who sports the derisive name Fleshly, looks like a mound of flesh without sense or intelligence, and is contrasted to a man named Leather Kid, who is protected by his uniform ("and your skin, it is like / a hide under hide" CP 281, ll. 29–30) as though to resist the assaults of Fleshly.[16]

The skeptical tone and boastful misogyny are ways for Gunn to hide his homosexual identity by assuming a heterosexual pose that he must have felt

> ① came to peace with his homosexuality rather late, so early 'sexual' poetry is inevitably inauthentic

was a renunciation of his artistic integrity. He called the attitude adopted in his early poems "a mixture of dishonesty and ignorance,"[17] aware that this "dishonesty" was also based on the fifties cultural code condemning inclinations that, for Gunn, were natural, and consigning him to a double lie, a double "act" in his erotic poems. In the poetry of Gunn's youth, passion passed through double cultural and ideological filters which obligated him to feign something he did not feel, and relegated him, willingly or not, to deceit and inauthenticity.

Between Tradition and Innovation

Gunn's movements between two realities and literary traditions, English and American, are reflected in his poetic praxis, in his continual passage from traditional meter to free verse, from a poetry of ecstatic vision like Blake's, to a more intellectual, philosophical reflection. His is a stylistic exercise of confronting the poetic tradition, sometimes to imitate, sometimes to modify, and sometimes to contest it. Oscillation between the two extremes, though he is ultimately in search of balance through synthesis, is a major trait of Gunn's poetry. His journey could be described as that of a wanderer in search of a full life and true artistic expression, who is open to every type of experimentation. In these contradictions and self-challenges he found fertile soil, because within his self-contradictions there were personal coherencies; there was substantial continuity to a discourse that, without any severe break, developed dialectically throughout the course of his collections. The titles of the collections show this continuity and tension. Though oriented towards a point of balance and calm (which was never fully reached and repeatedly up for discussion), the poems always questioned the paradigm of movement. This shows at a physical level by real, material progress towards a place, and at a psychological one, by the dynamic of human interaction. This is the case in *Fighting Terms* (where it appears mostly in terms of conflict), in *The Sense of Movement* (in which action becomes an existential absolute), in *My Sad Captains* (which signals the first attempt to open himself to the outside world), in *Touch* (where the dynamic is one of union), in *Moly* and *The Man with Night Sweats* (where he presents his physical metamorphosis). It is also the case in *Jack Straw's Castle* (with its labyrinthine castles and relative movement), in *The Passages of Joy* (where it takes the form of *Streben*, or *élan vital*) and finally, in *Boss Cupid*, the collection whose title is related to *Fighting Terms* in opposite but analogous ways, suggesting the image of Cupid in the role of a "boss" who dictates the rules, and against whom one may not rebel.

The first two collections, *Fighting Terms* and *The Sense of Movement*, taken with the first part of the third collection, *My Sad Captains*, have been described as a "unicum,"[18] an expression of the initial phase of Gunn's work.

The phrase "fighting terms" emphasizes the encounter between two entities which are substantially identifiable, despite the deliberate vagueness of the phrase, as the self and external reality. The title suggests the idea of Eros as an antagonistic relationship, as in "Tamer and Hawk" ("I lose to keep, and choose / Tamer as prey" *CP* 29, ll. 23–24) and in "The Beach Head" ("Or shall I wait and calculate my chances / Consolidating this my inch-square base, / — Myself a spy, killing your spies-in-glances—" *CP* 27, ll. 37–39). The word "term" has a triple meaning, showing simultaneously the relationship between two people and, at the linguistic level, suggesting "words" and "terminology," and Gunn's reflections on the act of creating poetry, as well as the third meaning of "end" or "limit."

The individual is caught in the vice of a dualism at various levels, such as the contrast between reason and instinct, the real and the ideal, past and present, a tendency towards isolation and need for contact with others. In the poem "Lofty in the Palais de Danse," the protagonist Lofty is a Hamlet-like hero, who is worn down by his isolation, incapable of communicating with others; his name suggests he is "dignified" and "proud." He resembles many other characters in this collection, such as the speaker in "Wind in the Street" and the lighthouse keeper in "Round and Round," poems characterized by obsessive repetition of the same line in the opening and closing of each stanza. The repetition itself reveals the speaker's stasis, disorientation, and existential paralysis:

> I may return, meanwhile I'll look elsewhere:
> My want may modify to what I have seen.
> So I smile wearily, though even as I smile
> A purposeful gust of wind tugs at my hair;
> But I turn, I wave, I am not sure what I mean.
> I may return, meanwhile I'll look elsewhere.
> [*CP* 6, ll. 19–24]

In these lines (the final stanza of "Wind in the Street"), the uncertainty of the individual who is incapable of finding meaning in his life or a goal to accomplish ("I am not sure what I mean"), is contrasted with the gust of wind which has direction and even purpose. The wind itself, then, substitutes for the speaker's will in the role of "engine," pushing the human being forward to grope towards something indeterminate.

The obsessive repetition of the same line or its parts at the beginning and ending of every stanza creates the effect of an endless spiral, recalling the automatism of surrealist poetry as well as certain aspects of Dylan Thomas's work. Belonging to the generation before Gunn's, Dylan Thomas left his mark on the young poet, even though the poets of the fifties rejected the linguistic virtuosity and apocalyptic imagery of the Welsh poet:

> I did actually admire Dylan Thomas, and still do, but a friend of mine said the other day, "What the poets of the Movement had in common was a reaction against Dylan Thomas," and I think that's probably right. I didn't want to write like Dylan Thomas.[19]

The Prison of the Intellect

In "Round and Round," the speaker is a lighthouse keeper whose duty is to supply to others a valuable reference point, yet he is unable to identify himself with the job he performs. He feels imprisoned within the lighthouse (the tower is, for Symbolists, the perfect emblem of isolation). In the lighthouse, his movements carry him in a spiral direction up and down the stairs, giving the tower the connotation of a Dantesque Inferno with no exit.[20] He vaguely yearns to break the chain of his utterly inhuman solitude, but the only voice he hears is that of the boundless sea, which is an archetypal symbol for the unknown and for adventures that frighten him. He limits himself to "...a little exercise," and never actually moves very far from the tower, constantly circling this prison (obviously the prison of self), which is also a totem or cult object: "Where thoughts dance round what will not shift —/ His secret inarticulate grief" (*CP* 11, ll. 23-24). Isolation infects not only the realm of language and communication (rendering his grief "inarticulate"), but also the body, which is unable to distance itself from the lighthouse. The tower rises to the level of an almost sinister pagan divinity, exerting upon him a hypnotizing effect ("But all he does is fix his eyes / On that huge totem he has left" *CP*, 11, ll. 21-22).[21] The fear not only of venturing into the unknown, but even of gazing at it, is apparent in the images of faces turned towards the outside, like the condemned beings sculpted upon a totem, who are reflections of the self multiplied endlessly: "But there things dance with faces out —/ ward turned: faces of fear and doubt? / He wonders, winding up the stair" (*CP* 11, ll. 16-18). These multiple refractions of the human figure, like the acknowledgment of inanimate and animate, or nonhuman and human parts ("things" and "faces") remind us of the decomposition or fragmentation of the self in T.S. Eliot's poetry, and the cloning of selves in certain surrealist paintings, such as Magritte's *The Time of Harvest* and *Galconde*.

A similar experience is had by the protagonist of the sequence "Jack Straw's Castle,"[22] who is prisoner of a castle that is a projection of the body. He is unable to open to the external world, to accept all of its aspects, especially the un-poetic ones[23]: "why can't I leave my castle / he says, isn't there anyone / anyone else besides me" (*CP* 270, ll. 4-6). A series of nightmares, whose subjects range from the Furies and Medusa to the American serial killer Charles Manson,[24] assume the aspect of an initiatory descent into hell. Only after his self has split into a series of personalities which allow him to assume a range of viewpoints (even though these threaten his ontological unity),[25] does Jack Straw finally manage to accept the presence of the Other and break the shell of his isolation. He transforms the nightmare into a dream of union and confronts external reality: "— Thick sweating flesh against which I lie curled —/ With dreams like this, Jack's ready for the world" (*CP* 279, 11, ll. 37-38).

An analogous psychological situation — the problem of exiting the labyrinth that imprisons the human being—shows up in "A System" (*Boss Cupid*), where the terror of living manifests not only at the intellectual level, but also the physical, taking the form of an actual sickness, an obsession that makes the protagonist crazy:

> Squatting ass-naked in some corridor,
> A ringing in his ears like distant cries.
> [...]
> He dreams at the center of a closed system,
> Like the prison system, or a system of love,
> Where folktale, recipe, and household custom
> Refer back to the maze they are of.
> [*BC* 35, ll. 7-8, 17-20]

The speakers in the two poems "The Court Revolt" and "The Right Possessor," both characterized by elaborate metaphors and an historical setting, are also exiles who choose and cultivate their own condition of solitude. The images suggest a person who is estranged from the world, as in the last stanza of "The Court Revolt":

> Though on a larger scale, see in his case
> A problem which is problem of us all:
> His human flames of energy had no place—
> The grate that they were lit for would not hold,
> The vacant grates were destined to be cold.
> [*CP* 18, ll. 26-30]

These lines recall the cosmic pessimism of Thomas Hardy,[26] the idea that nature is indifferent to human passions and aspirations. The place where the human being should put down roots turns into a prison deprived of human warmth and signifies his condemnation to death.[27] The human being is nothing if unable to integrate into the surrounding environment; his or her energies are inevitably destined to atrophy or consume themselves in self-destruction. In this poem we already see Gunn's distrust for the heroic gesture which, though attractive, is destined to end in nothing ("His human flames of energy had no place—"). As we shall see in Chapter IV of the present study, this will happen in *My Sad Captains*, particularly in the beginning poem, "In Santa Maria del Popolo," which ends significantly in the lines "— For the large gesture of solitary man, / Resisting, by embracing, nothingness" (*CP* 94, ll. 31-32).

CHOOSING INERTIA

Solitude, or shutting oneself inside one's egoism, is a refusal of life, a choice of death-in-life. In the ballad "Lazarus Not Raised," as in "Wind in the Street" and "Round and Round," the implacable repetition of the refrain with minimal variations confirms the ineluctable condition of estrangement.

The last lines of "Lazarus Not Raised," "Without that terrified awakening glare, / The scheduled miracle would have taken place" (*CP* 8, ll. 34–35), refute the Biblical episode, suggesting that the miracle of Lazarus's resurrection could have taken place if he had been capable of wanting it, if he had not been overwhelmed by the angst he associated with living, if he had not opted for the prison of his tomb, if he had not refused life:

> He chose to spend his thoughts like this at first
> And disregard the nag of offered grace,
> Then chose to spend the rest of them in rest.
> [*CP* 7, ll. 21–23]

Note the phonetic and iconic correspondence between the first and second "rest," which accentuates Lazarus's meaningful choice. The first "rest" has a temporal connotation, indicating the flow of days and of life, the succession of thoughts ("He chose to spend his thoughts like this at first"); it is negated and reversed in the second, which immobilizes the moment, rendering it inert and paralyzing both Lazarus's mental activity and the progress of time. Lidia De Michelis emphasizes how Gunn visualizes in this poem "that which Kierkegaard already postulated and immediately denied in the introduction to *The Sickness Unto Death* [1849], the possibility that Lazarus could judge the offer of new life to be absurd, frightening, and useless: ... 'And what advantage would it be for Lazarus to be risen from the dead, since at the end he would have to die; what advantage would it have been if there were no He, He, who is the resurrection and the life for whoever believes in Him.'"[28]

To Martin Dodsworth, the figure of Lazarus represents the personification of the individual existentially confronting a choice and incapable of basing that choice on a rational foundation:

> As Gunn rewrites the Bible story, Lazarus so perfectly exemplifies the force of inertia that he is not even raised from the grave in order to return to it. Although he is said by the poet to choose, he is not seen to choose on a rational basis. The *rest* of his thoughts are spent in *rest*: they seem to exemplify a natural, necessary and inexplicable relationship to inertia, which is in ironic contrast to the orderly form of verse used throughout the book in which the poem appears.[29]

Inertia, which plays a central role here, is also pertinent to the situations delineated in the majority of the other poems in the collection; indeed, movement is always revealed as substantially illusory. Movement is a narcissistic oscillation around a point, as in "Wind in the Street" and "Round and Round"; it is an obsessive wandering in search of something nonexistent as in "Lofty in the Palais de Danse"; it is a haunting doubling of self and the voiceless fear of one's own shadow in "The Secret Sharer." This poem's title proposes to rewrite the shadowy figure in Conrad's novel (1909); it ends with the words "The wind turns in its groove: I am still there" (*CP* 13, l. 20), countering again, as in "Round and Round" and "Wind in the Street," the dynamism and finality of natural elements to the paralyzing inertia of man.[30] Lazarus's choice — or non-choice — seems much more negative when judged by a value system in which the positive term (even if not totally positive) is represented by "movement" and "fighting," by the resistance to inertia. This is also the case of the speaker in "Looking Glass," a poem whose title adumbrates the famous book of Lewis Carroll, *Through the Looking-Glass* (1871): though he does not pass through a mirror to enter another realm, the speaker sees in it a completely illusory world:

> I see myself inside a looking glass
> Framed there by shadowed trees alive with song
> And fruits no sooner noticed than enjoyed;
> I take it from my pocket and gaze long,
> Forgetting in my pleasure how I pass
> From town to town, damp-booted, unemployed.
> [*CP* 22, ll. 31–36]

He lives a double life, trying to escape his outsiderness, self-exile, and rootless nomadism ("...I pass / From town to town, damp-booted, unemployed") by contemplating, in a purely mental mirror, a garden overflowing with riches ("And fruits no sooner noticed than enjoyed"), a fictitious Eden, world of dreams, in which a never-realized desire takes form, and differences between thought and action, between reality and dream, are cancelled out.[31] The mirror offers the reverse image of the real life of the speaker, and gives him a temporary oblivion ("Forgetting in my pleasure how I pass").

In these years Gunn's existential vision manifests in the polarity between inertia and action, between closure and openness, between submission and challenge, generating a deep ambivalence which is partially overcome in the later collections (from *Touch* on), in which action leads to metamorphosis. This is the case in the title-poem "Moly," in which the speaker, completely imprisoned in the body of an alien creature "...Buried in swine" (*CP* 186, l. 18), *acts* to attain the change necessary for his regeneration:

> I root and root, you think that it is greed,
> It is, but I seek out a plant I need.
> Direct me gods, whose changes are all holy,
> To where it flickers deep in grass, the moly:
> [*CP* 186–87, ll. 19–22]

Action as Existential Absolute

Action is useless, vain, and unproductive, yet there is no alternative to it. One cannot opt for inertia, because only through consciously choosing action can man enter into that dimension of risk-taking that alone (according to Sartre) gives him free expression of his own potential. The description of choice and action as "existential absolutes" (which reflects Sartre's profound influence on Gunn during his first artistic phase) is so strong that in the poem "Lerici," Gunn labels Shelley "a minor conquest of the sea," insofar as "He fell submissive through the waves." In contrast, Byron "was worth the sea's pursuit" because "...His touch / Was masterful to water..." (*CP* 23, ll. 2, 9–10). Gunn prefers Byron to Shelley because he did not abandon himself to the "wave" of life, but like an indomitable "swimmer," confronted it with energy, refusing to be discouraged by defeats. This message returns in the final poem of *Fighting Terms*, "Incident on a Journey," where the persona is closed and isolated in a cavern, which is a metaphor for the prison of the mind. In a dream appears the figure of a soldier with a head wound. He has given up thinking; he privileges action over sterile reflection (most of the protagonists in *Fighting Terms* are victims of reflection); he has found wisdom and a reason to live:

> 'No plausible nostalgia, no brown shame
> I had when treating with my enemies.
> And always when a living impulse came
> I acted, and my action made me wise.
> *And I regretted nothing.*
> [*CP* 33, ll. 16–20]

Using the structure of the *ballade noir*, characterized by the refrain with only marginal variations on the theme of "regretting nothing," this poem recalls, in its setting, in the figure of the soldier, and also in the dream, the Romantic poetic tradition, in particular the poem "La Belle Dame Sans Merci" by Keats. Unlike in Keats,' however, the visit during this dream does not lead to prison and death, but to liberty, which in this case is figured as the choice of action and the refusal of inertia.

Because of the soldier's visit and his story, in which impulse and action play a strong role, the speaker is able to make a choice, something that Lazarus avoided, and to accept life without asking himself its meaning:

> Later I woke. I started to my feet.
> The valley light, the mist already going.
> I was alive and felt my body sweet,
> Uncaked blood in all its channels flowing.
> *I would regret nothing.*
> [*CP* 34, ll. 36–40]

The head wound links this, the last poem of the collection, to "The Wound,"[32] the first, where the wound itself signifies the doubling of a self incapable of finding its identity. "The Wound" is one of Gunn's most famous and oft-discussed poems; some consider it the best in the collection. Colin Falk, for example, calls it:

> the great exception in Gunn's early verse, the only poem where he commits himself straight out to poetic intensity.... "The Wound" ... is exceptional in that it manages the rare feat — almost impossible for the modern poet — of attaining the grand manner whilst leaving the personal foreground largely unoccupied.[33]

Parini, on the other hand, impersonality is a sign of a poet still in style, who is trying to achieve through dramatic monologue the necessary distance between himself and his material:

> The beginning writer rarely has sufficient space between himself and his material. The use of a persona helps, for it allows the poet to search for a sympathetic alter-ego, to study himself indirectly, safely. The poem acts as a grid through which the light of self-expression passes; with luck, something of the poet's true nature remains.[34]

For Clive Wilmer "The Wound" "is still a tremendous poem."[35] Referring to the close relationship between sexuality and death in the poem, Wilmer sees an extraordinary foreshadowing of the elegies in *The Man with Night Sweats*:

> Like the comparably wounded persona of "The Man with Night Sweats," he [the speaker] has "dreams of heat," and the poem is concerned quite as much as the AIDS series with death and friendship, vulnerability and defence, action and contemplation ... There was no way of knowing in the 1950s ... that sexual excitement would provide the occasion for premature death. Yet right at the beginning of his career Gunn was thinking of the proximity of sex and death and setting up the images and conceptions he would draw on for his response to the AIDS tragedy.[36]

For the author of the obituary published in *The Telegraph*, "*Fighting Terms* won immediate praise, particularly for the poem 'The Wound,' which drew upon *The Iliad* and demonstrated a muscularity and rigour in its metre which was out of temper with the times."[37]

In "The Wound," which Gunn considered "the best poem in my first book,"[38] the Trojan War is an opportunity to explore the psychological condition of anxiety. Although initially representing, according to Gunn himself, his response to reading Shakespeare's *Troilus and Cressida*,[39] and offering Troilus as a hero, a soldier, and a victim of love's deceits, the poem becomes symbolic of a more profound and general existential angst. Here the hero Achilles, in a way that anticipates the collection *My Sad Captains*, embodies the virile, stoic attitude of the man in the face of the wound of his existence, which reopens continually in his daily experience:

> I called for armour, rose, and did not reel.
> But, when I thought, rage at his noble pain
> Flew to my head, and turning I could feel
> My wound break open wide. Over again
> I had to let those storm-lit valleys heal.
> [*CP* 3, ll. 21–25]

Facing the alternatives of shutting down, of isolation, on the one hand, and action on the other, understood as having value in and of itself, regardless of its aims or effects, Gunn decisively chooses the latter. He identifies the choice of action with artistic duty, as we see in "A Mirror for Poets," which seeks to define, through extended metaphor, the role of the artist in a violent world such as the Elizabethan one, which mirrors our world of today. The serene Parnassus in which Gunn found himself writing (Cambridge in the fifties) must come to terms with preceding horrors, with the tragedy of World War II, with Auschwitz and the Holocaust, after which, to paraphrase Theodor Adorno, it is no longer possible to write poetry. One cannot ignore violence, which is part of human life, as Ted Hughes also believed; to repress it is only to deny a part of oneself which is destined to re-emerge in a destructive or self-destructive way. John Mander, though recognizing Gunn's distance from the direct political or social commitment of most other poets of his generation, argues that

> Mr. Gunn is not, as far as I know, particularly interested in politics, either as a poet or a private person. But the implications are, I think, there. His poems reflect certain attitudes of the postwar generation very accurately. Mr. Gunn is not the only writer to examine violence in our time.... But he is certainly the only English writer who, in a period of confusion and fear of commitment, has attempted to re-examine the very basis of commitment.[40]

James Michie has a different opinion, saying that Gunn's involvement in contemporary social problems is completely nonexistent. Even the way in which Gunn approaches the theme of violence shows him guilty of disingenuousness:

> Refugees, enemies, spies, frontiers, treaties, assassination — all the ghastly apparatus of our age is there. But in Mr. Gunn's hands they seem even less real than when Mr. Auden bandied them about with such schoolboy relish before the Spanish war arrived to make them seem in slightly bad taste. It is surprising to find Mr. Gunn using all the images of war as if they were part of a Buchan romance rather than the actual horrors of our lives.[41]

In Clive Wilmer's opinion:

> Gunn is not a political poet in the "committed" sense — he is primarily concerned with identities and relations we think of as pre-political.... But as Camus (one of his heroes) discovered, "freedom" and "choice" do not exist in abstract purity: once a man is oppressed, he discovers the political nature, whether he will or not.[42]

Referring to the poems in *The Man with Night Sweats*, especially those previously published in *Undesirables*, on the theme of the disinherited, Peter Swaab identifies in Gunn's poetry a particular type of political and social commitment:

> Even in the many poems where he describes people who are ill, or dying, or derelict, it is what they've made of themselves that he dwells on, together with their often surprising resources. There is an idea of community in this well-populated book, but it's unusual in being so little grounded in sympathy, nostalgia or shared purpose.[43]

In "A Mirror for Poets," whose title paraphrases that of a work appearing just after the middle of the sixteenth century, *A Mirror for Magistrates*,[44] Gunn relates the Elizabethan age to the modern world from the very first line, "It was a violent time..." (*CP* 24). The poem manifests an almost Eliotic vision of history (the Eliot of the early period, from "Prufrock" to *The Waste Land*) as a succession of tragic occurrences that condemn human beings to despair. Gunn seems to suggest that an age immersed in violence gives artists, not only reasons to reflect on the individual and civilization, but also material for art. Violence cannot be eluded, unless in precarious moments when the poet, absenting himself from his space and time, manages to retreat to a peaceful Arcadia outside of time[45]:

> In this society the boundaries met
> Of life and life, at danger; with no space
> Being left between, except where might be set
> That mathematical point where time and place
> Could not exist. Yet at this point they found
> Arcadia, a fruitful permanent land.
> [*CP* 24, ll. 13–18]

During a recording of his poems in the mid–1960s, Gunn had this to say about violence in the contemporary world:

> I think we live in an extraordinarily unviolent world really. I know this is not the cliché, but if you compare somebody's day in London, say, or in San Francisco, now, with what it would have been a hundred years ago, let alone two hundred years ago, it's extraordinarily mild and easy and pacific: you don't see any fights around you or anything. I think our particular generation is obsessed with the IDEA of violence. Maybe it misses it. It's a kind of nostalgia for violence. I think it's terribly unhealthy actually — like most nostalgias. I think it's a nostalgia for something it hasn't ever had and doesn't particularly want really — wouldn't particularly like if it had it. But it is around us. I suppose I'm rather typical in this way. I'm trying to be a bit more intelligent about it in my last book and in what I'm writing now, but I suppose I was extremely typical of the Fifties in what I was writing.[46]

Precisely because violence is *also* necessarily action, it becomes part of the artist's range of existential choice.

CHAPTER III
A Challenge to the Void

HEROES IN MOTION

The glorification of action as an end in itself finds its most intense expression in the collection *The Sense of Movement*, where no real sense of movement is found, and the direction of action is not defined, yet activity retains its existential value in the manner of Sartre or Nietzsche. Even the epigraph of the collection exemplifies this attitude; it is a passage from the play *Cinna* by Corneille, the father of French tragedy, whose protagonists, in obeying laws of honor, are compelled to perform acts of heroism which are sometimes inhumane.[1] Their virtue, their heroism, and even their belonging to the aristocratic class are not just hereditary qualities, but ones that must be won and constantly maintained through will and action. In the epigraph ("Je le suis, je veux l'être" *CP* 37), the ontological reality expressed in the first part (to be, to exist) is seen as an immediate and necessary consequence of the second part, the will and the duty to act. The heroic gesture as an end in itself is the only guarantee of being.

The interaction between will and action, or between mind and instinct, is what the title *The Sense of Movement* intends. It implies the need to invest movement itself with a rational justification. Gunn explains:

> By "movement" I mean the sort of actions one is involved in, whether voluntarily or not, through all one's life — unpacking in a new apartment, riding a motorcycle, writing a poem, murdering one's landlady. By "sense" I mean both "sensation" and "meaning." This is the only pun in the book, as I remember, but it indicates what I want to do in a poem — not only convey an experience but try to understand it.[2]

The only way to escape from the prison of the intellect, and from the drama of existence in a world without sense is action (as in the poem "Incident on a Journey"); however, this action cannot be a pure, instinctual reflex, but must involve the individual in his own interests, activating simultaneously his mind, body, intellect, and senses, making them part of the cosmic flux, even if the results of the action are often tragically disastrous.

The Sense of Movement is one of Gunn's best-known collections (certain poems, such as the renowned "On the Move," are often anthologized), but in reality, it is a second apprenticeship piece. Undercurrents of his new American environment flow, but an English sensibility and an English *forma mentis* prevail.

> It is still a very European book in its subject-matter. I was much taken by the American myth of the motorcyclist, then in its infancy, of the wild man part free spirit and part hoodlum, but even that I started to anglicize: when I thought of doing a series of motorcyclist poems I had Marvell's mower poems in my mind as a model [*OP* 177].

Critics reacted favorably to *Fighting Terms*, in which they recognized the voice of a promising poet, but *The Sense of Movement* elicited conflicting responses. For Lawrence R. Ries, this collection signaled a great step forward from the previous one:

> *The Sense of Movement* is a more satisfying and mature volume, in which we find Gunn's best poetry.... Where we had in his earlier attempts at objectivity and detachment retreated to unreal social context and difficult metaphors so that his poems frequently became challenging riddles, the newer poems take their metaphors from more immediate situations and their meaning is more easily discoverable. Although choosing characters like motorcyclists to carry his meaning leaves him open to dangers of melodrama and pathos, he finds in the modern tough a successful vehicle for the response to the dilemma of modern man. The success in his choice of material gives him greater control over subject and technique. The often stilted iambic pentameter of *Fighting Terms* becomes more pliable without losing the vigor that he needed to reinforce his theme. Language, theme, and form blend in these later poems with remarkable success.[3]

John Press, on the other hand, notices a lack of that vigor which made *Fighting Terms* successful: "The poems in *The Sense of Movement* may ... have lost something of the sharp tang that made *Fighting Terms* so exciting and memorable a first volume." At the same time, he recognizes that "the verse in this second volume is more weightily mature and harmonious."[4]

Frankly unfavorable is the opinion of John Mander, the mouthpiece of those critics, primarily British, who are suspicious of Gunn's "American contamination":

> America has, of course, developed an academicism of her own, particularly in poetry, that has no equivalent in this country. At Cambridge, Empson and the Metaphysicals were in the air, they were felt presences: but they were not held up for emulation in Creative Writing Classes. Two weaknesses of the second volume would appear to be traceable to this source: a certain derivativeness, and a new preoccupation with the poet as poet.[5]

Many poems in this volume glorify "all the toughs through history," violent heroes touched by a divine hand. Among them, "Lines for a Book" caused an animated debate, arousing accusations of totalitarian sympathies on Gunn's part, like those aimed at the late Modernist works of Ezra Pound, T.S. Eliot, and Wyndham Lewis. Aware of the political tendencies found in this poem ("there is a kind of weakness in the attitude behind 'Lines for a Book' because ultimately it can lead to Fascism, can't it?"),[6] Gunn asserted the predominantly sexual nature of his attraction for the "toughs through history," which he linked to cultural changes and a different type of masculine model presented by the media and especially by the cinema of the fifties: "suddenly, you got this wave of people, people like Marlon Brando and James Dean. There was a new kind of ideal: it was a blue-collar hero, it wasn't the gentleman hero."[7]

"Lines for a Book" is a single-stanza poem with thirteen rhyming couplets (an imitation of the heroic couplets of commemorative seventeenth and eighteenth-century poetry), which opens and closes with the lines: "I think of all the toughs through history / And thank heaven they lived, continually." In the lines, "I praise the overdogs from Alexander / To those who would not play with Stephen Spender. / [...] / I think of those exclusive by their action, / for whom mere thought could be no satisfaction" (*CP* 56, ll. 3–4, 19–20), the poet reifies action, expressing a profound admiration for "the toughs through history" who are capable of challenging its meaninglessness by putting their lives at risk. "Lines for a Book" is also a parody of Stephen Spender's poem which starts with the line, "I think continually of those...," but Spender's, unlike Gunn's, celebrates the "truly great," those who are not disturbed by the noises of the world and "Never allow gradually the traffic to smother / With noise and fog the flowering of the Spirit" (ll. 14–15). Gunn also refers to another of Spender's lines, "My parents kept me from children who were rough." Spender was also homosexual, but unlike Gunn, he did not cheer for "the toughs through history," and was not a "tough guy" himself. In Spender's poem, the character is not permitted to play with the rough, unmannerly boys ("They threw mud / While I looked the other way, pretending to smile, / I longed to forgive them, but they never smiled" ll. 10–12).[8] Gunn reverses this image in "Lines for a Book," where the rough boys exclude Spender by refusing to play with him. In the word "play," we can detect a sexual connotation.

The idea of violence as an end in itself which undoubtedly emerges in these lines, is interpreted by Martin Dodsworth not as proof of a totalitarian attitude ("the poem is very unlikely to make a Fascist where there was none before, and he himself has moved on to poems that do qualify his admiration for strength of will and so on in a way that we should find morally acceptable"), but rather as an expression of restlessness and "fantasies project[ed] into a void," which make the poem, despite its insistence on action, rather motionless: "despite its concern with action, despite its bravado, the poem is essentially static."[9]

The collection pulsates with violent heroes, whether "toughs through history," uniformed protagonists, or motorcyclists in some poems. Rarely does Gunn linger introspectively upon these men, or focus on their individual psychology. Their identity is primarily that of the group, determined by the uniform that they wear or by the instruments of their action. The motorcyclists of "On the Move," with which the collection opens, are unthinkable if detached from their motorcycles, which are like masks over their true selves, tools that provide a social and collective dimension to otherwise empty individuals: "On motorcycles, up the road, they come: / Small, black, as flies hanging in heat, the Boys" (*CP* 39 ll. 9–10). Riding without destination ("They ride, direction where the tyres press" *CP* 39, l. 19), they try to establish a relationship of self-confidence and challenge to the surrounding world, which seems to be their only recourse for consolidating the group identity, and giving significance to their actions: "And almost hear a meaning in their noise" (*CP* 39, l. 16).

For these uniformed heroes, or modern day centaurs, who are half man/half mechanical animal because of their motorcycles, which are extensions of their selves and metaphors of sexual energy, Gunn nurtures an admiration. This admiration does not lessen in later collections, even while he recognizes the limits of the artificial pose. He directs himself first, to defining a goal for action, and later, gradually, to the discovery of stillness and harmony with the surrounding environment. His somewhat fetishistic admiration for uniforms remains throughout all of his work, even though in the later years he learns to regard it with a certain ironic detachment. In the poem "A GI in 1943" (*Boss Cupid*),[10] Gunn exposes the illusory power, the meaninglessness, and even the cruelty that hide behind a uniform, seeing boys "armored in hide that / adorns to hide / every fallibility / cruelty or awkwardness / with the smooth look / of power..." (*BC* 55, ll. 17–22). He also reveals how morbid and sterile his own voyeuristic attitude seems to him, an attitude that has remained unchanged for half a century: "[my cock] has learned nothing / fresh in fifty-three years" (*BC* 55, ll. 34–35).

Already in "On the Move," it is possible to see a subtle vein of self-deprecation, an exposure of the mask, suggested by the adverb "almost" ("And almost hear a meaning in their noise"). Paradoxically, the meaning that the boys are looking for in their action is negated by the noise — which destroys any possibility of communication, at least verbal — produced by the instruments of their action, while their uniforms, the guarantee of their identity, are worn like dust-covered trophies, foreshadowing that other dust to which they will be reduced at death.[11] Their gesture is also a challenge to nature: "they scare a flight of birds across the field; / Much that is natural, to the will must yield" (*CP* 39, ll. 20–21). This is a violent action made possible by technological superiority, but one that seems to suggest, ultimately, their intrinsic sense of inferiority. In a state of total clouding of conscience, they try to approach the privileged condition of animal or saint, in which there is no distinction between intellect and instinct ("For birds and saints complete their purposes" *CP* 40, l. 37), but this approach, suggested by the final line of the poem ("One is always nearer by not keeping still" *CP* 40, l. 40) is in truth only an illusion.[12] In Gunn's *Weltanschauung* (at least in this phase), where, in Terry Eagleton's words, the poet "has been equipped with a myth from the outset ... of Sartrian existentialism,"[13] man is the result of a fall, not from Eden, but from a condition of happy animalism: his damnation consists in his liberty and the possibility of choice.

That distancing from Nature caused by the prison of the intellect and of thought, which thrusts before man a multiplicity of paralyzing choices, recalls Sartre as well as Eric Fromm in his famous book, *Escape from Freedom* (1941). To Fromm, while the animal exhibits an uninterrupted chain of reactions to stimuli, in humans, this instinctual chain is interrupted by thought. The role of the individual in relationship to the natural world changes from a purely passive adaptation and symbiosis to an active role of shaping nature, inventing instruments to confirm his own superiority and difference, with the paradoxical, destructive effect of steadily increasing his separation from nature. Modern man, liberated from the restrictions of a pre-individualistic society, restrictions which, at the same time, gave him security and self-limitation, has not found liberty in the positive sense of realizing his own being, that is, expression of his own emotional and sensory potential. Although bringing independence and rationality, liberty rendered him isolate and, worse, anxious and impotent.[14]

Gunn seeks a justification for the actions of the young centaurs in the fourth stanza of his poem, the only one with a meditative, reflective tone, which momentarily interrupts the action, seeking to give it meaning, even if only a vague and abstract one, as the insistence on the generic and impersonal pronoun "one," proves: "One joins the movement in a valueless world / [...] / One moves as well, always toward, toward" (*CP* 40, ll. 30, 32).

In a recent interview with James Campbell, nearly half a century after the publication of "On the Move," Gunn recognizes the excessive formalism of his composition, and the vagueness of the message, even calling it dated and "unnecessarily well-known and anthologized":

> There are many things to dislike about "On the Move." To begin with, there's the constant use of the word "one," which I find very stilted now. Now I would use the word "you" rather than "one." Then again, it's such a period piece. I say that, not because it's based on a short book by Sartre, or because it's also based on *The Wild One*, but because of its tremendous formality, which I really dislike. I'm also not sure that the last line means anything: "One is always nearer by not keeping still." Nearer what? Well, yes, the motorcyclist is nearer the destination, but what's the destination of human beings? Aha! It's a question that seems to answer itself but doesn't.[15]

According to Alan Bold, "On the Move" exemplifies the egocentrism of the poet, projecting it on "boys who are engaged in demonstratively negative action, action that solves their egocentric dilemma.... The poem does not move beyond a statement of the powerful appearance of the Boys and an admittedly skilful communication of their anguish.... This 'part solution' is totally self-indulgent. It does not acknowledge the inviolability of other individuals."[16] The critic does not appear to notice the vein of self-irony and Gunn's recognition of the illusory nature of the heroic pose, even though it had been, in this phase of his career, the only available way to challenge the void.

Alan Bold accuses the poet not only of tolerating and justifying certain "perverse" attitudes, but even of sympathizing with them. The critic refers to another poem, "The Beaters," whose title and epigraph suggest a cult of violence as an end in itself. The epigraph, "*None but my foe to be my guide*,"[17] indirectly paraphrases (by turning it on its head) the commandment, "Do unto others as you would want them to do unto you." Bold writes:

> Gunn insists that such people are not mere perverts but are also individuals in search of an identity, philosophers to some degree, that being the unique characteristic of the human species. So sadomasochistic perversions become dignified by Gunn who sees them as examples of action.[18]

Agreeing with this position, Edward Lucie-Smith describes "The Beaters" as a gratuitous glorification of pain, since "Gunn assumes that pain is for some a means towards the discovery of identity, and thus a means of achieving a kind of freedom."[19] For Alan Brownjohn, the poems in this collection demonstrate "a somewhat displeasing cult of romantic toughness showing a preference at heart for the brutal, the irrational and the willful instead of accepted humane standards."[20]

"The Beaters" compares the atrocious violence of the Nazis to the behavior of a youth gang, projecting into their viewpoint, emphasizing the indifference, superficiality, and even the subtle pleasure with which they execute certain atrocities. Gunn (whose distance from the poem is evidenced by the fact that he did not include it in *Collected Poems*, 1993)[21] on the one hand tries to filter, to withdraw any sentimentality from, the horrors of World War II, the subversion of all values, the paradoxical conciliation of hate and love, cruelty and tenderness. On the other hand, he insists on the intrinsic weakness of those who commit such violence, insofar as their identity, acquired only by the uniform that furnishes an alibi for gratuitous violence, is revealed as completely illusory:

> ... they confess
> A manacled desire, and this resort
> Both limits and implies their liberty.
> Ambiguous liberty! It is the air
> Between the raised arm and the fallen thud.[22]
> [ll. 14–18]

Action is an instinctive gesture, an expression of illusory liberty supplied by the mask that the Beaters don, the social and collective role conferred by their uniforms. The uniform is merely ornamental; it is used to boast an identity otherwise lacking ("the dandy's affectation," l. 7). The weapon too, like the motorcycle in "On the Move," is a surrogate for sexual energy that is repressed by a behavioral code (of military discipline), but erupts in violent, destructive gestures. The plain sexual connotations of the line "it is the air / Between the raised arm and the fallen thud" convey the act of ejaculation.

Analogously, the violent, isolated actions of the protagonist are meaningless in "Market at Turk," composed of three stanzas of six lines each, whose rhythm, accelerated by strong enjambment, suggests the extreme tension of the young protagonist.[23] On the one hand, his uniform, prepared with extreme care "Boots, jeans, and a curious cap" (*CP* 58, l. 4), seems to guarantee a goal for his actions. On the other hand, his will (in this moment of waiting, this anticipation of action) is quite uncertain, prey to a state of disorientation[24]:

> he presides in apartness
> not yet knowing his purpose
> fully, and fingers the blade.
> [*CP* 58, ll. 16–18]

The only certainty is the instinctive gesture, the touching of the blade, which corresponds with the peak of his bizarre cap "jammed forward," suggesting masturbation, the self-gratification of an onanistic nature. Also in this case the instrument of action (and the same goes for the motorcycles of the young riders in "On the Move" and for the weapons—"whip, cords, and strap"—in "The Beaters") is a surrogate for repressed and diverted sexual energy, expressed metonymically by the assumed mask.

These examples indicate a change in direction and technique: abandoning the elaborate, subtle metaphors of the literary tradition, Gunn adopts myths, images and aspects of the contemporary world, using a language in which both literal and metaphorical expressions freely unite.

Neil Powell writes:

> What impresses most about *The Sense of Movement* is the radicalism of subject-matter, a feeling that Gunn has firmly established his intellectual and technical abilities and is now able to go on to deal with the contemporary situation in a manner more confident than that of any other English poet writing at the time.[25]

An example of this new use of contemporary language and themes is the discourse that characterizes the poem "Elvis Presley," dedicated to the hero of fifties and sixties music. Gunn is more attracted to Elvis's pose than his music, to the pop singer image, a symbol of protest and challenge and a new musical world. Music loses its hegemonic role inside the spectacle; performance is the most important aspect. The assumption of certain poses, in this case, those of Elvis Presley, allude to erotic gestures (suggested by the line "crawling sideburns, wielding a guitar" [*CP* 57, l. 4], in which the guitar has clear phallic connotations). This poem is pervaded by a sense of the observer's ironic detachment, which casts doubt on the authenticity and spontaneity of certain attitudes, together with the substantial indifference of the public ("Whether he poses or is real, no cat / Bothers to say" *CP* 57, ll.13–14), which desires only the spectacle. Elvis's music appears lacking in content or message; it is the same old story repeated *ad nauseam* ("...hackneyed words in hackneyed songs," l. 10). The poet turns his attention primarily to the gestures, seen in action, as suggested by the ample use of the gerund form: "unreeling, crawling, wielding." These gestures confirm the sense of struggle as an end in itself ("He turns revolt into a style..." *CP* 57, l. 11), which is also, in Sartrian fashion, a choice of action, an intolerance of repressive and obsolete models.[26] The performance manifests a hidden identity ready to challenge the surrounding reality and conventions, and capable of creating an alternative life, a temporary model for the younger generations to imitate even if, at least for the moment, it is limited to evening hours spent in a discotheque or a bar. This happens in the poem "PETE" (*Positives*), when the character Mackie takes off his clothes and his work tools to transform himself into a gifted guitarist, like John Travolta transforms himself into an exceptional disco dancer in an iconic film of the seventies, *Saturday Night Fever* (1977).

Neil Corcoran writes:

> The poem ["Elvis Presley"] seems in a poised atonement to its historical moment, in no merely modish way. The restlessness, dissatisfaction and self-generation, all set resolutely against traditional ideas of nature and theology, are the very impulse of dissidence in the 1950s, whether in French existentialism or in the explosion of a youth culture inventing itself as "teenagers" and "teddy boys." Presley, Marlon Brando and James Dean were the major spurs to that invention, and there are, of course, famous images of all three in leathers astride motorbikes.[27]

Despite the evident influence of the new myths of the American environment present in this collection, Gunn maintains that Elvis is only a symbol drawn from the culture in which he is gradually being transplanted, but reproducible anywhere:

> Obviously one's subject matter does largely come from the place one lives in but I am not sure that the subject matter of America is that different nowadays from the subject matter of England. To take that rather over-famous poem of mine about Elvis Presley, one could just as easily have written that poem from England or France, or Finland. I'm not sure whether it is important that I have lived in America.[28]

The poem "The Unsettled Motorcyclist's Vision of His Death" unites the modern myth of the motorcyclist with the literary tradition, recalling both seventeenth-century poetry (particularly Marvell, but also Donne) and Yeats. The poem links to Marvell at both a stylistic level (Gunn uses the eight-syllable couplet that Marvell preferred) and a thematic one, adopting images of the growth, development and decomposition of vegetable matter.[29]

The title resembles "An Irish Airman Foresees His Death" (Yeats), where the Irish poet glorifies "A lonely impulse of delight"[30] by means of which the protagonist, alone in the sky, begins freely to challenge death while confirming his own capacity for self-control, opposing his destiny and hostile nature.

Echoes of Yeats are noticeable in much of *The Sense of Movement* in certain formal aspects, and they are apparent at an intertextual level. In its title, Gunn's poem "Jesus and His Mother" recalls Yeats's "The Mother of God," from which he borrows also the insistent use of a refrain, "I am my own and not my own" (*CP* 64), which closes, with minimal variations, every stanza.[31] As with "Lazarus Not Raised," in "Jesus and his Mother," Gunn offers a rewriting of a famous New Testament episode. In response to Divine Will, he gives voice, Bakhtinian-style, to multiple points of view of single characters and their deepest desires; they seem to proceed in opposite directions to those transmitted by tradition and imposed from on high. Maria's human dimension, her mother's anxiety and uncertainty, emerge when, with profound inner pain, she rebels against her destiny ("I cannot reach to call you Lord / Answer me as my only son. / 'I am my own and not my own'" *CP* 65, ll. 40–42). She is aware of the predominantly human nature of the son she gave birth to, and feels incapable of accepting for him a divine role — alien to her own body and identity — which would completely estrange him:

> I did not understand your words;
> I taught you speech, we named the birds,
> You marked their big migration then
> Like any child ...
> [*CP* 64, ll. 16–19]

According to Martin Dodsworth, Yeats's influence is not limited to form, since Gunn uses "a Yeatsian form to treat this Yeatsian theme" of the presence of the sacred in the real. The refrain "I am my own and not my own" mirrors, says Dodsworth, a characteristic Yeatsian quest of a hero, "who bends all his nature to becoming what he is not, that is, to donning the mask of his anti-self: 'Saint and hero cannot be content to pass at moments to that hollow image [of their opposite] and after become their heterogeneous selves but would always, if they could, resemble the antithetical selves.'"[32]

Gunn himself recognizes Yeats's influence, especially in this collection ("there is ... a fair amount of Yeats" *OP* 177), yet emphasizes the inimitability of the model. Every attempt at imitation inevitably ends in parody and affectation: "Yeats was a bad influence — for most of my generation, I think — in that one tends to pick up all the mannerism but none of the intensity."[33]

In "The Unsettled Motorcyclist's Vision of His Death," the protagonist notices from the outset that the only way to attain human dignity is to declare war on nature. Pain and suffering cannot be avoided or mitigated, but must be confronted as the only way to salvation, even if this means self-destruction:

> Into the walls of rain I ride.
> [...]
> The firm heath stops, and marsh begins.
> Now we're at war: whichever wins
> My human will cannot submit

> To nature, though brought out of it.
> [*CP* 54, ll. 2, 5–8]

A sense of dignity compels human beings to refuse to submit to nature, of which they do not feel a part, even though they owe their existence to it. Although in the first stanza the motorcyclist seems, like the characters of "On the Move," to give meaning to his life by choosing action ("Into the walls of rain I ride"), it is insufficient to overcome the dichotomy between intellect and instinct. On the contrary, it aggravates the condition, because in his imitation of and challenge to nature's brute force, the motorcyclist realizes tragically his difference from it and at the same time the impossibility of uprooting himself from it ("though brought out of it"). Approaching his death is, paradoxically, a movement between death and life, a chaotic and gigantic fight with the vegetation on an earth that he finds utterly alien: "Through the dark earth that is not mine, / Crowded with fragments, blunt, unformed" (*CP* 54, ll. 26–27). The last word in line 27, "unformed," brings up the Bergsonian dilemma between life and form. The absence of form signals the diversity of the vegetable world compared to the human one. Dying, the motorcyclist affirms his own dignity in opposition to nature, to plant life, though he is subject to its blindly destructive power, which transforms all human potential ("richness") into garbage ("dirt")[34]:

> Cell after cell the plants convert
> My special richness in the dirt:
> All that they get, they get by chance.
>
> And multiply in ignorance.
> [*CP* 55, ll. 41–44]

The space between lines 43 and 44 creates a pause, which suggests the inexorable slowness of vegetable processes compared to the speed of the motorcycle, which represents the human, the vain but self-conscious choice, unlike the "ignorance" of nature. Nature's slow action, which in the end gets the better of him by causing his death, is at a lower level than human action in the speaker's hierarchy of the world. Unlike what happens in "On the Move," where the "birds and saints complete their purposes," in this poem the Hardyesque "Immanent Will" underlying natural processes is shown to have no recognizable aim, but follows a blind course such that living things "multiply in ignorance," "serving" this will. Nature's lack of self-awareness makes it servile, whereas consciousness ennobles mankind, even though it is also the source of his anxieties. Gunn appears to want to reverse the Cartesian statement "*cogito ergo sum*" into "*sum ergo cogito*": I am a person, and as such, I am condemned to think. To think means to create a scheme of the world, that necessarily implies a scheme for one's life, subduing blind impulses that are as present in man as they are in nature. To think means to affirm one's own humanity, even by means of violent, destructive, and self-destructive acts, reclaiming, according to Lawrence R. Ries, "the role of the assertive will in a valueless world."[35]

Unlike Philip Larkin, who believes that retreat, compromise, and escape from the world are the only ways to survive in the contemporary reality, Gunn (according to Ries) "was insisting that one must impose form upon the amorphous world, and physical action, especially in some violent form, is the safest guarantee of attempting to come to terms with the world."[36]

Man lives a double life, one part intellectual, which makes him superior to nature's chaos, but also condemns him to the anxiety of existing as an individual, and the other part instinctive and intuitive, which brings him very close to the natural world. In this intensely existential phase, however, Gunn sees Nature as lacking meaning, as being alienating and imprisoning.

The theme of being "condemned to humanity" recurs in the poems of *The Sense of Movement*, for example, in "Legal Reform," which opens and closes with the lines:

> Condemned to life, a happier condemnation
> [...]
> The sentence is, condemned to be condemned.
> [CP 77-78]

Here the poet speaks of an actual convict doing forced labor — identified with the incessant labor of thinking — who tragically realizes that his jailer, his taskmaster, is none other than his *doppelgänger*, the other face of himself who, in his desperate search for an existence beyond the law of brute nature ("hope, happiness, life"), condemns himself ("...a simple law / Passed by ourselves..." CP 77, ll. 7-8) to existential angst. In this poem the awareness of human guilt begins to emerge, the idea that we indirectly create our own prisons in the attempt to affirm our humanity, a guilt that, like Joseph K's in Kafka's *The Trial*, cannot be expiated by action or challenge.

SHAPING THE FOG

The theme of self-condemnation also occurs in the poem "Puss in Boots to the Giant" ("We condemn to Thought" l. 25),[37] and in "Human Condition,"[38] where the human condition is a desolate wandering in the fog. This vision does not cause Gunn to choose passivity or resignation. On the contrary, by will and discipline, aware of their being the only touchstones of reality, he forces himself to impose order on the disorder that surrounds him, to control his passion with the self-dignity of a thinking man:

> Particular, I must
> Find out the limitation
> Of mind and universe,
> To pick thought and sensation
> And turn to my own use
> Disordered hate or lust.
> [ll. 19-24]

In Gunn's poetry, the fog (wandering in it evokes the inferno of Eliot's hollow men) and the moonlight in which the boy in "The Allegory of the Wolf Boy" undergoes his torturous and lacerating metamorphosis, are symbols of insecurity, inner turbulence, and self-schism in which the psyche cannot rebuild its own wholeness. The moonlight is also expressive of a state of passivity and dreams, of turning inwards, in contrast to sunlight, which is synonymous with energy and action. Sun and moon reflect the duplicity of the protagonist in "The Wound," his simultaneous tendency toward introspection ("For joy I did not move and dared not speak,") and action ("I called for armour, rose, and did not reel" *CP* 3, ll. 4, 21).

In "The Silver Age," the stanzas end with the obsessive image of moonlight, in a sinister refrain that affirms the ineluctability of alienation. The image of moonlight as a mirror of one's anxious solitude re-emerges in the later collections, like the return of a nightmare which California's sun cannot eradicate. In "The Goddess" (*Touch*), the solar image of the goddess Proserpine, the incarnation of Mother Nature and symbol of the life force that pervades the universe and upon whose arrival the entire plant and animal world freely reproduce, contrasts with man, represented by the figure of a soldier who waits alone in the moonlight for the arrival of a woman.[38] The frenetic rhythm of lines, which proceed without pause from the first to last stanza by enjambment, celebrates (in what appears to be a 180-degree turn in Gunn's poetry) the regeneration of the world, but the soldier remains an isolated figure, unable, despite his desire, to actively participate in the awakening of nature that surrounds him. Touched by the goddess and encouraged to give free expression to his sexuality ("...waiting all evening for / a woman, any woman" *CP* 155, ll. 18–19), he, unlike the plants and animals ("breeding, breeding, in their nests" *CP* 155, l. 15), remains condemned to isolation and waiting. The embrace is only an illusion, and his uniform suggests his separation from the outside world ("and the soldier by a park / bench with his greatcoat *collar / up* ..." *CP* 155, ll. 16–18, my emphasis). This soldier is not unlike various isolated heroes in *Fighting Terms*: he is ready for action (his outfit confirms this), but condemned to waiting, to inertia. "For Signs" (*Moly*) is also dominated by the moonlight that pervades the protagonist's dream. He is obsessed by the image of an old self ("Dream mentor, I have been inside that skull, / I too have used those cindered passages" *CP* 189, ll. 28–29). Even in a volume like *Moly*, which is characterized by the brightness of California landscapes bathed in sunlight,[39] there are several references to the moon. Moonlight seems to bring up an old nightmare that the poet wishes to exorcise:

> But now the moon leaves Scorpio: I look up.
> [...]
> I lean upon the fence and watch the sky,
> How light fills blinded socket and chafed mark.
> It soars, hard, full, and edged, it coldly burns.
> [*CP* 189, ll. 30, 40–42]

Gunn's glorification of discipline and control, his attempt to find a balance between thought and action, between intellect and instinct, find their highest expression in the poem dedicated to his teacher, Yvor Winters:

> You keep both Rule and Energy in view,
> Much power in each, most in the balanced two:
> Ferocity existing in the fence
> Built by an exercised intelligence.
> [*CP* 70, ll. 30–33]

In order to fully express its potential, thought needs action, which alone allows it to reach that balance between "Rule" and "Energy" that Gunn attributed to his teacher. This balance should result not just in rules for living, but also in a sense of artistic duty, an awareness of the necessity of discipline in poetic activity, the ability to impose form on the most elusive material and sensations. "To Yvor Winters" is, for Neil Powell,

> A lucid statement of faith in intellectual sanity as opposed to romantic looseness and sentimentality: the ideal of "an exercised intelligence" is unexceptionable. The poem's conclusion is a vindication of Winters' criticism and may also be seen as something of an apologia for the excesses of "Lines for a Book."[40]

The idea that a balance between passion and intellect is the essential principle of poetic activity is confirmed in many self-reflexive poems in which Gunn comments on the process of composition, as in the cycle "Confessions of the Life Artist" (*Touch*). The poet realizes that his art, "...immersed in despair" (*CP* 161, 5, l. 1), is indefinite and abstract. Only through constant contact with reality, with concrete experience, can he impose a discipline capable of giving order where disorder reigns. Paradoxically, this order, or balance, leaves room for passion and instinct, for the immediacy of experience.[41] Art must anchor itself in the *hic and nunc*, satisfied to give expression to ongoing life, and renouncing every pretext of immortality. In the last stanza, in lines that recall Thomas Gray's "Elegy" ("But what of the unchosen? / / They are as if dead. Their deaths, / now, validate the chosen" *CP* 160, 4, ll. 1–3), Gunn is aware that his work is destined to oblivion because of a process of transformation and destruction that nothing can escape. In other words, art can assume a deep existential meaning, becoming rule and style for life, but it must renounce every oracular pretence, and all ambition to speak eternal truths. Though it is a means to confront the void, art does not offer an escape from the death to which we are all condemned. Although for Thomas Gray, death created, before God's eyes, a type of equality denied in life by a society structured in an apparently immutable hierarchy, for Gunn, this common destiny (death) is proof of the meaninglessness of existence, which not even poetry can escape or even less explain:

> The art of designing life
> is no excuse for that life.
> People will forget Shakespeare.

> He will lie with George Formby
> and me, here where the swine root.
> Later, the solar system
> will flare up and fall into
> space, irretrievably lost.
> For the loss, as for the life,
> there will be no excuse, there
> is no justification.
> [*CP* 163, 10, ll. 1–11]

This is not a renunciation of the ethical function of poetry which, in his own way, Gunn tried to express, as seen in "A Plan of Self Subjection," which questions much of the earlier work, and in particular the poems of *Fighting Terms*, through its reference to heroic figures of the past (Alexander, Mark Antony, Coriolanus). The refrain ("My circle's end is where I have begun" *CP* 47) suggests that the undertakings of these heroes have meaning only insofar as they challenge the void. This refrain, with its clear echoes of one of the leitmotifs in Eliot's *The Four Quartets* ("In the beginning is my end"),[42] implies that no undertaking significantly changes reality and that the poet's activity, his imposition of order on the world, represents only an illusory conquest:

> ... my verse
> Imposes form upon my fault described
> So that my fault is worse —
> Not from condonement but from being bribed
> With order ...
> [*CP* 46, ll. 9–13]

These lines confirm the need for balance between art and life, between "rule" and "energy," between material and form, emphasizing the liminal position in which Gunn finds himself as he must continually oscillate between the source of inspiration (where life pulsates) and the poetic creation. Paradoxically, writing is an action that, through form, ends up proving the imperfection of the material ("Imposes form upon my fault described / So that my fault is worse —"), as if order itself and the filtration of experience through language were a trick, a delusion, rather than a way of communicating truth ("...bribed / With order ..."). The lines, "As Alexander or Mark Antony / ... / I mask self-flattery" (*CP* 46, ll. 17, 19), suggest that the withdrawal into poetry always implies a mystifying intention, the assumption of a pose or mask. Art cannot avoid aspiring to the heights, but it must be satisfied with an illusory and precarious balance between paradise and hell, between light and shadow, material and form, between two poles, each of which looks paradoxically like the mirrored face of the other: "Because I have found that from the heaven sun / Can scorch like hell itself" (*CP* 46, ll. 6–7).

The glorification of will as spur to action is expressed particularly clearly in the philosophical poem "The Nature of an Action," divided into three stanzas of rhyming couplets in iambic pentameter, in which Gunn confronts the problem of perception of reality, and the individual's alienation from the world that surrounds him.[43] In the first stanza the speaker describes the room he is in, with its oppressively heavy furniture, some of which is eccentric and artificial ("...heavy-footed chairs / A glass bell loaded with wax grapes and pears" *CP* 41, 1, ll. 1–2). Guided by his instinct ("Directed by the compass of my heart" *CP* 41, 1, l. 8), which provides a lucid perception of the way, as the image of the compass suggests (echoing Donne's "A Valediction: Forbidding Mourning"), he tries to leave the room via the corridor, the crossing of which occupies all of the second stanza, twice as long as the other two,[44] until, summoning all his force of will, with a desperate gesture, he reaches the next room. The lines that describe the second room are the same as those in the first stanza, conferring a mirroring and circular structure to the poem. The surprise, however, is that, to the speaker's eyes, the second room does not appear identical so much as just similar, because by action, *he* has changed: "Much like the first, this room in which I went. / Only my being there is different" (*CP* 42, 3, ll. 9–10). Before, he was passive in the room, and therefore dominated by its reality, but by the gesture of acting on his will, he actively experienced his relationship with the second room. Though hardly changing place, he changes the way in which it is perceived, so that the ontological reality of things is brought into question. In the second stanza the labyrinthine world in which the speaker moves ("I groped to feel a handle in the mind" *CP* 41, 2, l. 10), feels like a suffocating and impervious reality that opposes his will with powerful resistance: "Although the narrow corridor appears / So short, the journey took me twenty years" (*CP* 41, 2, ll. 1–2). The temporal reference, as in "The Wound," is purely hyperbolical; it suggests the fatigue caused by a "penetration" into reality that occurs by a subjective perception of objects. Objects themselves, and the space in which they are brought together, lose consistency and seem unreal since they are part of the poet's perception (we could say, since they reside "statically" in his mind). Only by the force of will ("My cause lay in the will..." *CP* 42, 3, l. 1–2), can he overcome the schism between self and external reality; only by action can the world or self acquire ontological status.

The image of things that can become hostile, can transform into a nightmare if we are unable to find a way to live with them, and to define a space that welcomes both them and us, emerges in "Thoughts on Unpacking." The speaker is arranging certain objects, trying to create a livable space for himself and his companion, an attempt that is in reality quite difficult. His movements are slowed by his inertia, by something that blocks his free activity:

>   ... I clear,
> Or try to clear, a space for us, ...
> [...]
> ... But something hinders me:
> [*CP* 79, ll. 1–2, 5]

Every object is weighted down with the speaker's existential experience and ends up possessing the space around him, until it takes away his freedom of action: "...till I find / They have filled the space I carefully prepared" (*CP* 79, ll. 16–17). Organizing the space, even though limited to the arrangement of a few objects, is a metaphor and mirror of his existence, destined to be continually under analysis, as he tries to start from scratch and exorcise the ghosts of his past. While the speaker seeks to free the space which he has carefully prepared for himself and his companion, love is depicted, not as a battle without quarter as in *Fighting Terms*, but as a mere agreement, a mutual sharing of common space: "Now as I sweep it clean, / I realize that love is an arranging" (*CP* 80, ll. 29–30).

According to Alan Brownjohn the objects are the symbolic reflection of a particular psychological situation, the inability to communicate or overcome the barrier that divides self from other:

> This poem is about certain obstacles and embarrassments which threaten a relationship — not only minor, tangible things but more serious difficulties.... If we are not careful, he [Gunn] is saying, these things become all-important obsessions ... and they will obstinately resist any attempt to banish them.[45]

The problem of the relationship between subject and object runs through the poem "The Corridor," whose title indicates those narrow spaces in which the self is forced to move (as in "The Nature of an Action"), that boundary that separates thought and action, being and becoming, and even life and death. The poem is structured in nine quatrains, whose rhyme scheme (*abba*) is a closed form suggestive of the protagonist's experience. His experience repeats itself infinitely in the succession of lines until the realization (which coincides with his liberation) reached at the ninth (a multiple of the perfect number) and last stanza:

> What could he do but leave the keyhole, rise,
> Holding those eyes as equal in his eyes,
> And go, one hand held out, to meet a friend?
> [*CP* 86, ll. 34–36]

At the beginning of the poem the speaker, incapable of a real contact in the outside world, succumbs to the mental (like Lawrence's "sex in the head") and onanistic pleasure of the voyeur, contemplating the embrace of two lovers through a keyhole. Being convinced that he is the only observer, he reaches the conclusion that the observation of pleasure is much nicer and more intense than the experience itself, confirming the idea that passion is "acted," which informs the poems in *Fighting Terms*.[46] The first line of "The Corridor," "A separate place between the thought and felt" (*CP* 85) seems like a rewriting of the "space between the thighs and head" of "Carnal Knowledge." The corridor itself and the keyhole are the symbolic thresholds between two spheres, two worlds, between intellect and action, between the physical pleasure of the lovers and the intellectual pleasure of the one who prefers to enjoy without being involved, without exposing his body to contact with the other.[47] The voyeur's sense of self-justification immediately decreases, however, when he notices two strange eyes watching him ("Two strange eyes in a fascinated face / That watched him like a picture in a book" *CP* 85, ll. 19–20). He in turn becomes the object of observation, losing his earlier position of superiority in regard to the lovers. His identity as observer is challenged by the two eyes in the mirror, which relegate him to the object of their perception, to a picture in a book without will or liberty, and therefore without true ontological consistency.

The speaker reverses his epistemological attitude after discerning his reflected image, or after the realization that he exists in that particular moment and in that particular place, not only as observer but also as observed, as simultaneously actor and character in someone else's play.[48] There are similarities here to Heisenberg's principle of uncertainty (enunciated in 1927), according to which it is not possible with physical experience, however ideally refined, to determine with precision simultaneously the position of a particle and its speed. This physical principle can be related to the philosophical one of defining one's ontological space, one's own *ubi consistam*.[49] The image reflected in the mirror ("Two strange eyes in a fascinated face / That watched him like a picture in a book"), which recalls Prufrock's obsession ("The eyes that fix you in a formulated phrase"),[50] attracts the speaker even more than the lovers' embrace, even to the point where the image completely replaces the lovers ("...they were clean gone / The couple in the keyhole; this would stay" *CP* 85, ll. 23–24). This relates also to the figure of the double or *doppelgänger*, which in this poem, despite the fact that it maintains that perturbing aura typical of much late nineteenth-century literature, loses the sinister connotations it had in Gunn's "The Secret Sharer," foreshadowing his opening to the outside world and contact with the Other which would characterize Gunn's later collections.

Poems such as "The Monster" (*My Sad Captains*), "Bravery" (*Touch*) and "Behind the Mirror" (*Jack Straw's Castle*) demonstrate that Gunn's later openness comes in part from exorcising the *doppelgänger* and reconstructing a sense of personal wholeness.

In "The Monster," where Gunn reworks the image of the individual trying to escape from his sense of claustrophobic reclusion in his room by wandering in the dark night in search of bought pleasure (and we should emphasize that here it is a woman who offers it), the "monster" is the personification of the self who suffers from isolation:

> At once I knew him, gloating over
> A grief defined and realized,
> And living only for its sake.
> It was myself I recognized.
>
> I could not watch her window now,
> Standing before this man of mine,
> The constant one I had created
> Lest the pure feeling should decline.
> [*CP* 96, ll. 17–24]

In "Bravery," where the speaker concentrates on a painting by Chuck Arnett, and specifically on the figure of a man who, turning his shoulder to the observer, is about to enter a landscape full of fog into which he will be completely absorbed, the observation of the painting has the effect of a mutual, vampirish possession of the object observed and of he who observes it: the observer sees in the painting the projection not only of himself but also of his desire:

> Giant vampire! If your
> back were not turned, I
> should have known you
> before, you are
> my monstrous lover, whom
> I gaze at
> every time I shave
> [ll. 26–32][51]

In "Behind the Mirror," Gunn explores the theme of the divided self, of himself and his image reflected in the mirror. In this revision of the Narcissus myth, the hero fearlessly denies the reflection, definitively erases it, manages to recompose his lost wholeness, and become part of the surrounding world:

> [He] would come to rest on a soft dark wave of soil
> to root there and stand again
>   one flower,
> one waxy star, giving perfume, unreflecting.
> [CP 293, ll. 20–23]

Mental appropriation of reality is also experienced in the poem "In Praise of Cities," one of the most tender in *The Sense of Movement*, where the "she" is not a woman, but a city that is anthropomorphically a type of Mother Nature created by man. She is the queen of a benevolent universe, capable of transforming, in the dark, into a lover who gives in lasciviously to every embrace:

> She presses you with her hard ornaments,
> Arcades, late movie shows, the piled lit windows
> Of surplus stores. Here she is loveliest;
> Extreme, material, and the work of man.
> [CP 60, 4, ll. 13–16]

The city is a woman, indifferent but not hostile ("Indifferent to the indifference that conceived her, / Grown buxom in disorder now, she accepts /— Like dirt, strangers, or moss upon her churches—" CP 59, 1, ll. 1–3), who welcomes human beings without expecting anything in return. She is better adapted to their rhythms than nature, which confronts the individual with an alien reality, one dominated by chaos. Even the city is subject to decay, to the metamorphoses caused by the invasion of brute nature ("moss upon her churches"), but she accepts change as an integral part of her identity, pulsing with life, incessantly alive with electrifying dynamism.[52] The "man made" is, in Gunn's value system, on a higher level than nature, and the city itself is seen as a place in which the individual does not lose himself, but finds himself and his roots.

For Alan Bold, "In Praise of Cities"

> indicates that Gunn finds the exploration of cities more rewarding than the exploration of other individuals because in them he can escape a definite commitment to another person. The city accepts him for what he is and asks nothing from him except his imposing presence.[53]

Another critic, John Press, notices something morbid in Gunn's attraction to the city:

> He praises the modern city, amorphous, broken, unfinished, precisely because its rhythms are alien to those of nature. There is something perverse, yet compelling in his total acceptance of the metropolis.[54]

Despite grasping a fundamental aspect of Gunn's work, which is the predominantly urban nature of his muse (after *Touch*, most of the poems are set in cities and reveal their many faces)[55] neither Bold nor Press recognizes that Gunn's desperate attempt to reach the outside world implies establishing contact, through the environment, with other people. Gunn himself occasionally said that his predilection for cities was due to the fact that they had a human imprint:

> It's a liking for the man-made, for the massive, for something that has the human imprint on it, rather than for the deserted, the provincial. The liking for buildings more than mountains. This is part of me, I suppose, and it is difficult to explain oneself.[56]

Contrary to what Alan Bold believes, then, his sense of communion with the city moves Gunn to participate in its life, both in the community which lives there and that of all humanity, as seen in "Back to Life" (the last poem in *Touch*), which has as background a city park where all people, young and old, share the same destiny. The macro-organism of civilization is symbolized by a tree whose leaves are like individuals who grow and then fall from the same branch:

> I walk between the kerb and bench
> Conscious at length
> Of sharing through each sense,
> As if the light revealed us all
> Sustained in delicate difference
> Yet firmly growing from a single branch.
> [*CP* 176, ll. 39–44]

In "Iron Landscapes (and the Statue of Liberty)" (*Jack Straw's Castle*), Gunn expresses his organic vision of the city in Whitmanesque terms, welcoming the strong pulse of life which hides under the apparent chaos of activity that occurs in cities, the personal form underneath the formless, the sharp, aggressive beauty of objects like "Block, cylinder, cube." He describes the manmade structures of the city with a terminology inflected by that of plant life, emphasizing simultaneously their perpetual and apparently uncontrollable mutation, but also their irreducible permanence[57]:

> No trellises, no vines
>   a fire escape
> Repeats a bare black Z from tier to tier.
> [...]
> But I'm at peace with the iron landscape too,
> Hard because buildings must be hard to last
> — Block, cylinder, cube, built with their angles true,
> A dream of righteous permanence, from the past.
> [*CP* 231, ll. 1-2, 13-16]

The opposition between human (comprehensible in that it is human) and nonhuman (nature, which is extraneous and hostile) finds expression also in the long poem (eight stanzas of seven lines), "Merlin in the Cave: He Speculates without a Book," placed almost at the end of *The Sense of Movement*. The line with which the long poem opens and (with a small variation) closes, "This was the end and yet, another start," "This is an end, and yet another start" (*CP* 81, 84), suggests that this is a landmark, that the poet has overcome the obsessive feeling of condemnation with which most of the poems of the collection are informed, and that he is trying to begin a new existential journey (even though in a rather hesitant way). Although the line suggests the obsessive repetition of the same journey that condemns Merlin to the prison of his intellect, symbolically represented by the cave which "...is empty, and is very cold" (*CP* 82, l. 42), a change of course and the definition of a new horizon are foreshadowed by the last stanza:

> Knowing the end to movement, I will shrink
> From movement not for its own willful sake.
> — How can a man live, and not act or think
> Without an end? But I must act, and make
> The meaning in each movement that I take.
> Rook, bee, you are the whole and not a part.
> This is an end, and yet another start.
> [*CP* 84, ll. 78-84]

The recognition of the inevitable end of movement results, not in the choice of stasis and death (like Lazarus), but in a conscious commitment to action, to the stoic fight to end the Sartrian anxiety of existence.

If seeking to impose a rational order upon existence (like Merlin tried to do) means to lose one's humanity, then — concludes the speaker after a reluctant journey through the past — it is necessary to accept the human dimension, with its limits and potentials, to be content with observing the world and understanding it within the limits of human possibility, via one's senses, without trying to penetrate the impenetrable, but seeking to intervene in it through action. This is not dictated by "the intelligence of instinct," which the human being has already lost ("I lost their instinct. It was late. To me / The bird is only meat for augury" *CP* 81, ll. 13–14), but must spring from a conscious choice and a constant search for meaning ("But I must act, and make / The meaning in each movement that I take").

In this poem Gunn reverses the symbolism of Plato's allegory of the cave, implying that man reaches true consciousness not by breaking the chains of physical being to welcome with the eye of his mind the reality that inexorably escapes the mortal eye — that method, long pursued by Merlin, was completely disastrous — but by harmonizing his own intellectual activity with the rhythms of the universe in which he finds himself. The final line of the poem, "This is an end, and yet another start," connects back to the first, as so often occurs in Gunn ("This was the end and yet, another start"). The change of the verb tense from past to present reveals, at the end of Merlin's intellectual speculations, his openness to the present, and indirectly, towards the future, suggested by the word "start." The other change in the refrain, the replacement of the indefinite article "an," with the definite one, "the," suggests the end of an obsessive cycle which repeats, indefinitely, the breaking of the circular movement which held him imprisoned in his cave. What Merlin achieves is a true aim: the possibility of turning the page and opening himself to a new world.

This theme is taken up and developed further in the last poem of the collection, "Vox Humana,"[58] which ends appropriately with the word "future," thus with an invitation to leave the past behind, anticipating a change on the poet's part. By describing a being as yet unformed, of indeterminate nature, a blur, Gunn emphasizes the need for courage to face the world; by naming things one might arrive at some understanding, albeit partial:

> as you name, ...
> I shall become more precise.
> [...]
> Or if you call me the blur
> that in fact I am, you shall
> yourself remain blurred, hanging
> like smoke indoors. For you bring,
> to what you define now,
> all there is, ever, of future.
> [*CP* 87–88, ll. 15–16, 25–30]

The poet affirms not only the importance of humanity, but especially the value of language as a tool of understanding, of communication, and also of intervention into reality, recalling an essay by Heidegger on the poetry of Hölderlin, where particular attention is given to the line "*dichterisch wohnt der Mensch auf dieser Erde*" ("poetically the human being lives upon this earth"). The "poetically," as Gianni Vattimo argues, "means ... that historically man's living has to do with living in an environment, but this living in an environment is experienced existentially as belonging to a language that is speech."[59] Language thus becomes a means of conscious action, an essential element for the definition of that "meaning in each movement" that Merlin proposed at the end of his meditation as the only glimmer of salvation. Naming things to know them and also, indirectly, to "possess" them poetically, is symptomatic, for Waltraud Mitgutsch, of Gunn's changed approach to his material. As long as nature is observed from a distance, says this critic, it is gifted with an existence and movement that does not necessitate any interference, no contact with the outside, so that the self feels completely alienated from it. In the moment in which the poet-self names objects existing in nature, he tries to make nature his own, to re-create it through language, and it is through this artistic recreation of external reality that his own ontological being is assured.[60] In other words, while the self suffers exile from the world in the existence of others who become testimony of his alienation from nature, through language, in the naming of the universe, the Self (à la Heidegger) finds itself and becomes part of the universe.

Opening with a poem like "On the Move," which glorifies the pose and the heroic challenge as ends in themselves, and closing with one like "Vox Humana," which emphasizes, not only the value of the human, but the necessity of gradually (not violently or suddenly) approaching reality, a slow and careful discovery of what is true, the collection is suspended between two opposite poles which also characterize the prevalent attitude of the next volume, *My Sad Captains*, that is, the opposition between the vain pose (of which Gunn will define the limits) and the need to approach nature, to face reality and one's destiny, to accept them for what they are, and to seek to know them, as much as a human being can.

CHAPTER IV

Surrender and Recovery

The Phenomenology of Defeat

The need to submit to the laws of nature, to accept existential angst (which is a sickness of the modern world), to make this acceptance the foundation of a stoical ethics—all take shape in the third collection, *My Sad Captains*. The title suggests the poet's parting from his captains, those divinely-touched heroes, who, besides being serious and thoughtful (the Elizabethan sense of the word "sad"), like those in Shakespeare's *Antony and Cleopatra* ("come, / Let's have one other gaudy night: call to me / All my sad captains, fill our bowls once more; / Let's mock the midnight bell"),[1] are also truly sad because they shine only in reflected light.

Critical reaction to *My Sad Captains*, which represents both a stylistic and thematic turning point in Gunn's work, was not very favorable. Those who had appreciated the energy and vigor of the first two volumes found this one more static, weak, and repetitive. John Fuller found the second edition of *Fighting Terms* "most welcome," and good enough to "compensate for the disappointment of *My Sad Captains*."[2]

For Lawrence R. Ries, the collection signaled the beginning of a regression that would increase in the later volumes:

> From a classical style on themes of assertion, force and violence, his poetry became gradually freer in form and more static and meditative in theme.... When the third volume, *My Sad Captains*, appeared, there was an initial note of praise for the new direction in which the still young poet was moving. The syllabic verse and the more placid subject were seen as a promise of mature poetic evolution, but the signs were misleading. The critics did not realize that Gunn was actually rejecting his earlier stance, and that his new poetry, carried further into still freer forms in *Positives* (1966) and in *Touch* (1968), was a regression for the poet rather than an evolution.[3]

The work is divided into two parts, the first of which Gunn calls "the culmination of my old style" (*OP* 179), while the second is a series of poems in syllabics, in which his tone is "a little more humane" (*OP* 179). The oscillation between the heroic pose of the preceding works and the openness to the world of the later ones is suggested by the epigraphs of each part, taken from Shakespeare's *Troilus and Cressida*, and F. Scott Fitzgerald's *The Last Tycoon*, as well as from the poems' titles. "The Monster," "Black Jackets," "The Byrnies," to mention a few, recall the uniforms and challenges of the centaurs in "On the Move," whereas "Waking in a Newly Built House," "The Feel of Hands," and "Considering the Snail," suggest quite clearly a change in direction.

His changed attitude already emerges in the opening poem of the volume, "In Santa Maria del Popolo," which refers to a picture by Caravaggio, *The Conversion of Saint Paul* (1601), displayed in the Roman church that Gunn visited during a brief trip to Italy.[4]

In place of the shadows, dust, and moonlight that dominated *The Sense of Movement*, Gunn puts sunlight, which renders possible a "reading" of the painting. From the painting, which depicts St. Paul's mystical epiphany — his subject also has to do with light, as does the technique of Caravaggio, a painter who loved forceful chiaroscuro and scenes loaded with dynamic and dramatic tension — the poet in the last stanza addresses the humble, defenseless people praying in the church. This represents a change in perspective, which on the one hand might indicate his skepticism about the marvel represented in the painting, or the idea that miracles and religious visions can occur only in the illusory world evoked by works of art (in this case, all the more illusory because of Caravaggio's super-realist technique), and on the other hand, in a way that recalls Eliot's mythic method, it aligns the past and present, with the purpose of showing the desolate banality of the latter.

The poem has a regular metrical form — four stanzas composed of eight iambic pentameter lines in alternate rhyme (mostly monosyllabic, though in some verses it is actually assonance); except that in the last stanza, where the above-mentioned change in perspective occurs, polysyllabic rhymes balance the monosyllabic ones.[5] Each stanza is an independent unit expressing a self-sufficient thought, a separate meditation. The experience the poet projects in the poem takes place in a specific, concrete place, in the dark, almost claustrophobic interior of a Roman church, and, as suggested by the use of the present tense, and by recourse to a cinematic technique like a zoom lens, with which he first expands, then contracts, the surrounding scene.

Each stanza can be divided into two parts, the second of which can be read as a response to what is expressed in the first part. Only in the last stanza does a variation in the structural rhythm emerge, as the first part is composed of five lines, which are followed by a particularly expressive response concentrated in the last three lines. The final two, because of the dash that separates them from the preceding ones, seem to detach themselves visibly from the stanza to make an epigrammatic final couplet. This couplet is related, visually and verbally, to the final lines of the second stanza ("...what is it you mean / In that wide gesture of the lifting arms?" *CP* 93, ll. 15–16) and indirectly seems to furnish a response, at the end of the composition, to the question raised above (like those that run through Blake's famous poem, "The Tiger"), significantly placed in the middle of the poem.

Yet this answer is an elusive one, and, before providing it, what the poet offers is a problematic interpretation of the painting by means of an oxymoronic and ambiguous rendering of Saul's theophany. At first Gunn seems to question the origin of the light through which the divine power supposedly manifests itself, for, in spite of its dramatic effects, this light does not imply necessarily a supernatural source, especially if we consider that the source appears to be perpendicular to the horse's flank, maybe reflecting from here to the inside of Saul's arms. And although this power *seems* to be strong enough to overthrow Saul, who cannot *resist* the overwhelming impact with it, it remains almost invisible. That which the hero encompasses in the wide range of his extended arms is Nothing, the void; the experience intended by Caravaggio in the painting seems to be, from a Christian perspective, the humiliating defeat of human pride and at the same time an exalting mystical epiphany. For Gunn, on the other hand, it is the defeat of a yearning for the Absolute which is inevitably denied to man, so that Saul is not so much the incarnation of the human soul *raped* by God (as Donne would say), as a sort of defeated Faust, or, as Gunn would say, a "sad captain" destined to failure.

Even though the poem is set in a church, the religious feeling is utterly lacking. The poet does not see anything sacred in the painting or the building. The church seems to him a place in which people — in this case, old women — look for an illusory refuge from the menace of a hostile, incomprehensible universe.[6]

The absence of the sacred in Santa Maria del Popolo emerges in the first stanza where the speaker waits for a ray of sunlight which at the right angle will make visible "The painting on one wall of this recess" (*CP* 93, l. 3). The natural source of light is implicitly contrasted to the supernatural, which presumably is responsible for Saul's fall. The word "recess" (without the religious connotation of "chapel" occurring in the last stanza) suggests the total absence of the sacred in this building. Using the word "recess" associates the dark chapel with the oppressive places (caves, corridors, graves) of the first two collections, which are the objective correlative of the chains of intellect, which paralyze human action and are therefore responsible for man's deepest existential frustrations.

In the second part of the first stanza Gunn considers the effects produced by light and darkness in the church and painting, noting that the imposition of external darkness on the shadows of the painting render its reading so difficult ("Until the very subject is in doubt" *CP* 93, l. 8) that the observer is completely disoriented. Even though Gunn is aware that the strong chiaroscuro effects are the most typical feature of the pictorial school founded by the painter ("Caravaggio, of the Roman School" *CP* 93, l. 4), he cannot hide his disorientation when he sees that the main elements illuminated by the light in the painting are the limbs of horse and humans which dominate the painting by occupying its central part. Gunn does not further explore the reason why Caravaggio might have positioned these figures so boldly and disconcertingly, even though the first stanza suggests that it has not escaped his attention. In the second stanza the poet tries to decipher the painting, pointing out that his reading is dependent on the light: both outside light, which penetrates the church, and light within the picture itself. Only when his eyes get accustomed to the darkness of the image and a slanting ray illuminates it, does the poet manage to understand the gesture represented in it. Once again, in line with the glorification of movement characteristic of his poems before *My Sad Captains*, the poet's attention is caught, not by a face or a body, but by energy in action: he notices that while the face is "hidden," the emphasis is placed on the tension of the body, caught in the act of opening its arms as though it were unable to resist the force that has struck it. The poet suggests here that, whereas at a physical level, the violence Saul undergoes produces "the one convulsion" of his body — at a spiritual level, it causes a complete reversal of his whole life, which is somehow reflected in the "cacophony of dusty forms." The cacophony suggests the separation of Saul from other figures in the painting, his complete involvement in this experience, which generates the alarming "wide gesture of the lifting arms." The poet does not supply a direct answer to the enigma of this gesture, but in the next stanza obliquely offers a completely secular interpretation, which renders the gesture an expression of a kind of erotic convulsion, or perhaps of an experience that belongs to that realm — so mysterious, and thereby congenial to Baroque art — where the ecstasy of the soul becomes one with that of the body, where exquisite pains and bliss meet and merge. In other words, this gesture is the expression of a supreme, perhaps sinful desire, that cannot be ritually exorcized by the redemptive effect brought by Ananias, who in the Bible restores Saul's sight.[7] Deeply linked to Caravaggio's chiaroscuro effect, this gesture shows and at the same time hides the metamorphosis taking place in Saul, or as Gunn says, "the painter saw what was, an alternate / Candour and secrecy inside the skin"(*CP* 93, ll. 19–20). Paradoxically, an experience of divine revelation turns out to be a dark mystery that cannot be revealed ("secrecy") and remains incomprehensible to the observer, the painter, and to Saul/Paul. This unintelligibility is due to the fact that the external appearance is only a mask put on to hide one's true identity, as Gunn suggests when he directs his attention from the canvas in Santa Maria del Popolo towards other paintings by Caravaggio—like that alluded to in the line, "Young whore in Venus' clothes..."[8]— or those in which the artist used low-lifes ("...those pudgy cheats, / Those sharpers..." *CP* 93, ll. 22–23) as models to create great works of art.

Gunn is suggesting here that humanity's great myths, especially those arising from institutionalized religion, are only *masks* used to cover shameful and squalid realities, even though the masks themselves are not lies, but part of the intrinsic duplicity of life. This duplicity is shown not only in Caravaggio's works, or in the dichotomy between art and life, between culture and nature which is always present in them, but also in the life of the painter and especially in the violent death of this fascinating *accursed artist*.

As for the speaker of the poem, "The Unsettled Motorcyclist's Vision of his Death," all the energy contained in Caravaggio's heroic poses was destined to be extinguished ("was strangled") for paltry and venal reasons ("For money"). Being strangled "...by one picked off the street" (*CP* 93, l. 24) connects the painter's death to the violent deaths seen in some of his religious paintings, especially *Judith and Holofernes* (1607) and *David with the Head of Goliath* (1610).

As in aestheticism, Gunn identifies the gift of genius and creativity as the bright side of personalities who inevitably also possess a disquieting dark side; they can also be perverse, violent, and debauched, just as Caravaggio was in real life. In other words, heroism, whatever form it assumes, is the prerogative of people who cannot live a simple, insignificant life like the old women of the last stanza. These silent women, who seem to be devoid of any individuality and are presented as a group (in contrast to the solitary man of the preceding stanzas),[9] hide their tragic suffering in a poor gesture of containment ("...head closeted / In tiny fists..." *CP* 94, ll. 28–29), which is the opposite to Saul's ("...large gesture of solitary man / Resisting, by embracing, nothingness" *CP* 94, ll. 31–32). Echoes of Nietzschean attitudes emerge in this poem, especially in the last lines, where the people representing the flock or crowd, though deserving of compassion, are contrasted to isolated individuals (like most of the speakers in *Fighting Terms* and *The Sense of Movement*) who, even though morally suspect and destined to fail, are capable of a gesture of challenge to their desperate destinies. Their gesture, however, like that of the solitary man of the last lines—which corresponds to Saul in the picture and the "toughs of history" in earlier poems—is utterly in vain.

The poet recognizes the existence of gestures other than the heroic and the violent. Also the humble gestures of the ladies in the church suggest, in a quite different way, resistance to the nothingness that characterizes human existence.

According to Alan Bold, this poem demonstrates a changed attitude in the maturing poet:

> For the first time Gunn has placed the big dramatic gesture in human perspective by admitting to his poetry tired, disillusioned, poor, ignorant, old human beings. At last, Gunn sees that a life of unlimited choice and demonstrative will is only possible for a privileged few who do not have to cope with the physical oppression of poverty and cultural underprivilege. Dramatic gestures are merely a pose. The real human condition is, for the majority, a more tragic experience. For nothing these old women can do in the way of gesture could liberate them from a life tied to a squalid environment. As Gunn himself put it: "Here at last I begin some kind of critique of the Heroic."[10]

Even the gestures of the poor women in church are, as mentioned above, a way of resisting the nothingness of life, and it is the word "nothing" that begins the second poem in *My Sad Captains*, a lyric of philosophical character (in line with "The Nature of an Action" in *The Sense of Movement*), where Gunn, as the tautology of the title "The Annihilation of Nothing" suggests, tries to defeat the temptations of nihilism, enunciating the metaphysical premises of the collection:

> It is despair that nothing cannot be
> [...]
> Look upward. Neither firm nor free,
> Purposeless matter hovers in the dark.
> [*CP* 95, ll. 19, 21–22]

The poet contemplates a universe in which matter is "purposeless," lacking intention, and thus incapable of sustaining man in his attempt to give meaning to his existence. Yet it is precisely from this stoic awareness that the will to resist the void must arise, as well as the desire to construct an authentically human existence in a world which is alien to humans ("...I woke without desire, / and welcomed zero as a paradigm" *CP* 95, ll. 8–9). The expression "welcomed zero as a paradigm" suggests that the possibility of penetrating the void resides not in the heroic gesture of asserting one's will (which is, as in "The Unsettled Motorcyclist's Vision of His Death," self-destructive), but in the acceptance, the "welcoming" of the absence of meaning in life. The poet tries to escape from his despair that the void is an ontological paradox ("It is despair that nothing cannot be") by imposing significance on the objects that exist in the void, by showing respect for things (though "purposeless" and "neither firm nor free"). One vanquishes the void by emphasizing its undeniable existence and the indestructibility of those things existing within it.

Alan Bold proposes a comparison between Gunn's "The Annihilation of Nothing" and "Upon Nothing" by the seventeenth-century poet John Rochester. For Rochester's generation, the universe was suddenly created out of the void. For Gunn's generation,

> the Cambridge generation — the astronomical orthodoxy was continuous creation: the universe has always existed and always will. Man's dread of negativity, of total oblivion comes from his fallacious belief that there is a vacuum waiting to swallow him up. To Gunn, death is merely extinction of the body because even in death the body is organically prolonged. Taking Rochester's paradox to its illogical conclusion Gunn points out that Nothing is full of matter — gas condensing into stars, hydrogen becoming helium — waiting to be shaped by the will.[11]

For P.R. King, "The Annihilation of Nothing"

> is entirely successful in realizing a completely abstract, philosophical concept (related to existential philosophy and particularly the ideas of Jean-Paul Sartre) and it is achieved in an abstract language which is yet translucent and resonant. This negative poem seems to demand the more positive rejoinder of the poems

of the second half of the book which tentatively explore a different kind of relationship to the matter of inanimate nature.[12]

THE TWILIGHT OF HEROISM

Despite Gunn's changed attitude, there persists, especially in the first part of the collection, a tendency to focus on isolated heroes, some of whom, though they have a different uniform, could be the alter egos of the motorcyclists in *The Sense of Movement*. Gunn continues to be sympathetic towards them, revealing a quiet admiration, though it is accompanied by a greater detachment and a more vigilant, self-critical conscience. In "The Byrnies" ("byrnie" was the coat of mail worn by Vikings and warriors of the High Middle Ages), the men are openly presented as heroes—in one of the rare instances when Gunn actually uses that word. They are ready to conquer the surrounding country, but end up, when seen from a different angle, being only "a little group above the foreign wood" (*CP* 107, l. 32), something insignificant in an unknown, and disorienting place ("foreign"). Relativity of viewpoint and multiplicity of perspectives begin to emerge and are increased in several poems in the second half of the collection ("Considering the Snail," "The Feel of Hands," "A Trucker"). The universe is not unitary, but multiple, and its ontological reality, in terms of dimension, size, and power, varies according to the angle from which one views it. In Gunn's cosmological vision a dislocation of planes causes a continual questioning, a reversal of roles in the processes of metamorphosis that characterize the collections *Moly* and *Jack Straw's Castle*. In place of the divided self, who was compelled to confront his *doppelgänger* in the mirror ("The Secret Sharer," "The Corridor," etc.), Gunn gradually posits a Self that assumes and contains the Other in itself while maintaining its own individuality. The poem "Back to Life" (*Touch*) attests to the need for openness to the world, that does not, however, imply the annihilation of the Self in the Other. In this poem, Gunn observes the life in a city park during the daytime hours and contrasts it to the sense of solitude and anxiety that troubles people once evening falls ("The branch that we grow on / Is not remembered easily in the dark" *CP* 176, ll. 46–47). By means of a nature metaphor quite common in poetry (the image of life as a large tree on which we are the different leaves), the poet realizes that we are part of the whole and yet separate from it: "As if the light revealed us all / Sustained in delicate difference / Yet firmly growing from a single branch" (*CP* 176, ll. 42–44).

The epigraph to the first part of *My Sad Captains*, taken from Shakespeare's *Troilus and Cressida*, reveals the poet's awareness of an archetype of human behavior and the danger of viewing heroic actions as ends in themselves:

> The will is infinite and the execution confined, the desire is boundless and the act a slave to limit [*CP* 91].

These words recall the conflict between nature and culture, intellect and instinct, passion and its realization, that is present in the poems of *Fighting Terms*. Oppressed by the feeling of the impossibility of carrying out one's infinite will, the human being tries to realize an "absolute" through grand gestures which risk contempt for other beings, gestures of self-destructive and destructive violence like those of the motorcyclist (see "The Unsettled Motorcyclist's Vision of his Death") and the soldier in "Innocence."

Particularly significant to this problem are the poems in the first part of the collection, "The Byrnies," "Black Jackets" and "Innocence."

In the first, the heroes, unlike the boys of "On the Move," are afraid of the surrounding environment ("That dark was fearful — lack of presence —" *CP* 106, l. 9), and they look for light. Illumination assumes an important role in the entire collection while the poet/speaker searches for balance between darkness and light by means of a gradual journey towards the latter, unlike Lazarus, who preferred the dark of the tomb to the brightness of life. Leaving darkness, "the byrnies" try to escape a disturbing sense of "lack of presence" and light becomes an integral part of their identity and guarantee of their existence, as their uniform "...combined / Safety with virtue of the sun" (*CP* 107, ll. 26–27). Sun is, not only the source of warmth, a vital element, but also the means of communication between self and surrounding universe.

At the end of the poem they do not rise up in heroic challenge to their environment, but desperately seek a balance between intellect and instinct (related to the one between light and dark), making an effort to remember, when they hear the clanking of their mail (which recalls the "noise" of the motorcyclists, intended as a drowning out of the conscious self), the purpose of their gesture, even if this is never completely understood. Their identity and existence are closely related to their uniforms, even to the point where thought and action are mirrored by their outfit ("Thus concepts linked like chainmail in the mind" *CP* 107, l. 28):

By remaining "a little group above the foreign wood" (*CP* 107, l. 32), they incarnate the value of existence as resistance to a hostile world. The void that the individual must face is not just brute nature but also the unknown, a place not yet marked by human intervention and for this reason "dark." The darkness of an outside, mysterious world attracts, but at the same time remains indecipherable and impenetrable. With the figures of the "byrnies" who venture into the forest to confront its dangers, Gunn explores the archetype of the hero confronting for the first time the monsters who hide in the wilderness: "Barbaric forest, mesh of branch and root / [...] / Darkening the land, in quietness absolute" (*CP* 106, ll. 6, 8).

Both the "barbaric forest" and the "quietness absolute" evoke a primordial dimension in which the individual faces the surrounding world; although the world is hostile, foreign, and full of evil, there is no other solution than to adapt to it, accepting a re-dimensioning of self, from the hero who believes himself capable of dominating and incorporating the world, to the "little group" that measures itself against the surrounding forest and adapts itself to that reality. Encountering the unknown in nature is the first step towards growth, a vehicle for realizing human limits, and at the same time, a guarantee of identity. Franco La Cecla notes the importance of man's dialectical relationship with the unknown, which reinforces the bond between the individual and the group; in primitive cultures, the forest beyond the place of community is essential to that objective, insofar as it permits people to consider their environment from a different viewpoint, to judge it in relation to the entire cosmos, to discern its weaknesses and the possible threats from the outside.[13] In the essay, "The metalanguage of typological descriptions of culture," Jurij M. Lotman demonstrates that the border, the threshold between internal and external, between known and unknown, is an essential element in the spatial meta-language of cultural descriptions. By this language every society or cultural model defines the world of good and order, versus the world of evil, chaos, and disorder.[14]

"Black Jackets," also composed of quatrains with alternating rhyme like "The Byrnies,"[15] focuses on the re-dimensioning of a modern-day anti-hero, who already, before any action takes place, is destined to defeat, "Born to Lose."[16] The poem is characterized by a somewhat ironic attitude, mixed with a tacit compassion for the "red-haired boy" with his pretense of toughness, which he puts on for his Sunday activities.

A much weaker character than the boys of "On the Move," this young man announces his outsider status by having red hair, which is associated in literature with the demonic (for example, red-haired witches) and/or different (as in "Rosso Malpelo" by Giovanni Verga). Like the speaker in "The Allegory of the Wolf Boy," and Mackie in "PETE" (*Positives*), the boy in "Black Jackets" lives two lives; but neither one is a true manifestation of his nature or instinct. Unlike "wolf boy," who undergoes a nocturnal metamorphosis in which he abandons the social pretexts of daily ritual, this boy wears two masks, each adapted to the "dance of daily life."[17] During the weekend, he substitutes his work clothes for an over-sized Sunday outfit ("...shoulders grown to it" *CP* 108, l. 16) which makes him part of a community whose members deceive themselves, by their clothes and initiation rituals ("on his shoulders they had put tattoos" *CP* 109, l. 30), that they are recovering what they think is a lost identity, but in reality is an identity they never possessed:

> If it was only loss he wore,
> He wore it to assert, with fierce devotion,
>   Complicity and nothing more.
> [*CP* 109, ll. 25–27]

The uniform itself is not an intrinsic part of whoever puts it on, but is something extrinsic to the "character" ("...no more than leather / Which, taut across the shoulders grown to it" *CP* 108, ll. 15–16), something superimposed.[18] Nonetheless, the uniform guarantees their bond with a group ("Complicity and nothing more") in which, emerging from his isolation, the boy finds some security and even an assurance, however false, of identity.

It is interesting to note that, unlike the boys in "On the Move," the protagonist of "Black Jackets," though he lives completely in the present like they do ("The present was the things he stayed among" *CP* 108, l. 24), does not commit himself to action, nor does he fight against the void around him ("If it was only loss he wore"), but satisfies himself by passively sitting in a bar with friends whose actions consist only in drinking beer and telling jokes. The name they choose to call themselves, "The Knights," evokes a world of noble ideals, assuming ironic significance by reference to an anachronistic historical dimension appropriated to their condition, as suggested by the slogan, "Born to Lose."[19] Beyond the commitment to action, the space in which the individual can now act is greatly reduced.

J.H.J. Westlake proposes a comparison between the "fictitious knights" of today's world and the real ones of Arthurian legend:

> These knights on motor-cycles are the complete opposite of the knights of chivalry. Far from upholding the classical virtues they are, it is implied, petty criminals. They are quite incapable of defending the weak, since they are unable to come to terms with the world themselves. This is not really their fault, since they are born to lose, whereas their medieval counterparts regarded themselves as called upon to win.[20]

By carefully analyzing the boys' behavior, this critic discerns the rites of a congregation, and attributes to Gunn the desire to explore the intrinsic need of human beings to feel part of a group, to be effective members of society, in order to give meaning to their lives:

> The members of the group meet together to carry out certain functions, such as drinking beer and telling jokes. It is a closed society, and nobody may take part who has not been properly initiated. The adherents of this religion wear special clothes and meet in a special place to hold their "services."... In an age and a society where most people have rejected the established and sophisticated religions it is very easy to say that religion has been rejected altogether. Thom Gunn shows in this poem that there is, however, a fundamental need for religion which must be satisfied.[21]

The attempt to draw meaning from this sense of community is, however, illusory and therefore completely unsatisfying: "Instead of being brought together, the members of the group are made conscious only of their own individual isolation. Instead of deriving strength they are made to feel their own emptiness and futility."[22]

In "Innocence," Gunn describes the total indifference of a German soldier towards a Russian partisan who is being burned alive.[23]

> Could watch the fat burn with a violet flame
> And feel disgusted only at the smell,
> And judge that all pain finishes the same

As melting quietly by his boots it fell.
[*CP* 100, ll. 21–24]

The closed attitude here is extreme, an atrocious denial of the most sacred bonds that link every human being to his neighbor. "Innocence" is here a synonym of inhumanity, as the poet soberly denounces the violence inherent in every type of extreme ideology.

For Neil Powell this represents Gunn's critical attitude towards every "cult," not only of gratuitous violence, but also cults that glorify will as an end in itself. Powell believes that this absolves Gunn from the unjust accusations of Fascism directed at the early works:

> The construction of the poem makes it far more wide-reaching than any mere attack on Nazism. "Implicit in the grey is total black," writes Gunn in "To Yvor Winters, 1955"; implicit in any militaristic system is this kind of "innocence." We are moved and astonished by the poem as by a stunning dramatic denouncement: it succeeds exactly where "The Unsettled Motorcyclist's Vision of his Death" and "Black Jackets" fail, partly because the subject is more deserving of our concerned attention, partly because the verse is handled so carefully, the argument unfolded so deliberately.[24]

Gunn speaks of "Innocence" in an interview:

> In this poem, I try to show how the exaltation of energy can lead to a kind of action where one discovers that energy is not destined to fall into a vacuum, but often implies the destruction of the other's energy and it is therefore not absolute energy. I think this is one of the most important existential problems; how can we show the best of ourselves, or whatever you call it, without destroying the best of others.[25]

The image of the soldier who, obeying an inhuman code, becomes insensitive to the suffering and feelings of others, returns with an attitude of total detachment on Gunn's part, some years later in "The Corporal" (*Jack Straw's Castle*), where the vitality of soldiers' bodies is compared to their death mission, to the point that even the show of their primal instincts such as the sex drive ("Girl-hungry loutish Casanovas" *CP* 233, l. 13), is only a means to distance themselves momentarily from their destiny, to deceive themselves that they can escape it. The poet compares their obvious physical energy with the rigidity of the code: "Yet something fixed outlined the impulse. / His very health was dressed to kill. /[...]/ Against the uniform space of death" (*CP* 234, ll. 26–27, 30). These lines recall "The egotism of a healthy body" in "Innocence," revealing in the use of the word "death" (recurring at the end of each stanza, which reproduces the tight structure of some poems in *Fighting Terms*), the indissoluble link between the role of the soldier and death.[26] The use of past tense, however, accentuates Gunn's conscious distancing from myths which, as he himself knows, informed his youth:

> Half of my youth I watched the soldiers
> [...]
> Grey black and khaki was their look

Whose tool and instrument was death.
[*CP* 233, ll. 1, 4–5]

In "Clean Clothes: a soldier's song," Gunn remembers his military experience, and shows the discomfort he felt, especially at a physical level. The song is in reality a confession, a reflection on the loss of identity caused by the alienating uniform that the poet had to wear. By means of the image of clean clothes, the title suggests his desire for a reality entirely different from the one he is living and recalls one of the small pleasures that make military life a little less heavy and mortifying:

> And now that smell I hate:
> [...]
> My body stewing in its close-fit casserole.
> How else then could I stay
> Adequate day by day
> [...]
> Without the thought of change into
> Dry clean clothes that renew
> The anonymity which holds me in one piece?[27]

In contrast to the soldier in "Innocence," who was both accomplice to and victim of the homicidal irrationality of war, Claus von Stauffenberg,[28] in an eponymous poem that closes the first part of *My Sad Captains*, incarnates the dignity of defeated heroism in a statue-like pose. The poet takes as his example the great myths of the past, and freezes the heroic gesture in the lasting dignity of a statue:

> And though he fails, honour personified
> In a cold time where honour cannot grow,
> He stiffens, like a statue, in mid-stride
> — Falling toward history, and under snow.
> [*CP* 111, ll. 21–24]

By means of this heroic figure, who rises disobedient against the blind and delirious Nazi power ("Across from Hitler, whose grey eyes have filled / A nation with the illogic of their gaze" *CP* 11, ll. 18–19), Gunn confirms the paradoxical superiority of defeat, which is here an honorable action, "beautiful" for itself, and not for its consequent effects, an idea that links ancient stoic ideals with Sartre's modern glorification of the gratuitous gesture. The line, "In a cold time when honour cannot grow" (which echoes "It was a violent time" of "A Mirror for Poets"), and the last line of "Claus von Stauffenberg" "— Falling toward history, and under snow," reveal a vein of subtle irony, a bitter awareness that every gratuitous gesture, even though heroic, is destined to fall into the vacuum of a valueless world where there is no place for honor, while the hero himself, despite his statuesque size, will be completely impotent in the face of the blanketing and nullifying effect of the snow that buries him.

According to P.R. King, the snow and ice which form the background to von Stauffenberg's heroic gesture serve to immortalize the gesture itself by preserving the body "at the moment of redemptive courage." For this critic, von Stauffenberg "is predestined to take the role of a modern Brutus. Gunn makes him the symbol of the rational man who gains honour and redeems history in the act of destruction which, although it fails, nevertheless allows him to emerge as the very image of vigour and valour."[29]

In a radio program in the mid-1960s, a few years after the publication of *My Sad Captains*, Francis Hope said:

> I think that what's important about this poem isn't just the obvious way in which it rebuts the charge that Gunn's poems play with politically dangerous ideas. It gives us an insight into the kind of action he respects, and the ends to which this much-praised will should be directed.... The poem as a whole is surely a success; even its difficulties convey the extreme difficulty of any decent gesture.... it takes courage to write a heroic poem, just as it takes courage to be a hero when faced with something like the Third Reich. Gunn's poetry sets out to resolve such values as courage and resolution which might seem altogether too simple, too much abused and devalued, for the modern world or modern poetry.[30]

The contrast between the dangerous (because inhuman) will of the infinite and the awareness of the will's limits occurs in two poems of the same title (mentioned earlier in Chapter II), "Modes of Pleasure," where the poet takes up his familiar theme, the vanity and transitory nature of every erotic "triumph." Both are centered on "pathetic heroes," who are irremediably defeated in their illusion of heroism, their will reduced to an act of mere lust, and therefore destined to exhaust itself by repetition of the same mechanical gestures, much like T.S. Eliot's tragic view of history. The human will and passion are nothing more than expressions of a "machine" destined for the performance of physiological functions. In the first of the two works called "Modes of Pleasure," the hero, the "Fallen Rake," arouses acute fear in the speaker ("I jump with terror seeing him" *CP* 101, l. 1). He has no past, no system of values to anchor him (since his past consists exclusively of single mechanical gestures, and repetitive sexual encounters). The terror that he arouses does not come from his strength, but instead from the exhaustion of his energy (physical as well as mental, "...being fallen from / The heights of twenty to middle age" *CP* 101, ll. 5–6). The last stanza shows his self-destructive paralysis consuming him: "Rigid he sits: brave, terrible, / The will awaits its gradual end" (*CP* 101, ll. 23–24).

In the poems we have examined we detect the profound contrast between the vain pose with its illusions of heroism, and the simultaneous stoic refusal of the pose and its rhetoric — that is, the ironic self-awareness of the limits and loneliness of human beings along with the glorification of this same loneliness. These profound contrasts inform the whole collection and reach their highest expression in the final poem "My Sad Captains," which is also the volume's title. In this piece, Gunn says farewell to his captains, those isolated heroes whom he admired and took as models, and who were a source of poetic inspiration.

In his words, "'My Sad Captains'" is "a good sad serious poem that rounds off this part of my poetry, poetry in much of which I emphasize the will as an end in itself. From now on, a bit more flexibility."[31]

The sad captains, serious and sorrowful, withdraw to a faraway place, and probably represent not only the heroes previously exalted (despite their failed destiny), but also literary models that Gunn used as reference points. They will continue to shine like the stars, and indirectly exert their influence, but now, from a greater distance:

> True, they are not at rest yet,
> [...]
> they withdraw to an orbit
> and turn with disinterested
> hard energy, like the stars.
> [CP 129, ll. 13, 16–18]

Like stars, they retain light (one of the major symbols of the collection's second part), and endure through time, so that they continue to lend meaning, even though the poet knows that, like stars, they can exist in the universe without being able to light it fully, unable to cast out the darkness and the shadows of doubt and existential angst.

The relationship with early models, declared explicitly in "My Sad Captains," was anticipated in the first part of the collection by the self-reflexive poem "Readings in French," made up of five aphoristic epigraphs by which Gunn steps back from "father figures" who had formed him, to paraphrase Harold Bloom.

> III
> *Nothing Unusual about Marcel Proust*
> All are unmasked as perverts sooner or later,
> With a notable exception — the narrator.
> [CP 98, ll. 9–11]

Despite his ironic detachment from past models, the poet ends by recognizing, in the last stanza (at least in the first version of the poem, published in the 1961 edition of *My Sad Captains*),[32] the impossibility of totally withdrawing from the tradition which weighs, according to Bloom, on the poet's ability to freely express his artistic creativity, while also constituting an essential part of it: "I start from here. But where then did I learn / The terms that pose the choices I discern?"[33] (ll. 17–18).

FROM SENSES TO SENSE

In the second half of the collection (where Gunn is "taking up that humane impulse in a series of poems in syllabics" *OP* 179), the background of California's wide open spaces, observed for the first time in their vastness and brilliance and contrasted to the caves and corridors of his earlier poems, is anticipated by the epigraph from *The Last Tycoon* of F. Scott Fitzgerald.

> I looked back as we crossed the crest of the
> foothills—with the air so clear you could
> see the leaves on Sunset Mountains two
> miles away. It's startling to you sometimes
> —just air, unobstructed, uncomplicated air.
> [*CP* 113]

Here the poet contemplates, with ecstasy and yet precision, an external world which is no longer felt as hostile; he projects upon it, rather than assimilating it into his own personal universe. He gives himself completely, abandoning himself in an anti-intellectual way. Gunn thus creates a new type of poetry that is no longer a self-assertion, but rather an exploration, a quest, a gradual approach to his surrounding reality, which necessarily involves a change in his viewpoint. From the gaze of the solitary hero who dominated his surrounding world, Gunn moves on to that of the poet who projects himself into things, and tries to penetrate them, as in "Considering the Snail," a work that recalls the animal poems of Marianne Moore (among them "To a Snail"),[34] "The Fish" of Rupert Brooke, and the story "Kew Gardens" by Virginia Woolf. The poet enters the universe of a snail, who slowly, but with surprising determination, makes his way through the world. The nature of exploration changes too, from one that was predominantly intellectual (think of the icy line, "Even in bed I pose ...") to one that is predominantly physical, and involves all the senses.[35] Despite this new openness to the world around him, it is difficult for the poet to reach a total physical freedom (LSD and the artificial paradises of the sixties play important roles in this process); he continues to filter his sensory perceptions through his intellect, listening to them with his mind, but finally *lowering* himself to their level. *Lowering* implies an attitude similar to that of the undefined being in the poem "Wodwo" by Ted Hughes. Beginning *in medias res*, Hughes has this creature gradually explore the "jungle" of the surrounding world, trying to give meaning and explanation to its actions so that it might understand the essence of its identity ("What am I? ... / [...] / what am I doing here in mid-air?").[36] In Gunn's poem, intellect and reason are tools for understanding and deciphering the language of the senses and not mechanisms of repression and negation.

The second part of *My Sad Captains* opens with a poem, "Waking in a Newly-Built House" that clearly signals a metamorphosis (though slow and still painful) in the poet's attitude. Waking in a new environment is a metaphor for Gunn opening himself to a new type of poetry, and his adoption of syllabics, which characterize the second part of the collection. The new house offers a privileged point of observation, being built on the top of a hill. The house marks a new start, a completely different way of ordering reality and establishing a new set of priorities inside it:

>   ... the neutral sections
>   of trunk, spare, solid, lacking at once
>   disconnectedness and unity.
>   [*CP* 115, ll. 10–12]

    The poet accepts the existence of the objects around him as they are, without imposing intellectual criteria of wholeness or fragmentation ("disconnectedness and unity"), thus reaching an understanding that their reality consists precisely in being what they are, and not in the "meanings" that the human mind tries to put upon them.

    Gunn opens himself to a peaceful exploration of the world ("calmly"), without violence or a spirit of self-assertion that tries to define it. He wishes to discover the essence of things, analyzing and lingering on minutiae such as "...the neutral sections / of trunk...." Yet, unlike the undefined being "wodwo" of Ted Hughes' poem, who is completely immersed in the surrounding world and whose exploration proceeds in a language without punctuation (reproducing paratactically the apparently chaotic succession of the speaker's questions), Gunn experiences his rebirth while still protected by an envelope, a den, a niche — which is the house.[37] Like Virginia Woolf, he approaches the external world, which he finds attractive, through the protective veil of an intermediate space, from a point between the self and the unknown, in this case provided by the window. The poem starts with the lines: "The window, a wide pane in the bare / modern wall, is crossed by colourless / peeling trunks of the eucalyptus" (*CP* 115, ll. 1–3). The world is like a painted image, filtered across the windowsill. The sill represents the separation between the poet and the world. Gunn is like a blind man who, as soon as he recovers sight, marvels at the world's shapes and colors (despite not being able to define them and seeing only purity and rarefaction, "colourless," "raw sky-colour,") without yet being able to touch or feel it as fully part of himself. The image of the window recalls "High Windows" by Philip Larkin, which in turn echoes the theme of "Erfüllte Leere" by Stéphane Mallarmé. The high windows that seem to open upon the infinite, end by blocking the sun, not offering a possibility of escape from the nothingness of existence, but confirming the abyss that surrounds human life ("The sun-comprehending glass / And beyond it, the deep blue air, that shows / Nothing, and is nowhere, and is endless").[38] In Gunn's poem, on the other hand, the emptiness of the world is annihilated (as in Rainer Maria Rilke) by thing-ness, by the outlines of things ("their precise definition"), by that dichotomy between absence and presence which constitutes the very essence of their being. Objects exist and are without significance; the human being is wrong to impose an identity on them, or to conform them to his will.

    The theme of discovering objects, feeling their presence in one's surroundings, which can become obsessive and claustrophobic (as noticed in the poem "Thoughts on Unpacking"), continually recurs in Gunn's poetry, especially in "Pierce Street" (*Touch*); here Gunn, from an initial state of disorientation and apprehension ("Nobody home..." *CP* 177, l. 1), moves gradually to a sense of recognition of the environment, naming its objects, and accepting them for what they are. The external environment is a metaphor for the mental terrain, its exploration a journey to the poet's past, which is overflowing with ghosts; these are identified with figures of soldiers, an entire garrison impressed upon the wall who, despite their armor, seem to have lost the meaning of their existence:

> in line, in groups, aloof,
> They all stare down with large abstracted eyes.
> [*CP* 177, ll. 23-24]

Gunn distances himself from these figures immortalized upon the walls but not blessed with real life (like Saul in Caravaggio's painting): "They are the soldiers of the imagination / Produced by it to guard it everywhere" (*CP* 178, ll. 26-27). In contrast to their abstract permanence ("Where the painter reached to make them permanent" *CP* 178, l. 33) he posits the fleeting flux of life:

> The house smells of its wood.
> Those who are transitory can move and speak.
> [*CP* 178, ll. 35-36]

The line, "The house smells of its wood," clearly expresses the poet's change in view; liberating himself from the ghosts of his intellect, he begins to feed his imagination, not with abstract ideals, but with the power of his senses (here, touch and smell), finally ready to listen attentively to the world which shows in all its naturalness (it is important that the house is "natural," being made of wood and illuminated by "...long threads of sunlight..." *CP* 177, l. 1).

The soldiers with "large abstracted eyes" recall some of the defeated heroes of earlier poems, like "Rastignac at 45." The poem's protagonist derives from the poor but ambitious student in the "human comedy" of Balzac (*Papà Goriot*), whose memorable experiences of Paris life "among the oversexed and titled" (*CP* 122, l. 16) have marked his body and face till he looks like a madman who cannot be believed, deserving only ironic compassion. The repetition of actions similar to those of the "fallen rake" in "Modes of Pleasure" transforms the mask he has put on (to satisfy his thirst for success) into something grotesque, pressed indelibly, like a tattoo, upon his body:

> But this: time after time the fetid
> taste to the platitudes of Romance
> has drawn his mouth up to the one side
> secretly, in a half-maddened wince.
> [*CP* 123, ll. 25-28]

A sense of discovery informs other poems in the second part of *My Sad Captains*, in particular "The Feel of Hands," whose title anticipates that dimension of awareness of the outside world, of oneself and others, through using all the senses, especially touch, which is the central theme of the volume *Touch*.[39]

Gunn moves gradually, freeing himself slowly from the protective shield that characterizes his attitude in the early collections, orienting himself towards a kind of interpersonal relationship that accepts the physical and mental presence of other people, trying to harmonize with other elements of the world, making physical and mental awareness not separate, but mutually reinforcing even if that goal remains distant.

One step in this direction is documented, as mentioned above, in "The Feel of Hands," where Gunn concentrates in four quatrains the development of a tactile experience. The lines proceed incessantly, by strong enjambment aimed at reproducing the hands' movements of discovery, sometimes delicate and uncertain, other times frenetic and violent. In the first stanza the poet is almost distracted by the contact even though his attention, concentrated on the source of the touch, is still predominantly intellectual. From the light and almost familiar contact ("I connect them with amusing / hands I have shaken by daylight" *CP* 120, ll. 7–8) of the first two stanzas, he moves through a sudden metamorphosis ("...they are grown / to cats, hunting without scruple" *CP* 120, ll. 11–12) to a state of disorientation of the speaker, who goes from being the subject of the experience to its object. The hands, like the objects in the poem "Thoughts on Unpacking," become gigantic and uncontrollable. They change in size, become indomitable hunters, thirsty for their prey. Metaphorically, they reflect the poet's search, which moves from the prison of intellect to knowledge of the body, discovering it gifted with a life of its own. The speaker draws pleasure from the sensual touch of these hands, as the fluidity of the lines running into each other suggests; a touch that, despite the violation of intimacy announced at the end of the poem ("I do not know whose hands they are" *CP* 120, l. 16), continues to produce a sense of wonder, stimulates further questions, suggesting that the body and senses are given a time and rhythm decidedly different from mental and intellectual ones. Touch becomes a vehicle for knowledge, even if for the moment it is only hinted at.[40]

In "Lights Among Redwood," sensual exploration entails the admiration of the forms and colors of things, together with attention to the tricks of light and shadow upon them, which reveal not precise outlines, but multiple aspects and tonalities ("a muted dimness coloured / with moss-green, charred grey, leaf-brown" *CP* 124, ll. 9–10). The poem closes on a moment of drunken, ecstatic vision:

> ... we stand
> and stare — mindless, diminished —
> at their rosy immanence.
> [*CP* 124, ll. 16–18]

A similar attention to chromatic detail (which replaces the blacks and whites in the earlier collections) informs a poem in the first part of *My Sad Captains*, "The Value of Gold," where the poet for the first time does not contrast himself to nature, but, making himself "insect size," discovers the power to enjoy its impenetrable innocence. Basking in light ("And I am gold beneath the sun" *CP* 110, l. 2), the speaker feels like an integral part of the external world, of its beauty and fullness that is subject, like himself, to the natural process of birth, growth, decay, and death:

> Then from one high precocious stalk
> A flower — its fullness reached — lets fall
> Features, great petals, one by one
> Shrivelling to gold across my walk.
> [*CP* 110, ll. 21-24]

The word "gold" in the last line links it to the first, where the poet-speaker describes the effect of sun on his skin ("The hairs turn gold upon my thigh" *CP* 110, l. 1), defining the true value of gold, as foreshadowed by the title of the poem: the continual metamorphosis that by solar energy links man to all of nature, making every small detail part of the greater whole.[41] In this poem overflowing with light, in which Gunn attempts a true immersion in nature, we see a fluorescence of words related to the prison of the intellect, such as "speculate" (which recalls the poem "Merlin in the Cave: He Speculates without a Book"), as well as several introspective questions by which the poet interrogates himself on the vital flux around him and his role in it.

Gunn takes a step forward in his slow process towards openness in "The Rooftop" (*Moly*), where, by a succession of quatrains of short lines, tetrameters rhyming *abba*,[42] he opens himself to perception of the world ("And to sit here for hours, / Becoming what I see" *CP* 203, ll. 7-8), letting it penetrate him without trying to contain it in his intellect. By immersing himself in the as yet unknown nature of the park, the speaker manages to perceive from the inside (as if he were experiencing it directly and not as an outside observer) the creative process of a growing seed, which includes the decay from which life arises. Here Gunn explains, as a living experience, what in "The Value of Gold" was still just a rhetorical question:

> ... The seed
> Bursts, bare as bone in going.
> Bouncing from rot toward earth
> Compound of rot, to wait
> An armoured concentrate
> Containing its own birth
> [*CP* 204, ll. 27-32]

The poet describes the epiphanic development of the universe, a latent force waiting for the actuation of its being, the cycle of life-death-rebirth that always and uninterruptedly continues "From seed to dead to seed / Through green closed passages" (*CP* 204, ll. 35-36), by means unknown to man.

In *My Sad Captains,* an inebriation like that in "The Value of Gold," obtained, however, not by immersion in nature but by separation from it, emerges in the two poems "A Map of the City" and "Flying Above California," placed in the first and second parts, respectively, of the collection. In "Flying above California" the speaker observes the world below him from an airplane (which recalls metaphorically the prison of the intellect, the existential closure of caves, suggesting that the barriers of separation and foreignness to the outside world are only partially overcome).[43] Despite his distance from it, the observer sees the landscape in fragments that strike all his senses (even taste: "valley cool with mustard, or sweet with / loquat..." CP 116, l. 3), evoking sensations of fullness and richness that transport him in imagination to faraway places with fantastic associations, from the mythical, sunlit Mediterranean to the glamour of the Nordic sagas.[44] Again the enjoyment of beauty accompanies the perception of the lack of intrinsic meaning of things touched by light:

> ...That limiting candour,
> that accuracy of the beaches,
> is part of the ultimate richness.
> [*CP* 116, ll. 12–14]

In "A Map of the City" the object of contemplation, once again seen from on high, is the city. Observed from the top of a hill (as if the poet aimed to make it his own, to possess it, "I hold the city here, complete" *CP* 103, l. 9), the city retains its Baudelairean perverse glamour ("I watch a malady's advance, / I recognize my love of chance" *CP* 103, ll. 15–16), but it changes, in a Whitmanesque way, into an organism pulsating with life and loaded with "endless potentiality": "The crowded, broken, and unfinished! / I would not have the risk diminished" (*CP* 103, ll. 19–20).

Contact

This feeling of pulsating life permeates "Considering the Snail," in which, assuming the size of an insect, the poet turns his attention—in three stanzas of lines that flow without interruption, almost reproducing the described action—to a small being, a snail, which he tries to understand from the inside. He wants to capture the extraordinary energy that moves the animal, despite the apparent slowness of its body, but he again runs into the resistance of beings to letting us know them. The movement of the snail, perceived as a "concentration of desire," is patient, stubborn, implacable, and engrossing to the poet:

> ... I would never have
> imagined the slow passion
> to that deliberate progress.
> [*CP* 117, ll. 16–18]

Unlike the boys in "On the Move," the snail is not purposeless, but seems the very incarnation of determination, possessing an inflexible will to reach its goal. The morbidly sensual exploration of reality that Gunn achieves in this poem, trying to penetrate the inside of the observed creature (although of course his point of view remains outside), and to make himself part of the self of the other, shows that his poetry is casting off its limiting intellectuality, in contrast to the abstract reason of his mentor, Yvor Winters.

"Considering the Snail" has been the object of many interpretations and differing critical judgments.

For David Holbrook, for example,

> The poem seeks to involve us in the poet's awe at the snail's "slow passion." It speaks extravagantly of the "snail's fury"; but this, again, is a mere touch of *hwyl*, of depressive-sentimental exaggeration: what can it mean? Only "poor us, like snails." But the poem has no rhythm — not an iota of the rhythmical excitement or metaphorical freshness one would obtain from any class of children aged 9–14 writing about a snail. It is expressed in language which is at the lowest level of colloquial small-talk.[45]

Contrasting to Holbrook's bitter criticism, Neil Powell, who also rewrites the poem in prose (which reveals intolerance for Gunn's experimentation with the technique of syllabics), observes the interesting differences between the two versions:

> On one level, the verse forces us to pause, ask questions, search out possible ambiguities.... What is certain is that the syllabic metre in "Considering the Snail" gives to the poem a tentative, hesitating, questioning movement which mirrors the movement of the snail itself.[46]

Very interesting observations, directed not only at Gunn's technique but also at the symbolic meaning of the composition, are voiced by a non-western critic, Emeka Okeke-Ezigbo, who finds in the patient movement of the snail a metaphor for poetic creation:

> The snail's "slow passion" is the travail that accompanies serious creation; the perseverance and fastidiousness that go into creating an artistic piece and satisfying the creative impulse. By laboring and pushing gently through the dense night, the snail, as if contending with primordial forces, emerges triumphant, making a *bright* path where "rain has *darkened* the earth's dark." The snail's accomplishment, then, is a vindication of the technique of forbearance; the ultimate superimposition of mind over matter.[47]

With the expression, "superimposition of mind over matter," the critic relates "Considering the Snail" to one of the recurring traits of Gunn's poetry, the effort to impose form on the chaos of nature, assuming the role of "artifex."

The metaphor of poetic creation, that from darkness, wet and therefore palpable, makes a clearly defined and determined sign ("...the thin / trail of broken white across / litter..." *CP* 117, l. 15), links this poem to one of the early works of Ted Hughes, "The Thought-Fox." As the neologism of the title suggests, Hughes compares the intent animal concentration of the fox ("...an eye / A widening deepening greenness,")[48] to a poet's inspiration and creation, that is to say, to a type of activity that uses the senses and instinct, more than the intellect, and whose final result is a completed work of art:

> Till, with a sudden sharp hot stink of fox
> It enters the dark hole of the head.
> The window is starless still; the clock ticks,
> The page is printed.[49]

The prints of the fox in the snow[50] correspond to the "printed" page, marked and not simply written. Similarly, the "trail of broken white across / litter..." in Gunn's poem signifies the determined, relentless hunt of the snail through the darkness of matter which lets itself be penetrated and molded. Another interpretation is also possible, suggested, among other things, by the personification of the snail (the subject is the masculine "he") and by the use of words like "wood of desire," "hunts," "fury," "slow passion." The metaphor is that of sexual initiation, of a physical impulse, sometimes violent and uncontrollable ("a snail's fury") that manifests in the darkness, obeying only its instinct ("with purpose, knowing nothing" CP 117, l. 10). Even the broken white mark has a clear male sexual connotation and is the fruit of that hunt in which all of its body was consumed. The sexual reading is confirmed by another image of the snail in a poem of the eighties, "At the Barriers," where Gunn, remembering the experience of a San Francisco fair, compares human inhibitions to the absolute freedom and sexual expression in the relationship between two leopard slugs:

> On the TV screen I saw two Leopard Slugs mating.
> They are hermaphroditic, equally taking and giving,
> overspread with a pattern of uneven spots, leopard-like.
> By a strong thread of mucus reaching from their tails,
> which suspends them from a branch of the Tree,
> they hang — in air — nothing impeding them
> as they twine upon one another, each body
> wrapped at every point about the other, twisting in embrace,
> in a long slow unstopped writhing of desire,
> wholly devoted to the sensual ecstasy.
> Glistening, they exude juices from their mutual pressure.
> [CP 399, ll. 14-24][51]

In "Considering the Snail," Gunn tries to capture the movement of the snail from inside, moving toward a type of poetry in which, in the manner of William Carlos Williams, he recognizes inside himself and simultaneously transmits, moments of experience, a type of poetry that expresses the movement towards and into undifferentiated beings.

This effort to project himself into things and their viewpoints by a perceptive process can be associated with the theories of Maurice Merlau-Ponty, and the capacity to imagine the primitive encounter with the world that Edmund Husserl called "primordial constitution," that horizon of experience lived in an intuitive and natural way. Another example of the process is offered by "A Trucker," where Gunn tries to capture the essence of a truck by animalizing it, transforming it into a living organism, part of the *Lebenswelt*[52]:

> .... the cabin is lofty
> as a skull, and all the rest
> extends from his foot as an
> enormous throbbing body
> [*CP* 126, ll. 3-6].

The title refers, not to the machine, but to the driver, whose identity is the same as his instrument (a huge uniform), to the point of annihilating himself in it, making himself a mechanical body vibrating with life, by a process of deformation, expansion, and contortion of the human figure. The interpenetration of human and truck, especially the decomposition and re-composition of the human body, recall the experiments of Expressionist, Cubist, and Surrealist painters, where the human figure expands, contracts, and recomposes in a series of planes. Especially in Futurism, the body is a living machine, surprised and captured in its frenetic and unstoppable movement.

The attempt to penetrate the existence of another, nonhuman, being reaches its greatest heights in two poems of the collection *Jack Straw's Castle*, called "Yoko" and "The Cherry Tree." In the first, the poet tries to enter into the mind of a dog (as Virginia Woolf did in *Flush*), sometimes humanizing it, describing from the inside its sensations, and its disconnected succession of discoveries during its walk with its master ("leader" and "love"), to whom it shows a total devotion, even to the point of representing them as lovers ("...I try to lick his lips, / I care about him more than anything" (*CP* 299, ll. 16–17), and to feel lost and disoriented in his absence ("I am confused, I feel loose and unfitted" *CP* 299, l. 9). The dog constantly observes its master, and imagines his thoughts:

> with bowels emptied, feeling your approval
> and then running on, the big fleet Yoko,
> my body in its excellent black coat never lets me down,
> returning to you (as I always will, you know that)
> [*CP* 300, ll. 43–46]

The walk is a moment not only of discovery ("I investigate tar and rotten sandwiches..." *CP* 300, l. 29), but also of happy and immediate immersion in the diversity of the world, in the flux that involves humans, animals, and all of nature ("I stand with you braced against the wind" *CP* 300, l. 49), in the infinity of its details, even the most minute and insignificant, perceived especially through the senses—for it is by means of these that the world shows its rich fullness. The poet tries to make the dog talk, gives it a voice, concentrating especially on its sensations that involve taste, touch, and smell, and accepting all the physiological functions with naturalness. These are the vehicles of openness and contact with the outside world, the recognition of signs left in the environment, proof of other beings who earlier passed this same spot, impressing on it part of their life:

> Here on a garbage can at the bottom, so interesting,
> what sister or brother I wonder left this message I sniff.
> I too piss there, and go on.
> [*CP* 299, ll. 21–23]

The celebration of innocence and the recovery of bodily intimacy, although they do not conquer fears of the Other, nor eradicate the menace of the outside world, as seen by the anxious visions and nightmares in *Jack Straw's Castle*,[53] do bring Gunn further along in his exploration of the nonhuman world. In "The Cherry-Tree," he rediscovers a kind of completely natural maternity, alien to any form of selfish possession, which he conceives as a relationship somehow similar to that existing between a tree and its fruits. In this poem Gunn tries to discover and feel "what it is like to be a Cherry Tree," as he said at a reading. He captures the tree in the moment of gestation, the production of fruit, and then later, in the moment of losing it ("she loses them all" *CP* 295, l. 56). Gunn chooses the feminine pronoun, as if the tree were a personification of Mother Nature, a synthesis of all fertility myths. This is a fertility conceived in exclusively physical terms, foreign to any moral system or hierarchy of values which humans inevitably place on reality, experienced as a natural manifestation of inner energy, of a physiological impulse which, once the reproductive cycle is over, leaves no signs, no satisfaction, no regret:

> That's why she made them
> to lose them into the world, she
> returns to herself,
> she rests, she doesn't care.
> [...]
> She knows nothing about babies.
> [*CP* 296, ll. 57–60, 65]

Though the tree is clearly immobile ("as unmoving as the statue / of a running man..." *CP* 294, ll. 4–5), the poet captures the life and uncontrollable energy that pulses inside it (described as a "need to push," suggesting a gestation similar to that of the maternal womb), which, from the inside of her being she propels toward the outside, with the definite objective of producing fruit, like babies one must feed until they reach maturity and their life cycle is complete:

> ... a need
> to push
>   push outward
> from the center, ...
> [...]
> But she is working still
> to feed her children,
> [...]
> bringing up all she can
> a lot of goodness from roots
> [*CP* 294–95, ll. 16–19, 38–39, 41–42]

The being and identity of the tree do not change and are not disturbed by the new role: the cherry tree remains intact, complete, and indifferent to the tumultuous generative process it has undergone, which repeats itself with the changing seasons.

In "Yoko" and "The Cherry Tree," the flow of free verse and the succession of stanzas of different lengths take the place of syllabics and traditional meter, as Gunn moves towards further openness to the outside world with respect to "Considering the Snail" and "A Trucker." In these poems he played the role of observer who projected himself onto observed objects, as the word "considering" suggests, breaking objects down (as in "A Trucker") and reconstructing them from the inside, or trying to capture their vital energy (as in "Considering the Snail"). But in "Yoko" and "The Cherry Tree" his penetration into the creature/object is such that he annihilates himself in them, reducing to zero the distance between viewpoint and object, and becoming a direct participant in the Otherness of the tree's life.[54] The process is one of interpenetration between the self and that which the self observes, of interaction between subject and object, similar to that in certain of Cézanne's late–nineteenth century paintings, especially those of Mt. Saint Victoire,[55] an interpenetration found also in Rilke's *Dinggedicht*, in his poetry of thing-ness and objectivity. Rilke was constantly trying to break down the boundaries between the subject and the world, and "expanding musically in the silence of things to enjoy the omnipotence of the word."[56]

The syllabics that Gunn begins to use in *My Sad Captains* (of which "Considering the Snail" and "A Trucker" offer clear examples), while giving more force to the individual word, at the same time allows in its fluidity, a greater spontaneity of language with respect to traditional meter. With syllabics, Gunn finds a less restrictive poetic language without falling into the trap of writing prose in verse:

> I suppose my own attempt to write free verse is in writing syllabics, which is probably cheating, but I find that in writing syllabics I can get certain free verse effects which I certainly can't get in metrical verse. There is a great danger in syllabics, that it will just fall into a mass of prose written differently, but I don't think good syllabics should do this any more than good free verse.... I find that in syllabics I can much more easily record the casual perception, whereas with metrical verse I very often become committed to a particular kind of rather taut emotion, a rather clenched kind of emotion.[57]

Regarding the influence of American poetry on his use of syllabics, it is interesting to note the poet's words on the occasion of a radio program during the sixties:

> The cliché nowadays in the literary reviews in America is that free verse is essentially American and that metrical verse, traditional metre is essentially English. It seems to me that there is an element of mysticism in this distinction in that, you know, the English can speak colloquially as well, just as colloquially as the Americans. And it's very difficult to say why very few of the English have writ-

ten good free verse. I mean, there is a real contrast here. The good writers of free verse in England you could number on the fingers of one hand. There's Eliot, there's Lawrence, and there's a few there, and it's a very specialized kind of free verse. If you contrast this with not only Wallace Stevens and William Carlos Williams, but often very minor poets who write good free verse, the contrast is incredible. I think this is maybe something to do with tradition rather than with something innate in the language. I think it's more to do with people's traditional attitude though.[58]

For Gunn, syllabics represents a means to "get certain free verse effects,"[59] a step towards greater fluidity, a liberation from form, that reaches its highest expression in the later collections from *Touch* to *Boss Cupid*.

What I *have* given up is syllabics: I find the virtues of syllabics indistinguishable from those of free verse, so one might as well write free verse and trust entirely in the rhythms rather than partly in the number of syllables.[60]

Freeing himself from the requirements of form, simplifying syntax, distancing himself from pre-formed systems, from the collection *Touch* onwards, Gunn continues to develop his personal style. *Touch* is a transitional work, a moment of reflection in his career. In the same period, he experiments with images and verse, photography and poetry, co-creating (with his brother Ander) the book called *Positives*. Gunn is in search of a direction, and he engages with a series of themes and languages, which range from the long "Misanthropos" cycle, to the fragments that he places next to photographs in *Positives*. In many poems in *Touch*, including the title poem, the lines are irregular and flow into each other almost without pause:

> you are already
> there, and the cat
> got there before you, yet
> it is hard to locate.
> What is more, the place is
> not found but seeps
> from our touch in
> continuous creation, dark
> enclosing cocoon ...
> [*CP* 169, ll. 40–48].

The period placed in the middle of the stanza is not a real pause, because the beginning of the next line, "What is more," almost neutralizes the interruption, creating the impression of uninterrupted continuity.

According to Clive Wilmer:

Each line acquires a different significance if isolated from its syntactical context, yet each of them has the kind of line-ending which compels us to read on within that context. This method of versification enables Gunn not only to describe the world, the incompletion that he loves, but at the same time to dramatize the ways in which we come to know it, in terms which point ultimately to his own beliefs about its nature.[61]

The freedom from syntax is even more accentuated in *Jack Straw's Castle* and *The Passages of Joy*, where some poems, like "The Plunge" and "The Cat and the Wind," are in free verse composed of small fragments (often the lines are only one word or part of a word) almost completely lacking in punctuation, and running into each other by strong enjambment:

> each
> nerve each
> atom of skin
> tightens against it
> to a gliding
> a moving with —
> ["The Plunge" *CP* 253, ll. 11–16]
>
> twigs, leaves,
> small pebbles, pause
> and start and pause
> in their shifting,
> their rubbing
> against each other.
> ["The Cat and the Wind" *CP* 329, ll. 17–22]

In this type of poem, attention is concentrated not on rhythm but on the individual word or fragment which renders, in the manner of William Carlos Williams, even the smallest perceptions and sensations in the moment of their occurrence.

The syllabics of the second part of *My Sad Captains* represents a step towards free verse, which does not, however, mean a complete abandonment of traditional forms. Gunn still uses these with expertise and a nearly classical precision.

> I don't see free verse ... as permanently replacing my metrical verse. I want to continue writing both, to keep them both available.... It is nonsense to say that meter is dead. It was never alive, it is an unbodied abstraction: it's the poem that has to be alive.... I like Lawrence's description of meter as belonging to the past and the future, and free verse to the present. Meter is attracted to thought-out, pondered subject matter, its passion tends to be more durable, it cuts deeper, it is more determined.... Free verse is attracted to the subject matter of the present in that it admits of the unforeseen, the ephemeral, the spontaneous more easily — the image floating in front of our face, the rhythm suddenly discovered. There is a sense of improvisation, of its happening while you are reading it.[62]

The poems in *Moly* are mostly in traditional meter, rigorously structured with tightly-controlled rhyme, which permits the poet to filter and communicate an experience like that of artificial (drug-induced) paradise, the effects of which are impalpable and ineffable, giving form and outline to the indefinable. In "The Bath House" of the sequence "The Geysers" (*Jack Straw's Castle*) — where the poet tries to render the gradual crumbling of consciousness that leads him to a "galactic" regression to the womb — the irregular lines divided into fragments separated by white space replicate the slow, painful nature of the experience itself. However, once recomposed, the lines likewise regain a sense of wholeness, by means of a regular metric structure (mostly rhyming iambic tetrameters and pentameters):

> I give up
>   hope   as they move in on me
> loosened so quickly from it   I am free
> I brace myself light strong and clear
> and understand why I came here.
> [CP 246, ll. 109–13]

"The Bath House" shows at a formal level the alternation between openness and closure typical of Gunn's work, through the contrast between the fluidity of often fragmented free verse and the formality and control of traditional meter.

The adoption, first, of syllabics, and later, of free verse, aroused differing reactions from critics, some of whom thought them failed experiments, while others praised the greater fluidity that they provided.[63] For Lawrence R. Ries, "the last half [of *My Sad Captains*] forsaking the accustomed strict verse forms for syllabics, introduces Gunn's more static and meditative poetry."[64] Clive Wilmer shares this opinion: "what Gunn has discovered through free verse has affected his standard meter, sometimes to its detriment in the rhythms and the organization of content. A surprising gaucheness is apparent in the rhythms. I find that Gunn's use of meter is most effective when he sticks to the rules."[65] Similarly, Colin Falck describes Gunn's move to syllabics as an experiment which works only when "the inner movement of what he is expressing manages to coincide or co-exist with the mechanical demands of the syllable-count, so that the syllable-count itself simply drops out of consideration as irrelevant." Otherwise, he says, "what Gunn does ... is to fall into another, more modern, but in the end no less mechanical system of verse making."[66] Neil Powell on the other hand, as we saw in his discussion of "Considering the Snail," favors this type of experiment, saying of "My Sad Captains" that "one is immediately struck by the way in which the supposedly neutral syllabic form carries here an intense tone of reverie...: the poem demonstrates forcefully that if syllabic metre can make a poem seem prosaic it can also, and for much the same reasons, add fluency and continuity."[67]

CHAPTER V

An Experiment in Artistic Collaboration

PREMISE

Interaction between literature and the visual arts (painting, design, printing, photography, etc.) has a very long tradition. In English literary history there are many instances of collaboration between the arts, whether between two artists, like Virginia Woolf and Vanessa Bell,[1] or by one author, such as in William Blake's poetry, the Pre-Raphaelites' paintings, or John Ruskin's designs. So many texts in recent decades have taken up the subject of this interaction between literature and visual arts that it could be called a trend—consider Michel Tournier's novel, *La goutte d'or* (1985) (of which we will speak more later); A.S. Byatt's collection, *The Matisse Stories* (1975), which uses Matisse's paintings as references inside and outside of the text; and John Banville's novel, *Athena* (1995), which contains invented pictures of seventeenth-century Flemish painters. Sometimes (as in the case of Vanessa Bell's drawings for Virginia Woolf's stories) the written text is the source for the images that accompany it, sometimes the reverse is true, while it is more rare when the text and images arise simultaneously.

There are many examples of photography's influence on literature;[2] in Proust's *Recherche*, the narrator "imagines himself in a photographer's shoes, feeling his gaze lovingly turned to his grandmother, suddenly becoming as detached as a photographic lens."[3]

As Roberto De Romanis observes, "in the era of incipient realism, a conspicuous number of writers demonstrated a great interest in the new medium, using it often to plumb the depths of realities which risked escaping the eye. Consider Verga and Capuana, Hugo and Zola, to mention a few. Some of these decided to use the new equipment, sometimes building it at home..., often dividing their time between the two activities."[4]

Initially seen as a tool for capturing aspects of reality, and therefore a guarantee of that realism from which painting was gradually departing, photography began to be considered an art at the turn of the century (when Alfred Stieglitz founded the magazine *Camera Work*),[5] with noteworthy effects on artistic experimentation, and on the individual and collective imagination.[6]

Many novelists drew inspiration from the new technology, and photographs accompanied many new texts. The first edition of *Alice's Adventures in Wonderland* is "a sort of photography album, 'illustrated' and digressing from the fantasy story, written in a childish hand.... It is therefore a story constructed *around* pictures of Alice and her companions."[7] Among more recent writers the French Michel Tournier, who had particularly intense, multifaceted relationships in the world of photography, made trips to Canada and Japan with photographers, writing books in which he explored all aspects of the photographic image and all of its possible relationships with literary representation[8]; the novel *La goutte d'or* (1985) is entirely constructed around photographs.[9]

We live in a time when images are substitutes for reality, and when being participants in an experience means capturing it in memory by means of photographs[10]; photos offer testimony not only of something bound to decay and be lost forever, but also, as Roland Barthes says, testimony of *that which was*.[11]

According to Roberto De Romanis, from the complex relationship between photography and literature, there radiate

> two principal tendencies. The first is that which tends to synthesize in one image (photographic or literary) all possible reality: a kind of *haiku* or *koan* or illumination (references which we find in Cartier-Bresson, in Minor White, or even in certain reflections on photography made by Roland Barthes); the second concerns narration, playing with inscriptions, captions, duplicating the same cliché image many times, trying to give depth, movement and action to photography. We are talking about Andy Warhol and David Hockey.[12]

The contribution of Thom Gunn's brother, Ander, to *Positives* combines the two tendencies mentioned by De Romanis, since every independent image (except for the last three which show an old woman from various distances) is a self-contained nucleus to which the poems connect through commentary or caption,[13] and also takes part in a discourse or narration that embraces the whole range of human life.

POSITIVES

Among the above-mentioned collaborations between literature and photography (and many other examples that could be given), that of Thom and Ander Gunn — the fruit of a period Thom spent in London in the mid-sixties[14] — offers something new, in the sense that the photography came before the text. It is not intended to document or reveal aspects of the text, as, for example, is the case in the illustrated edition of Vittorini's *Conversations in Sicily*.[15] The images in *Positives* existed before the poems: against the background of sixties London (though it could have been any other city), they show moments of human life in a sequence. The people who attracted Ander's attention belong to various social classes; rarely, however, do they appear in a group. The individual is—with few exceptions—isolated and captured in the shell of his environment, which is rendered through details—at times simply fragments—of interiors or exteriors.[16]

As Thom Gunn writes in a letter quoted by Lidia De Michelis, "there is nothing much to say about *Positives*: it is a book about London, and my brother's pictures were almost always the starting point for my comments. Often, though, I was present when he took the pictures—it was a real collaboration."[17] Since the images focused in Ander's lens already existed, Thom's job was rather complex; he had to capture their essence by adding a verbal complement that was poetic, and not mere commentary or caption. Since poetry is also expressed through images, there is a risk that the photos will clip the wings of the poet, whose role is ancillary to that of the photographer.[18] This situation certainly explains the less than excellent quality of some of the poems, which descend into banality and whose meaning depends upon the images they accompany. The volume's title, *Positives*, seems to want to privilege the photos over the poems, even though it clearly refers not only to the final result of the photographic process, but also to the predominantly positive *Weltanschauung* emerging from the succession of moments photographed by Ander and in part also from the poems themselves. It should be noted, however, that, as if to revalue Thom's compositions, they are published on the left-hand pages of the book, and therefore come before the photos, even though this is probably a publisher's choice, given the greater visual impact of photos placed on right-hand pages. Nevertheless, each poem is a complement to the photo accompanying it on the right-hand page.[19]

Critics have shown little interest in *Positives*, or have made strongly limiting judgments; those who tried to salvage it mostly noted the overcoming of the cynicism of his earlier volumes. In a review of *Positives*, however, William Hunt insists on the overall bleakness of the work:

> There is a pervasive bleakness in this collection of poems and photographs by Thom and Ander Gunn. Bleakness itself is an apprehension of unacceptable limits. Throughout this collection, although poignant exceptions are present, the poems are very nearly mute. It is as if they deferred to the photographs.... What we see, hear, and feel does not satisfy.[20]

Neil Powell's judgment is likewise unfavorable:

> One might have suspected that Thom Gunn would allow the photographs to do the descriptive work and tackle more abstract matters in the poem; but this is not the case. Most of the poems are descriptive, often rather flatly, and they are mostly brief and desultory in manner.[21]

For Martin Dodsworth, on the other hand, "*Positives* marks an important stage in Gunn's development as a poet and has a special value for the reader in helping him to understand the kind of poetry Gunn writes."[22] Even Alan Bold, who insisted on the egotism of Gunn's early collections, receives this new experiment favorably:

> The fact that the poems had to interrelate with the photographs meant that Gunn had to pin his thoughts down on the surface of reality. There was simply no justification for Metaphysical self-indulgent free-association. There was no place in the book for striking heroic poses. For once we could *see* the people he was writing about. They existed, they were not introduced to make philosophical points.[23]

For Alan Bold, *Positives* is "a superb minor achievement, a plain-speaking meditation on the wastage of so much human life."[24]

We cannot deny that many of the poems descend to banality, often evidenced by a decidedly colloquial language that makes the poem simply a caption. In some cases, however, Gunn succeeds in giving the poem independent life, especially by evoking images different from those in the photo. This occurs in a poem placed next to a close-up of a smiling girl:

> or the laugh is like a prelude:
> the ripples go outward
> over cool water, ...
> [*Positives* 22, ll. 8–10]

In another poem, "PETE,"[25] referring to the picture of a youth playing the guitar, Gunn adds other images, trying to capture what is behind the image itself, which is the boy's dream of escaping from the gloomy routine of his daily job and becoming a pop star, like John Travolta in *Saturday Night Fever*: "But those clamps for a spade / turn, at evening, / [...] / ... to delicate / and precise instruments (*Positives* 26, ll. 7–8, 10–11).

In poems like this, the poet departs from the image, from that which is represented externally and the context in which it is presented, trying to penetrate the subject to see his thoughts, sensations, and passions, to bring out, by words, what the image indirectly reveals.[26]

In other poems, such as "SYON HOUSE," (one of the few with a title),[27] Ander's lens captures the image of a man in the background who looks upward from a boulevard flanked by columns in the foreground. The visual contrast between the man and the columns offers Thom Gunn an inspiration to express his vision of the human condition in the modern world: "I am oppressed by a sense of columns" (*Positives* 44, l. 8). This poem demonstrates the difference between Thom and Ander's *Weltanschauung*. Whereas the man in the photo is looking upward beyond the columns, which are placed in a way that gives a sense of openness, of possible freedom, Thom sees a man/column opposition and uses it to stress the struggle of man in a hostile universe ("...their pressure / is continual because / they have no mind or feeling / to vacillate" *Positives* 44, ll. 9–12).

Many images are not completely consonant with the verses: the photos celebrate life despite its difficulties (the fears of childhood, the responsibilities of adulthood, the fatigue of work, especially in an industrialized metropolis, the isolation of old age). Ander has a positive attitude to the world he portrays, whereas Thom's lines convey a feeling of exhaustion, of the individual's battle against fate. Often the poetic text does not match the picture (this is especially true of the best poems) because Gunn does not fully share his brother's positive attitude, his personal acceptance of life; Thom's existential angst prevails, and he reads it into the images.

Nevertheless it is abundantly clear that Thom Gunn is trying, though only occasionally succeeding, to put himself in his brother's shoes and especially trying not to override him: the subdued tone of the poems, which often lack punctuation, suggests an attempt to make them a part of the images, following their flow. Except for three poems, all are untitled, but the photographic image functions in a certain sense as the title. Each poem flows into the next, like a cell in a large being; short captions reflect the entire arc of human life from infancy to youth, from maturity to old age, to death, capturing particularly intense and meaningful moments. All of the photos show people in different moments of life: at work, at play, and at rest.[28] The main idea seems to be the recognition of the great loss of energy as we gradually approach death, shown through recurring images of rippling water, which is used as a metaphor for human energies that gradually exhaust themselves with age.[29] These energies are also renewed, insofar as death itself is only a dispersal of energy into the cosmic flux, as Gunn argues in "The Annihilation of Nothing":

> the ripples go outward
> over cool water, losing
> force, but continue
> to be born at the center, ...
> [*Positives* 22, ll. 9–12]
>
> the ripples which course out from that
> center, ridged with strength.
> [*Positives* 30, ll. 9–10]
>
> ... and if ripples
> touch the base of its arches,
> he cannot feel them, ...
> [*Positives* 72, ll. 1–3]

These verses make intertextual reference to Shakespeare's "Sonnet 60," where the poet uses the image of waves moving towards shore to symbolize the inexorable, unstoppable flow of time and human beings' total impotence in its regard: "Like as the waves make toward the pebbled shore, / so do our minutes hasten to their end."[30]

The image of water in *Positives* is closely tied to the omnipresence (in the volume) of the river that crosses London, the Thames; many of the photos are shot in the East End near the old neighborhood of the docks. The last verses cited above refer to a close-up photo of a large bridge upon which, in the background, walks an old man with a bundle on his back.

Gunn realized that many of his poems were inseparable from the photos, and for this reason, he chose only two, calling them "The Conversation of Old Men" and "The Old Woman" for *Collected Poems* (1993), which are in the section called *Poems from the 1960s*.[31] The poem "The Old Woman" closes *Positives*,[32] next to the close-up of an old woman with a scared look on her face. She seems to be contemplating the horror of death and holds her hand tightly to her chest as if to protect herself, not only from cold, but also from the darkness that will soon engulf her. The poem, which we will discuss later, confronts the horror of death ("Something approaches..." *Positives* 78, l. 1), trying to render the concept—consisting especially in the bodily sensations of which old age is gradually made ("Her deaf ears have caught it..." *Positives* 78, l. 3)—and the worrisome sense of mystery that it arouses ("...Will it hurt?" *Positives* 78, l. 10).

The other poem, "The Conversation of Old Men," is next to a photo of two old men talking on a park bench, whose words seem to disperse in the air: "...touching / then leaving what it / lightly touches; ..." (*Positives* 70, ll. 7–9). The title relates to the photographic image, as did the previous poem (the face of an old woman in close-up, almost hazy due to the extreme closeness of the lens, and two old men seated on a park bench concentrating on a small object that one of them holds in his hand), whereas the poetic verses diverge from the photo (in one of the rare cases in the collection), focusing not on the image, but on the melancholy mumbling of one of the men. Despite the title, the poem is not about a real conversation, but rather a silent monologue in which the words linger on in the sounds of the breeze, in the tactile, corporeal sensations that it arouses, and on the ripples of the water produced when the wind comes into contact with it, metaphor of the flow of life that continually touches human beings and then leaves them.

The last three poems refer to details of the same figure (the last photograph is a close up of the preceding one),[33] who is photographed with increasing degrees of closeness. They present the last gasps of the life of an old woman who is homeless, like most of the characters in Gunn's late poems, and in constant search of something in the garbage around her ("Poking around the rubbish / she can't find what she wants" *Positives* 76, ll. 1–2). She obstinately refuses death, and the destiny of the dry leaves around her[34]:

> Outside the abandoned house
> where she slept on old papers
> she stirs in the sun.
> [*Positives* 74, ll. 11–13]

Despite her attempts to cling to life, her memory wanes, her mind, labile and confused, loses meaning, wholeness, and continuity[35]:

> ... But Tom
> took something! What was it?
> [*Positives* 76, ll. 11–12]

Images of warmth that demonstrate the pulse of life contrast with those of coldness and aridity ("chill in her feet"), both associated with death.[36]

The theme of menace is presented here as moonlight, a symbol of insecurity, fear, and anxiety in contrast to the vitality of the sun and light. In this poem, however, Gunn exorcises the threat of death, even though he feels its terror, seeing it as the necessary conclusion of a cycle, like the arrival of a longed-for time that will end the fatigue of living:

> Let it come, it is
> the terror of full repose,
> and so no terror.
> [*Positives* 78, ll. 11–13][37]

The idea of death as a reality that one should try to accept with strength because it is part of the existential agenda, informs "Faustus Triumphant" (*Jack Straw's Castle*), a poem in which the speaker is a heroic figure at the opposite extreme from the old woman captured in Ander's lens (as Caravaggio's Saul was the opposite of the old women praying in the church in "Santa Maria del Popolo"). Faustus welcomes death almost complacently, seeing it as a reunification with the primal elements, especially fire, which, like in T.S. Eliot's *The Waste Land*,[38] acquires a purifying function:

> My joy so great
> that if hell threatens, the
> memory alone of flame
> protects me. There is
> no terror in combustion.
> I shall rejoice to
> enter into him
>   Father-
> Nature, the Great Flame
> [*CP* 268, ll. 31–39]

The regenerating power of fire, which makes the speaker part of the surrounding world, is an internal energy that guarantees salvation. It challenges the laws of nature which imprison man in his shell, promising a return to the cosmic oneness that negates separation.

After the publication of *Positives*, Gunn's poetry becomes dense with images of death and the theme of its painful acceptance often returns. Like D.H. Lawrence's phoenix that rises from its ashes, acceptance of death is the basic premise for a resurrection into the cosmic flow.

In "Breaking Ground," placed at the end of *Jack Straw's Castle*—where the succession of free and sometimes fragmentary verses appropriates, recalling them intertextually, the notes and rhythms of the Beatles' famous song "Let It

Be"—death is a metamorphosis of the self that, in melting into the universe, disassembles and reassembles to acquire new life. The poem is about a female figure dear to the poet, presumably his aunt, whose fatigue, like that of the old woman in the last pages of *Positives* is described in the poem's first part, called "Kent": "she's too old now to / dig, ..." (*CP* 303, l. 10–11).[39] In the second part, "Monterey" (from the famous rock concert held at Monterey, California, in 1967), far away in time and space from the image of the aunt, the poet remembers her during a Joan Baez concert[40] (which includes the Beatles' song, "Let It Be") and sees her reincarnated, through continuous metamorphoses, into the thousand faces and people attending the show. The exhaustion of the first stanza, the annihilation of the beloved figure in the ground which engulfs her ("lost, forgotten in / an indiscriminate mulch, ..." *CP* 304, ll. 27–28), change into something extremely alive, in the joyful movements and overflowing energy of the crowd at the concert:

> Let it be. It
> comes to me at last that
> when she dies she
> [...]
> is dispersed—but dispersal
> means
>   spreading abroad:
>   ..., she
> is distributed
> through fair warm flesh
> of strangers
> [*CP* 305, ll. 21–23, 27–29, 31–34]

The extension of her person till it embraces the whole universe is suggested also by the use of the feminine pronoun "shee" with the elongated vowel, which reproduces phonetically the sung melody ("shee" rhymes with "Let it be"), as if the beloved figure were in continuous expansion, able to re-emerge simultaneously in all the spectators:[41]

> ... renewed again
> and again ...
> [...]
>   Shee
> is gonn, Shee is lost,
> Shee is found, shee
> is ever faire.
> [*CP* 305, ll. 38–39, 42–45]

The last word, "faire," which echoes the final word of line 41, "here," suggesting the presence of eternal beauty in her, refers to a commemorative poem of Elizabethan times, "The 11th: and last booke of the Ocean to Cynthia" by Sir Walter Raleigh ("Shee is gonn, Shee is lost! Shee is found, shee is ever faire!"), which is dedicated to Queen Elizabeth.[42]

Whereas in the first half of *Positives* the leaps in age are rather large, later, the poet and photographer linger on images of old age, with the effect of slowing down the rhythm of the collection and suggesting the steady exhaustion of energy over the course of a lifetime.

The first poems stress the eruption of an undifferentiated élan vital, an almost sexless newborn human, from a completely instinctual fetus:

> She has been a germ, a fish,
> and an animal; even now
> she is almost without hair
> or sex. ...
> [*Positives* 6, ll. 1–4]

From its state of unconsciousness the baby gradually opens to the exploration of self and world, whose details become parts of its consciousness:

> Precarious exploration
> from coast to interior:
> [...]
> a triumph, a triumph.
> [*Positives* 8, ll. 6–7, 13]

But infancy is not only a time for gradual discovery of the surrounding environment. For Gunn, it is also a state of weakness, inferiority, and vulnerability towards adults, from which arises that sense of oppression that we saw in "SYON HOUSE" and the relationship between human being and column.

Thus Gunn comments upon the image of a child who, sad and worried, worn out by his own energies which he cannot understand, hugs a rag-doll as if to derive protection from it:

> Something is feeding on you,
> and it is what you feed on.
> The source of your strength guts you.
> [*Positives* 10, ll. 2–4]

After infancy, the lens focuses on children having their first experiences with social life, whose "...bodies are increasing / in secret society" (*Positives* 14, ll. 13–14), a period marked by great concentration and full activation of individual potential. The poet reconnects to the world of the motorcycle gangs[43] and the tough guys at the center of *The Sense of Movement*, to the idea of a challenge to the world by expressing vital energy: "all things are means to wheely ends" (*Positives* 16, l. 2). The line refers to a detail in Ander's photo, of a youth in the act of mounting his bicycle, and it anticipates his action. The rest of the photo shows in close-up a row of bicycles and in the background a young man leaning motionless against the wall, whose look is directed elsewhere, towards a reality that he has not yet managed to grasp: "...and dreams of cars" (*Positives* 16, l. 7)

In his glorification of youth, Gunn inevitably falls into clichés, writing lines that go no further than the image, which already expresses the potential and energy of the photographed subject. For example:

> Youth is power. He knows it,
> a rough young animal, but
> an animal that can smile.
> [*Positives* 20, ll. 1–3]

These lines accompany a close-up of a young man overflowing with bold confidence while making a lewd, challenging gesture with his hand, accented by a smile on lips that clutch a cigarette.[44] This pose connects back to the behavior of the boys in *The Sense of Movement* and the theme of opposition to the world by which they seek to confirm their identity.

Three later poems arise from a different relationship to Ander's images; the photos show musical events, young people who sing and play guitars, inspiring Thom to comment, not so much on what he sees, but on what he imagines hearing, capturing the essence of a music that has the power to express the inexpressible, to discover a sense of beauty in the disorder of experience: "...For the clear voice / has discovered, ... / ..., the bubbling source / of both joy and lamentation" (*Positives* 30, ll. 2–5).

In one of these three poems,[45] Gunn tries to render the effect of musical notes, beginning the poem with a treble clef and infusing it with the lyricism, melody, and syncopation typical of sixties music, with its strongly repetitive character.[46] The poet's attention is directed not to the image (a half-length portrait of a young man playing the bass) but to the effect of the music on the audience around him, rendered by the paratactic succession of the uncoordinated clauses, in a language lacking the logical links typical of verbal communication. Gunn tries to transform poetry into a musical composition, both—as mentioned above—by opening with a treble clef and by the pauses in the middle of the first, fourth, eighth, and eleventh lines. Describing not the image (youth playing bass) so much as the audience who listens, the poem reproduces the gradual formation of the notes and their impact on the listener, beginning with the present tense "The music starts" and ending with the present perfect tense, "they begin to recognize / that || the music has started" (*Positives* 24, ll. 10–11). By telling a story, "...a song / about life by the Mersey" (*Positives* 24, l. 9), the music emphasizes the enormous success of Liverpool's counterculture—the Mersey Poets and the Beatles.[47]

The spectacle of the flower-girls that Ander's lens captures in action in a city street, inspires one of Thom's rare initiatives. He describes two young girls, already aware of their femininity, and turns them into flowers (until this point it is a cliché, but now the symbol becomes more original). They await the contact of bees, which will desecrate them with their "black hairy legs." The image of hairy legs conjures up new pubic hair (recall "the familiar itch of close dark hair" *CP* 61, l. 21 in "The Allegory of the Wolf Boy"), and the deflowering itself is presented as a necessity, for the girls must perform their vital function:

> compact segmented buds
> bees will come to them
> and pollen will encrust.
> [*Positives* 18, ll. 6–8]

Lidia De Michelis sees a link between Gunn's poem and some famous models of American tradition: "the coupling woman-flower in combination with the figures of bees is already present in Whitman.... This assumes symbolic significance in William Carlos Williams, where it links man's aspiration to marriage with flowers, feminine symbols of all that gives birth."[48]

Later images point to another central experience of life — marriage — seeing it as an inevitable decline of love into daily routine. Even though the nuptial path can degenerate into monotony and exhaustion of the passion previously felt during youth, it is also seen as a necessary step, as the only way to escape isolation. The "big tea" that the spouses share when, as Gunn imagines, the woman captured in Ander's photo returns home bearing the weight of many shopping bags, is in fact also the symbol of communion and contact, as the expression "our own table" assumes the metaphorical quality of the bridal bed: "...I will give you a big / tea on our own table (*Positives* 38, ll. 6–7).

From this point on, the figures in the book are more isolated; they emanate a strong sense of loneliness, and are mostly associated with squalid scenes, vignettes of degradation and urban grey (photos of people at work; dockyards and sidewalks covered with smoke and fog).

The next lines accompany an image of a silhouette seen behind a demolished house, who raises a pick with fatigue, but also indomitable skill:

> ... Through an arc the point
> falls as force, the human
> behind it in control
> tiring, but tiring slowly
> [*Positives* 52, ll. 11–14]

The last words bring out one of Gunn's common themes — a painful gesture of resistance and tenacious opposition to a hostile world.

Like dust, which is a dominant image in the sequence "Misanthropos" (*Touch*), where it is the only thing that remains "...yet to be shared" (*CP* 151, 17, l. 16), the city's smoke is what brings men together. They must accept the smoke and try to bear it together, realizing their humanity in the surrounding environment, in that urban world which they partly constructed, there being no alternative. The smoke is constantly there, everywhere, it is "unescapable," "an inhabited confusion." These words are linked to a photo of a huge cloud of smoke. In the background, almost on the point of being submerged in it, are two silhouettes of faceless workers, about whom the only definite detail is, other than being together, the work tool upon which they lean, which is, like the uniforms of motorcyclists, an integral part of their beings. In this poem we see the need, however painful, to live with others in a communal dimension, in a city whose contrasts between rich and poor, joy and pain, cleanliness and dirt, continually testify to human action and community.

> ... People
> fumble toward each other through
> the greasy obscurity. On the downs
> one would be merely alone.
> [*Positives* 56, ll. 10–13]

There is a dichotomy between the necessary sharing of human space, which implies a sense of consensus and compromise with a series of difficulties (the words "people / fumble toward each other through / the greasy obscurity" recall Eliot's Hollow Men wandering in the fog), and the solitude and refuge found in the world of nature. But for Gunn, despite the desirability of escape, it is not a possible route. The volumes *Positives* and *Touch* signal the end of his existential phase.

The sense of respect for the Other, the need to define a space shared with similar people without trespassing upon them, informs one of the few poems with a title, "LEBENSRAUM" (German for "living space"), where Ander's lens captures from behind the silhouette of a man walking along a snow-covered road next to a row of huge, parked cars. The black of the figure contrasts strongly with the white of the snow, which, other than emphasizing the frigidity of existential solitude, testifies literally to the space invaded by human beings by placing their footprints upon it. Although coexistence with other humans is difficult, it is always preferable to isolation, to living inside a shell that leaves no room for contact and communication, as the second and last stanza of the poem emphasize: "...till / the bacillus of despair is / [...] / isolated and frozen over (*Positives* 46, ll. 11–12, 14).

Solitude causes a hopelessness that cannot be defeated, but only temporarily evaded. Gunn's *Weltanschauung* is still marked by existential angst, even though he tries to look beyond it, to find a glimmer of hope. The lines, "...in my every move / I prevent someone / from stepping where I step" (*Positives* 46, ll. 5–7) suggest his awareness of the need for a more humane attitude towards life and the world. One could say that a more "humanistic" Gunn is speaking to his old self. It is necessary to accept one's own humanity without invading the space of others, as the image of an old sweeper suggests. He is shot from behind and therefore, like many figures in these photos, without a face, thin and stationary as the broom that he holds in his hands (a tool that guarantees his identity and function and at the same time sustains him in a hostile universe). Gunn perceives the sweeper's almost aristocratic and philosophic detachment while he contemplates the lively body of a girl "in flower": "cataloguing an authentic / treasure in the quiet / collection of his mind" (*Positives* 66, ll. 19–21). The immobile figure of the sweeper contrasts strongly with the impetuous vitality expressed in the flight of a pigeon. Gunn compares the bird (which is not even present in the photo) to the old man, whose élan vital was once like the pigeon's, whereas now his face — as imagined by the poet — is furrowed by time, withered like the bark of a tree that bears the imprint of life's cycles: "...an old / man with a face like some gnarled / shiny section of black wood (*Positives* 66, ll. 7–9). The human being is compared to the animal because of an attitude that recalls the stoicism of the heroes in *My Sad Captains*, their ability to accept their destiny (in the sweeper's case, the decline of energy) with dignity and calm, and to appreciate, in the sight of the girl, the full self-expression of youth.

The next image and poem also recollect the stoicism of *My Sad Captains*. Here Ander's lens catches in close up the wrinkled face of an old man whose look shows neither joy nor pain but only the stoic tolerance of life and resistance to its imminent annihilation. From the image Gunn tries to reconstruct the long journey that made those wrinkles, to read them "...as / the ability to resist / annihilation, or as the small / but constant losses endured (*Positives* 68, ll. 5–8). Gunn returns to his common theme: man's constant resistance to "nothingness," his continuous and painful buttressing of himself against the void of the universe. The furrows on his forehead, and the wrinkles around his eyes, nose, and mouth, confer to his face the connotations of a mask, the essence of old age, the indelible signs left by time. Roland Barthes wrote about a 1963 Richard Avedon portrait of William Casby: "Since every photograph is contingent (and thereby outside of meaning), Photography cannot signify (aim at a generality) except by assuming a mask." In the Casby portrait, "the essence of slavery is here laid bare: the mask is the meaning, insofar as it is absolutely pure."[49]

Gunn never reveals his inner self in his comments on Ander's photos; the poems are strictly impersonal. The poet shares Eliot's idea of art as "the escape from personality,"[50] and said more than once that he wanted to write poetry "that can speak about anything at all, that can deal with the perceptions and concerns as they come up. I do not court impersonality so much as I try to avoid personality, which I'd prefer to leave to the newspapers."[51]

In *Positives*, Gunn contemplates the city (mid-sixties London) in its various aspects, accepting it for what it is without any egocentric appropriation or imposition of meaningful symbols. One of the last poems comments on the image of an old homeless man in the distance, bent under the weight of a bundle on this back, who is approaching a bridge which is in close up, and therefore gigantic in respect to the man. The image of the bridge recalls the poem *The Bridge* (1930), by the American modernist Hart Crane, which is dedicated to the construction of the Brooklyn Bridge in New York. Whereas in Crane's poem, the bridge is the symbol of union and communion between human beings (as it is for Walt Whitman), a possibility for encountering and surmounting barriers, in Gunn's poem, there is only the immanent and concrete sense of the bare stone, hard and heavy like the bundle that the old man carries on his back.[52] The call to life by the ripples of water under the bridge, which once again enter the flow of existence, the cosmic flux, does not touch the human figure, who is unable to find comfort and heat from nature or from other people: "...The wind / is cold, stone / hard, and Salvation Army / tea not sweet enough" (*Positives* 72, ll. 9–12). The reference to the English ritual of tea occurs in other poems in this collection, such as the one about the responsibilities of marriage and domestic cohabitation, and the one about the workers taking a break.[53] The ritual of tea, besides representing a motif of London life shared by all social classes, is also a moment of togetherness that provides foundation for that sharing of space, of respect and mutual exchange necessary for overcoming the barriers of isolation and existential angst.

In *Positives*, Gunn's attitude to the city is different from that in poems like "In Praise of Cities" (*The Sense of Movement*) and "A Map of the City" (*My Sad Captains*), where the poet humanizes the city, projecting a series of symbolic meanings, assuming the city within himself. Here, the city is real; it is the mid-sixties London captured in Ander's lens. Gunn said that in *Positives*, his intention was to distinguish "a form of fragmentary inclusiveness that could embody the detail and history of that good year ... and it contains a London I found hard to recognize only eight years after" (*OP* 181).[54]

At a technical level, *Positives* appears in a relationship of continuity to *My Sad Captains*, though it represents a step forward in free verse. Sometimes Gunn begins a poem with syllabics, then proceeds with a looser rhythm without any form; in the poem that concludes the volume, describing the image of the homeless old woman in close-up, the first eight lines are syllabics of seven syllables, while in the next ones, except for the penultimate ("the terror of full repose"), the form is broken, and the number of syllables changes. It is a movement to free verse via syllabics.

The poetic line in *Positives* is shorter, sharper, more severe, rhyme-less (except for internal rhyme), and uses alliteration and assonance, finding its consistency in the insistence on the single sound, recurring inside the line.

End rhyme is used only once, for ironic contrast, in a poem about a photo of three workers who gather for a tea break in the open space between piles of construction materials. Between the meditations of a middle-aged man, the poet inserts, in a central position and in italics, an ironic celebration of tea-drinking:

> *When God bade labour for our burden, He*
> [...]
> *... granted respite twice a day, for tea.*
> *O Teapot, heavenly maid, descend.*
> [*Positives* 62, ll. 5, 7–8]

Critics who were not overall favorably disposed to Gunn's efforts in *Positives*, redeem it in part because of its formal qualities.

Neil Powell says,

Many of the pieces in his [Gunn's] fourth collection, *Positives*, are more or less syllabic: this is without doubt the loosest collection of poems he has published, perhaps necessarily and therapeutically so.... The value of *Positives* is that Gunn has learned to write flatly, undemonstratively, and loosely in a metrical sense; some of these poems fulfil the promises of "Waking in a Newly-Built House" more clearly than anything in *My Sad Captains*.[55]

Alan Bold describes the work:

> Gunn's first book in free verse, and the sort of free verse he favours is that associated with William Carlos Williams: simple and conversational and rooted in the objects that are being described.... *Positives* is important from the technical point of view in that it demonstrated Gunn's ability to dispense with his metrical strait jacket.... Here he uses free verse in the style of William Carlos Williams and he uses it well.[56]

Gunn recognizes William Carlos Williams as his model in the collection as well:

> I was consciously borrowing what I could from William Carlos Williams, trying as it were to anglicize him, to help make his openness of form and feeling available to English writers [*OP* 181].

CHAPTER VI

The Liberating Sixties*

GAY PRIDE

One of the central problems in Gunn's poetry from *Fighting Terms* to *Boss Cupid* is the rendering of his homosexuality. In the atmosphere of Cambridge during the fifties, which was marked by a Leavis-like attempt to re-purify the "healthy" English tradition, to be gay was seen as socially and culturally unacceptable. In later years, this taboo weakened, though it has never entirely disappeared. Gregory Woods accurately pointed out that critics appreciated Gunn's poems when homosexuality was the source of elegiac laments, when it was something sad and tormenting like in the last part of *The Man with Night Sweats*. But his work went nearly unnoticed (or was negatively reviewed, with tacit disapproval of its joy) when, as in *The Passages of Joy*, the poet presented homosexuality and the life of gay couples shamelessly, in a carefree way, without inhibitions or fear of social restrictions.[1]

Although homoerotic inclinations can be seen in the early poems, in his almost involuntary admiration of violent poses of heroes in uniform pretending to be tough (soldiers, motorcyclists, and others), and in the sometimes obsessive battle between the sexes (as we saw in some poems in *Fighting Terms*), they never seem to be consciously accepted by the poet, never openly recognized as an integral part of his own nature. In these poems, the speaker is often observed at a distance, sometimes while entrapped in dark, gloomy places. Homosexuality is hidden, like the secret wounds of tough guys that they hide behind the shield of their aggressive poses and their uniforms.[2] The circular structure of these early poems suggests the constricted space in which the heroes act, while the insistent use of refrains assumes an oppressive and obsessive quality that reflects the speaker's lack of inner freedom.

Only through the liberating and cathartic experiences of the sixties ("the

---

*This chapter is a revised and expanded version of the essay, "Wrestling with the 'rappel à l'ordre': Thom Gunn and the New Modernism of the Sixties," in In and Around the Sixties, ed. by Mirella Billi and Nicholas Brownless (Viterbo: Settecittà, 2002) pp. 119–30.

fullest years of my life, crowded with discovery both inner and outer," *OP* 182), does the poet undergo a radical metamorphosis that profoundly influences his lifestyle and attitude to homosexuality. A brief poem in the collection *Boss Cupid*, called "The 1970s," suggests that the liberation was mainly of a sexual character: "For the sexual New Jerusalem was by far the greatest fun." (*BC* 44, l. 4)

The sixties mark a turning point in his life because they postdate his visit to the United States, far from England and its repressive culture. In the fifties, English culture was marked by conformism and bigoted, repressive morals. Although in the new environment he initially had to deal with another type of closed system, that is, the iron discipline and rules of Yvor Winters, Gunn soon freed himself from the restricting presence of another master and began gradually to discard his own inhibitions and to treat the theme of homosexuality in a more natural way. A central role in this struggle for emancipation and openness to new artistic experiments was played out in the ambit of the liberating experience of LSD in the sixties.[3]

The use of hallucinogens has a long literary tradition; opium played a large role in the nineteenth century, influencing Romantic poetry and prose. But it was especially in the sixties that drug use changed from elitist to communitarian, acquired a historic connotation, signaled one's belonging to a particular period and/or atmosphere. Its influence on literature and film — from the Beat Generation of the Fifties, to the climax of hippy culture towards the middle of the sixties, in the movies *Easy Rider* (1969), *Hair* (1979) and *Quadrophenia* (1979) — goes hand in hand with the growing success of music (consider psychedelic rock concerts like Woodstock in 1969 and the Isle of Wight in 1970). LSD was associated with the search for a new language, one closer to the rhythms of speech and, paraphrasing Kerouac, of breathing.[4]

In Gunn's poetry of this era (especially that collected in *Moly*, where many poems like "Rites of Passage," "Moly," and "At the Centre," have to do with metamorphoses), the caves and corridors of the earlier collections are replaced by wide-open spaces bathed in sunlight. The uniform is abandoned, clearing the way for nudity of a liberating kind. Gunn was gradually moving towards an acceptance of his own homosexuality, presented as a natural instinct that did not need to be concealed. He no longer experienced it as degrading or alienating (as in the poem "The Allegory of the Wolf Boy"), but as a way of being that implied, according to the later poems, affection, understanding, something that was not just sex ("It was not sex..." *CP* 407, l. 12; the poem "The Hug" in *The Man with Night Sweats* can be read and interpreted as a rewriting of John Donne's "The Extasie," "Wee see by this, it was not sexe").[5] The community experience and gay bars of San Francisco were the starting points for him to break barriers that had impeded him (and his uniformed heroes) from entering into direct contact with the surrounding world, permitting him to open freely to the redeeming, regenerating touch of other bodies.

The effect of the atmosphere of the sixties can also be seen in the poet's new way of relating to male and female identity. Whereas in the early poems the male seems to protect his maleness behind a hard, tough pose, covering himself with the mask of uniforms and motorcycles, after the sixties, the male gradually abandons the aggressive pose, the attitude of tough guy always ready to fight and to challenge. He re-values his feminine aspect, becoming capable of affection and open to gestures, not of aggressive challenge, but of tenderness.[6] Gunn's encounter with sixties culture gave the poet new ways to shape male and female identities that had been codified and passed down through tradition. While in the early collections, subconscious repression of his homosexuality caused sadomasochistic attitudes and poses, the poet now discovered new ways to express the coexistence of male and female identity in every individual. The tough guy pose and aggressive behavior gave way to a new attitude of sympathy for other people and their complexities, permitting Gunn to overcome the existential gap between mind and soul, intellect and instinct, masculinity and femininity, and find an escape from these paralyzing dichotomies that had prevented him from reaching inner equilibrium. The "beaters" and macho heroes, hostile to every type of contact in the early poems, gave way to surfers and swimmers who, embracing the waves, looked for a harmonious dialogue with them, immersing themselves in nature until they became a part of it ("The marbling bodies have become / Half wave, half men" *CP* 198, ll. 13–14). The quote is taken from the poem "From the Wave" (*Moly*),[7] which constitutes a kind of response to "On the Move" (*The Sense of Movement*). The image of the boys who try to overcome nature ("They scare a flight of birds across the field" *CP* 39, l. 20) contrasts with that of surfers who try to adapt themselves to its rhythms:

> Their pale feet curl, they poise their weight
>   With a learn'd skill.
> It is the wave they imitate
>   Keeps them so still.
> [*CP* 198, ll. 9–12]

Clive Wilmer observes:

> Even more striking is the contrast between "On the Move" and "From the Wave." To an English reader, the very title of the later poem reminds us of the earlier — preposition, article, monosyllabic noun, "move" and "wave" making a half rhyme.[8]

Completely taken up by his contemplations, the poet now observes with interest the smallest detail of the surrounding world, which is no longer experienced as hostile. Aggression and violence are replaced by tenderness, and frenetic movement is replaced by a state of calm imbued with the dynamic potential to realize a harmonious relationship to the outer world and its incessant flux. Instead of absorbing Nature into his personal universe, the poet lets himself dissolve in it, offering no resistance ("For though we have invaded this glittering place / And broke the silences, yet we submit: / So wholly, that we are details of it" *CP* 241, 2, ll. 28–30). This new mode of approaching the world leads to experiments with a type of poetry characterized by what T.S. Eliot called "extinction of personality," although for Gunn it did not mean a complete detachment from his own emotions. (Cf. Chapter V in this book.)

The LSD experience went in step with the discovery of new poetic voices (in 1963 a collection of American poets edited by Thom Gunn and Ted Hughes came out), which were completely unknown to the groups of writers gravitating to Oxford, Cambridge and the London literary scene. Among Gunn's discoveries is Robert Duncan, to whom he dedicates the poem called "Duncan" that opens *Boss Cupid*.[9] Read in the light of Gunn's recent death, the poem sounds like a prelude to, or announcement of, his own death, a testimony to a person who has entered his declining years and, unlike the hitchhiker in "Hitching into Frisco" (see Chapter VII in this book), seems to have "nowhere to go":

> In sight of a conclusion, whose great dread
> Was closure,
>   his life soon to be enclosed
> Like the sparrow's flight about the feasting friends,
> Briefly revealed where its breast caught their light,
> Beneath the long roof, between open ends,
> Themselves the margins of unchanging night.
> [*BC* 4, 2, ll. 28–34]

The poem is divided into two stanzas that compare the past (the extreme energy and creative powers of a younger Duncan, "When in his twenties a poetry's full strength / Burst into voice as an unstopping flood" (*BC* 3, 1, ll. 1–2), always in search of something new, always ready to look "...beyond conclusion"), and the present, in which, from the distance of forty years, the long-suffering body is gnawing at the spirit ("For since his illness he had not composed") (*BC* 4, 2, l. 27). Duncan, who from youth onwards never imagined the last word, looking always "beyond conclusion," was now reduced to "a posthumous poet," "In sight of a conclusion." The middle of the second stanza lacks all sentimentality; Gunn describes his friend's physical decay with a vein of subtle irony through the description of an event (Duncan's fall after a public reading) in which are woven the real and the imaginary, the physical life and poetic creation, a vein that is accentuated by the intertextual recall of a similar event that happened to the poet H.D. in the last years of her life. While the reality is the physical weakness of both poets (Duncan falls to the ground, Gunn is unable to break his fall), the imagination transforms the event into an act of love and tenderness: "— Fell he said later, as if I stood ready, / 'Into the strong arms of Thom Gunn'" (*BC* 4, 2, ll. 11–12).

Duncan's influence, along with the cultural freedom offered by San Francisco in the liberating sixties, certainly contributed to Gunn's changed attitude with regard to his own homosexuality, a change clearly visible in his own career. Whereas his early poems showed an imprisoned, masked homosexuality, he gradually learned to treat his sexuality in a more relaxed, open manner, and the later works celebrate this laboriously attained freedom.

Rebirth

"The Allegory of the Wolf Boy" (written in the mid-fifties) was a poem about his own youth,[10] in which he lead a double life, transforming himself at night not into a predator (like the name "wolf boy" would lead one to believe), but into prey, since he was victim of an uncontrollable power which made him blindly obey impulses, and act according to instinct. His condition was such that he could not choose, and for this reason he was unable to heal the inner wounds that he felt in both day and nighttime. The devastating effects of awakening to the homosexual instinct are emphasized in the final line, "Drops on four feet. Yet he has bleeding paws" (*CP* 61), where the wounds on the paws assume the connotation of stigmata. They evoke the image of crucifixion, testifying to the moral and social violence to which his homosexual instincts will be subject.[11]

Whereas in this poem the metamorphosis affects only his private life, that which takes place in "Rites of Passage" (the first poem in *Moly*) implies a radical refusal of all authority, thereby assuming a public dimension. The title of the poem refers to the moly plant, which, in Homer's *Odyssey*, Hermes offers to Ulysses to defend himself from Circe's spell, an episode explicitly referred to in the epigraph to *Moly*.[12] Metamorphosis brings about a degeneration of the individual from a human to an animal or vegetable state (such as Narcissus turning into a flower or Ulysses' companions turning into pigs) whether in the classical tradition or in fairy tales (*Beauty and the Beast*, *The Frog Prince*). The latter two examples of metamorphosis, however, involve changes from a lesser state (vegetable or animal) to a greater; thanks to the power of love, these beings revert to their former state. In Gunn's poetry and especially in "Rites of Passage," metamorphosis from man to beast is shown in a decidedly positive light, initiating a liberating process that ends in true regeneration.[13] The protagonist experiences the metamorphosis consciously in its making (as in Kafka's *Metamorphosis*, although here, the effect on him is diametrically opposed to Gregor's, that is, one not of shame but of liberation). He transforms into a creature that is half man, half beast, a sort of satyr or Pan, who enjoys a freedom never before experienced and appears proud of his new body that obeys only instinct. The speaker brings to light his own animal nature, while in "The Allegory of the Wolf Boy," the metamorphosis was observed from a distance, as though through the eyes of a voyeur, revealing an unspoken but profound shame that he was unable to overcome. Significantly, in "Rites of Passage," the metamorphosis of man into beast takes place not in the dark, but in full light ("horns bud *bright*," emphasis mine), suggesting that the individual has gained awareness of a freedom of choice that enables him to defy the father figure (incarnation of authority) and regress to a state of womb-like innocence. In this state, he can break from his old social self, and also from his old way of communicating, from his cultural inheritance of patriarchal language. Now he is able to communicate with the mother by a gesture of self-assertion ("I stamp upon the earth" *CP* 185, l. 22), leaving a mark on the bare earth and revealing, without inhibition or reserve, his sexuality.

The liberatory experience linked to taking drugs like LSD is the source of rebirth and rediscovery of innocence, in the light of which homosexuality can freely express itself and be realized. The lines "Behind an almond bough, / Horns gaudy with its snow, / I wait live, out of sight" (*CP* 185, ll. 16–18) in "Rites of Passage" announce a resurrection of which the speaker is proud.[14] Although "snow" means "drug" in American slang, the term here refers to the horns of an animal covered with the fallen petals of a flowering almond tree. With this image Gunn celebrates rebirth by a ritual that unites western Christian tradition (the angel holding an almond branch in the iconography of the Annunciation) to primitive rites of puberty in which young bodies are painted white and covered with ashes, alluding to the death of the child and the birth of a young adult.

Both "The Allegory of the Wolf Boy" and "Rites of Passage," though the effect on the protagonists is diametrically opposed, refer to puberty, to the physical transformation connected to the growth of pubic hair: "[he] Feels the familiar itch of close dark hair" ("The Allegory of the Wolf Boy" *CP* 61, l. 21); "— Skin that was damp and fair / Is barklike and, feel, rough" ("Rites of Passage" *CP* 185, ll. 5–6).

Experiences of regression to an animal state and of resurrection are the subject of many poems, for example, "The Garden of the Gods," "Being Born," "At the Centre," "The Discovery of the Pacific" (*Moly*), the cycle "The Geysers," "Saturnalia" (*Jack Straw's Castle*). In "The Discovery of the Pacific," Gunn renders the liberating experience of his encounter with American culture during these years,[15] by the image of conquest (evoking the frontier myth) of California and the ocean, on the part of a pair of young lovers. Diving into the Pacific takes on the meaning of baptism, an ablution that makes the characters part of a single being, generating a perfect union in total harmony with the movement of the waves in which their bodies tenderly immerse: "And come, together, in the water's motion, / The full caught pause of their embrace" (*CP* 222, ll. 23–24).

The long drive from east to west is a voyage of initiation, not only through contact with the unknown and the severity of nature ("the extreme chill"), but also through a questioning of their true identities, of their socialized selves:

> Kansas to California. Day by day
> They travelled emptier of the things they knew.
> They improvised new habits on the way,
> But lost the occasions, and then lost them too.
> [*CP* 222, ll. 5–8]

Gunn's encounter with sixties culture and the newly-achieved freedom of expression are at the root of most of the poems written in the following years, which culminate in the collection *The Passages of Joy*. The title attests to another rite of passage towards the achievement of complete happiness and freedom, a state of physical and psychic wholeness. This conquest permits Gunn not only to shake off old anxieties, to defend and openly maintain the dignity of his homoerotic relationships, but to approach them with awe and reverence as though they were part of a religious experience. "The Miracle" is extremely interesting from this point of view, for his audacious way (recalling Metaphysical poetry) of juxtaposing the sacred and the profane, hieratic language with counterculture jargon.[16] Composed of four stanzas with regular rhyme (*ababb*), each of which ends in a rhyming couplet, and in the form of a dramatic monologue interrupted only in the first and last stanzas by three questions uttered by an imaginary interlocutor,[17] the poem evokes the experience of a sexual encounter that took place in a McDonald's restroom. Yet there is nothing squalid nor shameful about this encounter — quite the contrary. What began as casual lust, a mere sexual instinct while the two lovers were going to the airport, acquires the sacredness of a rite because of the intensity of their desire. Desire transforms the restrooms of a fast food joint into a temple, and the urinal into which the speaker's companion stoops to ejaculate into an altar where one kneels to pray. Gunn is suggesting that even a casual sexual relationship, made decidedly unpoetic by the ambiance of a fast food restroom, can become sacred due to the passion and desire that transform the very act into a miracle, as the title suggests. But the poem does not insist on what may seem to be the mystical, sacred dimension of the erotic, à la D.H. Lawrence. Though Gunn does not exclude religious value from this experience, he simultaneously transforms it into a game by the ironic note introduced by the image of a sticky, wet mark left on his boot ("...that snail-track on the toe of my boot" *CP* 357, l. 15) at the end of the third stanza. Yet the lines, "I make it shine again, I love him so, / Like they renew a saint's blood out of sight. / But we're not Catholic, see, so it's all right" (*CP* 357, ll. 18–20), even though they could seem blasphemous, do confirm, however ambiguously, the religious nature of this experience.

The expression, "but we're not Catholic," highlights the religious uneasiness and evidences the problematic situation of gay men, who are banned from official Churches, but simultaneously evinces the profound freedom the poet has finally reached. He experiences this as rebirth, inner peace and artistic independence finally attained, something exclusively individual — and openly refuses to be considered a member of a particular social group. This vital need to defend his personal freedom is clearly expressed in an interview with Alan Sinfield, during which Gunn reveals one of the things that bothers him most, which is the tendency of many people to use, in a way he finds superficial and incorrect, the expression "homosexual life style" as if it were easily definable and therefore generalizable. One never hears, says Gunn, of a heterosexual life style; everyone is fully aware that there are a variety of ways to live as a heterosexual, and the same is true for homosexuals.[18] In other words, once Gunn openly admitted that he was gay, and that homosexuality was at the center of his work, he did not try to address an exclusively gay audience. The poet rebelled against the idea of being labeled and read as a writer of sexual propaganda, something which often occurs in the case of homosexual artists: "Much of the time I want to write for other people as well. I don't want to disown a gay audience, but I don't want to limit myself to that, because one can get very limited."[19] Like Duncan, Gunn uses poetry to explore new dimensions of individual identity in a way that is completely free of prejudice. According to Bruce Woodcock:

> Gunn's work since his first poems about gay experience appeared in *Jack Straw's Castle* (1976) has been not so much a record of gayness, as an exploration of unmapped territory, part of a process of gay self-creation, the charting of the imaginable potential in gay relationships.[20]

This search ultimately leads him to sublimate sexuality in love, as the poem "The Hug" which opens *The Man with Night Sweats* clearly shows. In this collection, being gay is intimately associated with AIDS and the devastating experience of facing the sudden, unexpected death of dear friends, as well as the atrocious suffering and deformation caused by the disease. In this vein, "Words for Some Ash" speaks of the day of Christ's birth, a day of joy and exultation for so many people, the symbol of the promise of a new world, and yet a day when his dear friend lies in agony: "Christmas Day your pupils crossed, / Staring at your nose's tip, / Seeking there the air you lost / Yet still gaped for, dry of lip" (*CP* 472, ll. 5–8). In "Secret Heart" the poet stresses the strident contrast between the joy of Christmas and the suffering of a dying friend whose agony evokes not the Nativity but the Crucifixion: "...Once in those weeks / You dreamt your dying friend hung crucified / In his front room, against the mantelpiece" (*CP* 473, ll. 12–14). The reference to Christmas, the religious festival par excellence, is particularly meaningful in that it evidences, as we saw in "The Allegory of the Wolf Boy," the social suffering, and in the case of AIDS, the physical and moral pain, to which homosexuals are subject. For them the birth of Christ is turned on its head, as the warning of a death without resurrection, the beginning of a long journey of pain.

In "The Hug," homosexuality involves a familiar intimacy, a mutual belonging consolidated by time and habit, as is suggested by the choice of the word "hug" instead of the more passionate term "embrace" that more accurately reflects the relationship between lovers.[21] The two stanzas of "The Hug" are composed of lines of differing lengths, whose disposition iconically suggests the interweaving of bodies during the hug (recalling the pattern poems of George Herbert), and at the same time evidences the lack of balance and instability caused by light drunkenness. At the end of a birthday party, after the poet and his companion are accompanied to bed by their host, the speaker "...broke on a hug, / [...] / Your instep to my heel, / My shoulder-blades against your chest" (*CP* 407, ll. 7, 10–11). At a figurative level the image recalls both the sculpture *Laocoon*, and the clasping bodies in certain works by Rodin.[22] As the words "instep," "heel," "shoulder-blades," and "chest" attest, the poet's attention is focused on physical contact between the two bodies, which does not necessarily imply sexual stimulation of organs and limbs (terms like "instep" and "heel" are not commonly associated with sexuality).[23]

The experience described in "The Hug" attests to the profound need of homosexual couples to become and feel part of a familiar microcosm in which cohabitation implies more than just sex. Nevertheless, the lines, "...locking me to you / As if we were still twenty-two / When our grand passion had not yet / Become familial" (*CP* 407, ll. 15–18), clearly evoke the poet's nostalgia for an intensity of desire and passion that has vanished with the passage of time.[24] But, stronger than nostalgia is the desire for human contact, as the last words show, when the poet declares that he only knew "the stay of your secure firm dry embrace" (*CP* 407, l. 22). This sounds like the desperate cry of a person who wants to escape isolation and the threat of solitude by his rapport with others (the adjectives "secure," "firm," and "dry" confirm this), but who at the same time is bitterly aware of the inevitable exhaustion of vitality and passion, as suggested by the use of the word "dry." Such bitterness is confirmed by the poem "Lines for my 55th birthday" (*The Man with Night Sweats*), where the love of old men is described negatively as "...dry even when it is hot" (*CP* 415, l. 2).

CHAPTER VII

The Body, Disease, and Death

*A healthy body is a guest chamber for the soul: a
sick body is a prison* — Francis Bacon

THE OUTSIDER

In Gunn's poetry—from *Fighting Terms* to *Boss Cupid*—the body always plays a central role, as seen by the struggling figures in the early poems who clutch each other, not so much like lovers as enemies, and the "toughs" in *The Sense of Movement* and *My Sad Captains*, who, even though unthinkable without their leather uniforms and motorcycles (like Marlon Brando in *The Wild One* by Laszlo Benedeck), give the impression of existing only by virtue of their active bodies. Again, the body is the focus of various metamorphoses and experiences of regression to the womb in the collections *Moly* and *Jack Straw's Castle*, ranging from the cycle "Jack Straw's Castle," in which the castle and its mazes refer in part to the prison of the body,[1] to *The Man with Night Sweats*, where we see physical decay and fragile bodies consumed and tormented by sickness, to the last collection, *Boss Cupid*, with its acts of cannibalism and libidinous homicides.

His continuous, obsessive attention to the body is also tied to Gunn's homosexuality, which, as we saw, he never openly admitted until the seventies, with the publication of *Jack Straw's Castle*.

The problematic confrontation of the impulses of a pubescent body is seen in "The Allegory of the Wolf Boy," in the sad double life of the boy who, during the day, plays tennis and takes tea, while at night he is the victim of shameful, uncontrollable impulses "written on" a body that is, on its surface, "open and blond," but inside its clothes, the victim of a tormenting itchiness ("...the familiar itch of close dark hair" *CP* 61, l. 21). The bloody paws at the end of the poem, after the boy's metamorphosis into a wolf has taken place, do not transform him into a strong animal ready to hunt his prey, able to reject and overturn the social and cultural codes that are so alien to his nature; instead, these bloody paws make him a symbol of suffering and sacrifice in that they become, as we noticed in the previous chapter, stigmata that crucify him. From a Platonic viewpoint, the metamorphosis that takes place in this poem represents falsity, not truth, insofar as to become is in some sense a negation of being, and it results in a staging of passion completely extraneous to the boy's nature, and therefore experienced as violence and the violation of his person, though it foreshadows several transformations that will supply the foundation for a future rebirth. From an anthropological viewpoint, on the other hand, the metamorphosis of the boy into a wolf recalls the gothic tradition of werewolves and the frequent image in popular folklore of a person who turns into a wolf on the night of a full moon,[2] loaded with the negative implications that metamorphoses assume in classical mythology, the degrading and painful transformation of man into beast. A psychoanalytical reading is also possible, in that the wolf could represent the boy's repressed id, which comes to light only in the nocturnal sphere, in a dream state. If the splitting is not overcome, the individual is subject to a continuous state of schizophrenia, with demonstrations of the aggressions latent in him.[3] The image of stigmata at the end of this poem, the blood on the paws, even the fur that covers the body, evinces a bodily "writing," an incision of his condemnation (for experiencing a sexuality not completely accepted by the cultural code) that recollects Kafka's story, "In the Penal Colony," where the condemned prisoner is judged by a machine which writes his guilt upon his body with needles. "The Allegory of the Wolf Boy" also evokes Kafka's *Metamorphosis* because we see the transformation in the making (Gregor Samsa wakes one morning realizing the change that his body has undergone). Like Gregor, the wolf boy is an outsider: whether the marks on his body are physical, or only a metaphor for inner discomfort, they make him an outsider who is excluded and misunderstood, and destined to be slowly distanced from his family's and society's affections.

The figure of the outsider, an alien in the eyes of bourgeois society, is a frequent one in Gunn's poetry. Even the early isolated heroes, like the lighthouse keeper in "Round and Round," felt excluded from the world and misunderstood by others. From metaphorical alienation — connected to his existential angst — the poet moves on gradually towards the outside world, focusing on real outsiders, poor marginalized people who live on the streets, who belong to the pitiless urban jungle, as we saw in *Positives* (the old woman at the end of the collection) and who emerge in the poems of *Undesirables*,[4] among them the homeless woman in "Old Meg," a poem whose title recalls the gypsy in Keats' "Meg Merrilies."[5] This allusion evidences Gunn's great debt to tradition, the constant presence in his work of a solid cultural, literary inheritance (mostly English) that interacts with stimuli from the modern world, the inexhaustible sample of faces, situations, joys and tragedies offered by American cities. We have already mentioned Gunn's debt to T.S. Eliot; here, reference to the seminal essay, "Tradition and the Individual Talent" is evident (see also Chapter I of this book), in that the masters of the tradition are tried out as contemporaries, as true interlocutors, and also reinterpreted and reread by the light of the present day. Keats' gypsy lives on in the homeless woman of Gunn's poem.

THE ANNIHILATION OF SELF

For a long time, Gunn continued to experience his homosexuality as a mark impressed upon his flesh, until he managed to rid himself from this feeling by discovering the free, nonconformist lifestyle that was spreading throughout the world, from a center in northern California, which would be his new home.

As "The Discovery of the Pacific" shows (cf. chapter VI of this book), the mythical journey to the west, the last frontier, becomes an experience of renewal. The exchange of warmth and tenderness between two intertwined bodies is not a challenge to the world. The warmth that is released in such a contact enables them to face nature, until they feel themselves part of a new Eden.

Although the experience in this poem refers to a heterosexual couple (*Moly*, like later collections, has many images of bodies who embrace happily), it is important to note that for the first time in Gunn's artistic career, in "The Discovery of the Pacific," sex becomes a means of discovery and renewal, an experience of giving and receiving, where the "fighting terms," the conflict between lovers in the earlier collections, is finally replaced by mutual tenderness.

The choice of a heterosexual couple in "The Discovery of the Pacific" confirms the poet's refusal to be identified solely as a gay poet who writes for a specific, exclusive audience.[6]

At the end of "Tom-Dobbin: centaur poems," the two creatures, or the two parts of the same creature (one of which is clearly Thom himself)[7] become a single body in full harmony with itself. Unlike the motorcycle centaurs of the early collections, these creatures enjoy fullness of being, and their encounter entails a fusion and immersion in the surrounding world: "Gradually closing in, until we enter / The haze together — which is me, which him? / Selves floating in the one flesh we are of" (*CP* 202, 5, ll. 4–6). The use of the word "haze" indicates, however, that the fusion, no matter how complete, has yet a margin of uncertainty, and can from one moment to the next, once the effects of the hallucinogen have worn off, be seen as the illusion it is. The drug gave the speaker a series of visions of beatitude and involvement with the surrounding world ("The cobalt gleam of peacock's neck, the course of a wind through grasses, distant smoke frozen in the sky, are extensions of self" (*CP* 201, 3).

Even when drug experiences bring tragedy, as in "The Colour Machine," where Gunn recalls the drug-related death of a friend, such loss is seen positively insofar as it is a way into intense experience which others (the survivors, those who came out of the experience and remain "visible") cannot know:

> Perhaps, for our vanished friend, the moment of giving made the fact of his disintegration something of negligible importance. Or perhaps his consciousness still lives in the intensity of that moment. I am visible and do not know [*CP* 205–06, 2].

"The Colour Machine," a poem dedicated to the vanished friend, Mike Caffee, is divided into two numbered stanzas; in the first, the poet describes the experience of the "color machine," a hallucinatory state in which everything melts together, familiar forms and dimensions are lost, and matter is in constant flux ("...Where it has thickened it starts to turn transparent; where it is almost transparent it starts to thicken. [...] it is in a state of unending alteration: we can name it only afterwards" *CP* 205, 1). From objective description of the experience, Gunn moves on, in the second stanza, to a commemoration of the friend (who presumably died during a hallucination from which he never returned, leading him to an involuntary act of suicide), transforming his openness to the hallucinogenic state into a gesture of love of which Gunn himself did not feel capable ("I too am a lover, but I am cowardly, selfish, and calculating..." *CP* 205, 2). The theme so prevalent in earlier collections here reemerges—the prison of intellect, the inability to abandon oneself to impulse, to open oneself completely to the world and others. Even if his resistance allows him to be, in this case, still among the living, it also causes him to reflect on his own inner transformation, which at this moment he feels is incomplete.

REGRESSION TO A PRIMAL STATE

The idea of regeneration of body and soul occurs in many poems in *Moly*. Gunn sometimes seems obsessed by the moment of his birth and tries insistently to relive it, as occurs, for example, in "For Signs": "I dream: the real is shattered and combined, / Until the moon comes back into that sign / It stood in at my birth-hour; ..." (*CP* 188, 2, ll. 7–9), where the poet, with an eye on the moon as though in search of a sign, achieves a dream state in which he has an acute sense of a past self that he wants to abandon but which always waits in ambush:

> Dream mentor, I have been inside that skull,
> I too have used those cindered passages.
> But now the moon leaves Scorpio: I look up.
> [*CP* 189, 2, ll. 22–24].

The theme of recovering the experience of the womb, returning to a prenatal state, an Eden overflowing with lights and colors in which he rediscovers his own origins, informs "The Garden of the Gods" ("Where my foot rests, I hear the creak / From generations of my kin, / Layer on layer, ... / [...] / This was the garden's place of birth: / I trace it downward from my mind" *CP* 213–14, ll. 21–23, 25–26).[8] The same theme appears more openly in "Being Born," as the rediscovery of union with the maternal womb before birth tears them apart, which the poet observes from the outside:

> I think of being grabbed from the warm sand,
> Shiny red bawling newborn with clenched eyes,
> Slapped into life; ...
>
> Must I rewrite my childhood? What jagg'd growth
> What mergings of authority and pain,
> Invading breath, must I live through again?
> Are they the past or yet to come or both?
> [*CP* 218, ll. 17–19, 21–24]

The origin of life is here experienced like a dream or distinct vision. The poem opens and closes with the image of a large ship ("The tanker..." *CP* 218, l. 1) which gradually moves away from shore, leaving behind a cloud of smoke ("...a formal S of smoke" *CP* 218, l. 2). In the infinite horizon that the image of the sea offers the poet (the aquatic environment links to the idea of the origins of life and to the experience of the womb), the movement of the ship breaking waves and the wake of smoke bring him back gradually to stage the moment of his birth, giving life to the people involved in it ("Midwife and doctor faintly apprehended" *CP* 218, l. 12), until he confuses, or rather, mixes, the past and the future.

The moment of being torn from the mother's womb recurs in "The Bath House" in the sequence "The Geysers" (*Jack Straw's Castle*):

> and bobbing in the womb, all round me Mother
> [...]
> caesarian lighting lopped me off separate
>
> and born in flight from the world
>   but through it, into it
> [*CP* 244, ll. 59, 69–71]

The poet has a true experience of splitting off, of physical disintegration, until he recovers his lost union, his physical and spiritual harmony, as the last lines suggest:

> I am part of all
>   hands take
>   hands tear and twine
> [...]
>   .. .. ..
> torn from the self
>   in which I breathed and trod
> I am
>   I am raw meat
>   I am a god
> [*CP* 246, ll. 115–17, 122–26].[9]

The theme of return to infantile innocence and a state of intellectual virginity is present also in the cycle "Three Songs" ("Baby Song," "Hitching into Frisco," and "Sparrow," *Jack Straw's Castle*) in which, in simple rhyming couplets ("Baby Song") and quatrains rhyming *abba* ("Hitching into Frisco") and *abab* ("Sparrow," with the exception of the first stanza, which is a nursery rhyme in *aabb*), Gunn's attention turns to song, to almost inarticulate language, like lullabies for three outsiders: a newborn who dreams of returning to the womb, a hitchhiker, and a beggar.

In "Baby Song," the newborn yearns for a return to that state in which it was part of its surroundings, before being violently separated: "Why don't they simply put me back / Where it was warm and wet and black?" (*CP* 247, ll. 3–4). Birth signals the beginning of suffering, and the ending of "The perfect comfort of her inside" (*CP* 247, l. 8); in the final couplet, the imagery of blood recalls "The Allegory of the Wolf Boy," and here it also means, not the flow of life, but pain and laceration.[10]

The poem "Hitching into Frisco" is the monologue of a hitchhiker who left behind a potentially tranquil bourgeois existence ("I was a gentle boy." *CP* 248, l. 9), motivated by the desire to discover absolute freedom, as seen by the last line — "And everywhere to go" (*CP* 248, l. 21) — which is separated from the previous stanza. The realities and otherness that he encounters on the road reveal lives of solitude and pain: "the homeless there." The homeless teem in the urban environment and contribute, in their transitory nature, to the formation and enrichment of the speaker's identity; his aimless movements are expressed in a rhythm typical of musical improvisation: "For all I leave behind / There is a new song grown" (*CP* 248, ll. 19–20).[11] This poem, like others in the cycle "Three Songs" and "The Discovery of the Pacific," recall, in their general atmosphere of desire for freedom so typical of the sixties, the ideas of the Beat Generation; consider the classic *On the Road* by Jack Kerouac, and his poem "Hitch hiker" of 1967, in which he uses, as is typical of the Beats, a truly colloquial language, overflowing with slang and ungrammatical sentences. Kerouac's poem is the dialogue between a hitchhiker (on his way "to sunny Californyy" like the protagonist of Gunn's poem) and the people who don't pick him up.[12] The sense of total freedom and scorn for social rules present in Gunn's poem (which makes his speaker close to the wanderer archetype so dear to Romantic literary tradition)[13] contrasts with the inhibitions created by the appearance of Kerouac's hitchhiker, who imagines, with subtle irony, the impression his garb makes on observers, who are suspicious and hostile to any show of "individuality" outside the parameters of social conventions: "Boom. It's the awful raincoat / making me look like a selfdefeated self-/ murdering imaginary gangster, an idiot in / a rueful coat, how can they understand / my damp packs— my mud packs—."[14] Despite the absence of any reference to the hitchhiker's external appearance, even in Gunn's "Hitching to Frisco," the character seems to put on a mask, or at least to be unrecognizable to those who know him: "Mom wouldn't know her son" (*CP* 248, l. 8). This line, which recalls "Jesus and his Mother" in *The Sense of Movement*, in which the mother will not resign herself to a separation from the son she birthed, who has become almost a stranger in her eyes ("He seemed much like another man, / That silent foreigner who trod / Outside my door with lily rod" *CP* 64, ll. 8-10), focuses on intergenerational conflict (so much an aspect of the sixties), the need to separate oneself from one's roots in order to find a new identity that for the moment is only hinted at (in the case of Gunn's hitchhiker it is made up of songs and "everywhere to go").[15]

In "Sparrow" Gunn's attention turns to a beggar, marked in body and spirit by the privations and bitterness of the life he leads ("I may look fifty years old / but I'm only thirty" *CP* 248, ll. 7-8), to the point that the unhealthy external environment has become one with his flesh ("in a leaky doorway in leaky shoes" *CP* 248, l. 14), in a way that recalls the old woman at the end of *Positives* ("Outside the abandoned house / where she slept on old paper" *Positives* 74, ll. 11-12). The life of "Sparrow" depends on alcohol, which can generate an illusory, temporary metamorphosis ("I'll be a daredevil then / [...] / a jewel among men" *CP* 249, ll. 21, 23), and depends also on the generosity of people, who in this case turn out to be completely deaf to his call and do not hear his lonely song: "I hope I see you cry / like Sparrow one day" (*CP* 249, ll. 27-28).

The cycle "Three Songs" heralds the characters in *Undesirables*, who are marginalized, living in the streets. Although they are always present in Gunn's work, the frequency of homeless people increases in the later collections. Like *Positives*, "Three Songs" encompass the entire span of human life, which is marked in every phase by situations of alienation and isolation. This is the case for the newborn (whose viewpoint Gunn projects himself into, reversing the usual atmosphere of joy and happiness commonly associated with birth), of the young hitchhiker uprooted from his own environment and desiring new experiences (despite the intimation, in "Hitching into Frisco," of feelings of uncertainty, lack of a stable base, loss of identity)[16] and finally, of the old-before-his-time homeless beggar in "Sparrow."

The consumption of hallucinogens brings to light another type of contact with the world, or, more precisely, an immersion in the world and all of its parts: the grass, flowers, sounds, colors, and odors of nature. This experience liberates Gunn from his existential angst, and assists his rediscovery of an Edenic innocence ("The first field of a glistening continent / Each found by trusting Eden in the human" *CP* 212, ll. 14-15). As in the works of William Blake and D.H. Lawrence, this rediscovered innocence means that nudity reacquires its original naturalness, and shame disappears. Such sensations come explicitly to light in the poem "Three," where Gunn's attention turns to a family on the beach in California (not coincidentally, it is a nuclear family with father, mother and child, like the Holy Family of Christian tradition), the symbol of a lost Eden that must be found. Even though "All three are bare," "Only their son / Is brown all over. / [...] / His three-year nakedness is everyday" (*CP* 195, ll. 1, 21–22, 24), it seems like the sun does not dare to touch those parts of the adult body of which they are consciously ashamed. As Gunn stresses at the end of the poem ("He still leaves it / And comes back to that pebble-warmed recess / In which the parents sit, / At watch, who had to learn their nakedness" *CP* 196, ll. 33–36), for the modern individual, the recovery of innocence cannot occur immediately and spontaneously — through a simple change of habits, like lying nude on the beach. It must be learned gradually by returning to that state in which shame is absent and there is no separation between intellect and instinct, in which the body is part of the self and not a simple shell which contains it (as is the case for the wolf boy and many other characters in Gunn's early poems, most of whom are "...condemned to be condemned" *CP* 78, l. 30).[17] The sacredness of natural, innocent nudity is suggested also by the title "Three" (instead of any other word connected to the idea of family or group) which, besides being the perfect number, the trinity — confirming the linkage to the Holy Family — is phonetically related to the word "tree," thereby uniting these persons (like Adam and Eve in the earthly paradise) to the branches of a tree, of which they are becoming part (even though the journey is, at least for adults, very long), a tree that is destined to be the source of new awareness and a more natural lifestyle.[18]

THE TORTURED BODY

In the subsequent collections, especially *The Man with Night Sweats*, the body loses the freedom and strength it had so laboriously acquired, and becomes something that imprisons the spirit; this happens because of an illness (AIDS, the plague of the century) that slowly but tenaciously devours the body. The sensation of imprisonment of the human spirit in a body that seems to obey needs different from its nature is already present in the poem "Moly" ("Oh a man's flesh already is in mine. / Hand and foot poised for risk. Buried in swine" *CP* 186, ll. 17–18), where the metamorphosis of a man to an animal makes possible the reacquisition of a long-lost unity between body and spirit ("From this fat dungeon I could rise to skin / And human title, putting pig within" *CP* 187, ll. 25–26). The theme of conflict between body and spirit recalls one of the central subjects of seventeenth-century poetry, which had such a profound influence on Gunn. In "A Dialogue between the Soul and the Body,"[19] Andrew Marvell creates a dialogue between soul and body, in which each laments its own prison, the difficulty of living with the tyranny of the other: "*Soul.* O who shall, from this Dungeon, raise / A Soul, inslav'd so many wayes? / With bolts of Bones ... / [...] / *Body.* O who shall me deliver whole, / From bonds of this Tyrannic Soul?"[20] In the end, it is the body that comes out better, after having seen in the soul the origin of all of its weaknesses: "*Body.* What but a Soul could have the wit / To build me up for sin so fit? / So Architects do square and hew, / Green Trees that in the Forest grew."[21]

As Susan Sontag points out in "AIDS and Its Metaphors," unlike other diseases such as cancer, tuberculosis and syphilis, AIDS reveals an identity (homosexual) that otherwise would have been hidden from relatives, colleagues, and neighbors. Especially in the years of its diffusion in the western world and the United States, to have AIDS was, for homosexuals, a particular experience of isolation and persecution, but it also kindled their sense of being part of a community, and their awareness that they might find understanding, support, and *compassion* in everybody else who was potentially at risk.[22]

The poems in the latter half of *The Man with Night Sweats* are elegies for friends who died of AIDS, mostly young people who, before the disease, were full of energy, but were slowly deprived of the strength of their bodies and their ability to control their vital functions; some of them were unable to exercise the simplest of daily "rituals," such as eating, as occurs in "The J Car":

> But though the crusted pancakes might attract
> They did so more as concept than in fact,
> And I'd eat his dessert before we both
> Rose from the neat arrangement of the cloth,
> Where the connection between life and food
> Had briefly seemed so obvious if so crude.
> [*CP* 480, ll. 17–22]

Gunn realizes that the body of his friend, devoured by the disease (the eyes which can hardly see, the mouth that cannot swallow, the legs that can hardly hold him upright) has nothing to look forward to. There is no future nor hope for those who are infected by AIDS, exhausted and tortured by disease ("I'd leave him to the feverish sleep ahead, / Myself to ride through darkened yards instead / Back to my health" *CP* 481, ll. 33–35).[23] Yet the poet can identify with his friend, can project himself into the friend's point of view, to perceive in his state the end of will and desire, whether erotic or poetic: "He knew he would not write the much-conceived / Much-hoped-for work now, nor yet help create / A love he might in full reciprocate" (*CP* 481, ll. 44–46).[24] Unlike what happened in Romanticism and Aestheticism, in which illness was seen as the price paid by the artist for an excess of interiority, sensitivity, and creativity, today there is nothing that redeems the condition of AIDS patients: they fight daily against the darkness that slowly but tenaciously erodes every vital function.[25]

Particularly meaningful is the poem "Still Life," whose title suggests the attempt to exorcise death and transform it into new life. Written in three stanzas of six lines rhyming *abab*— the first line "I shall not soon forget" (*CP* 470) recurs in the next stanza like a refrain —"Still Life" is about the image of the face of a dying friend which is indelibly impressed upon the poet's mind. The consuming illness causes a painful disintegration of the body and metamorphosis of the face. At the end of the poem, the face is the metaphor (as in some of Kafka's stories) of an indomitable spirit that wants to challenge his destiny, like Prometheus: "Back from what he could neither / Accept, ... / Nor, ... / Consentingly let go, / The tube his mouth enclosed / In an astonished O" (*CP* 470, ll. 13–18).

While in this poem, the body and spirit become one and the same, and the horror of death is rendered in the vision of a body that emits its last cry before dying (the final "O" is both the image of the deformed mouth and the cry of stupor, horror, and desperation emitted during the passage to another life), in "The Man with Night Sweats," the symptoms presumed to belong to the disease (the poet was never afflicted with AIDS) transform into a paralyzing nightmare where parts of the body that are yet under control (like the hands) try desperately to hold it together, to protect it (like a baby with its favorite toy) from the unknown avalanche of the disease that is overtaking it:

> Hugging my body to me
> As if to shield it from
> The pains that will go through me,
> As if hands were enough
> To hold an avalanche off.
> [*CP* 462, ll. 20–24][26]

The disease becomes owner of the body, transforming it into a cage for the individual, who can no longer eat, breathe, or move.[27] There is no indulgence of sentimentality in these elegies for friends dead and dying of AIDS, but rather the attempt to understand what really happened to them without any type of mystification, to understand how their relations with others and also their daily lives were transformed and ruined, to grasp what still remains, whether for the dead, or for the living who were spared, without any pretence of consolation.[28] As Deborah Landau wrote, "if the traditional functions of the elegy are to praise, lament, and console, Gunn's contemporary adaptations of the form consist mostly of lament with a measure of praise and blunt withholding of consolation. [...] Gunn depicts the physical and emotional effects of AIDS-related illnesses in concrete detail."[29]

"I find no escape," writes Gunn at the end of the poem "The Missing," fully aware that death is not sublime, and that there is nothing uplifting in it. The loss of loved ones to AIDS — a risk that the living continue to run — disorients the survivors, making them feel suspended in a void, and subject to the humiliation of decay: "But death — Their deaths have left me less defined: / It was their pulsing presence made me clear" (*CP* 483, ll. 17–18). From this poem emerges the sense of belonging to a community, a group connected not only by love and passion, but also by friendship and mutual support, that becomes a place of belonging, a family (it is one of the rare times that the poet uses this word): "...The warmth investing me / Led outward through mind, limb, feeling, and more / In an involved increasing family" (*CP* 483, ll. 6–8).[30]

Proposing a comparison between this poem and Thomas Gray's "Elegy," Tyler Hoffman says:

in contrast to Gray's elegy, which ends in the poet's epitaphic script (an assertion of class distinction that sets him apart from the anonymous, illiterate villagers whom he mourns), Gunn's poems inextricably link mourner and mourned, as the death of his community entails his own entombment.[31]

In the poem "In Time of Plague," Gunn compares the apparent vivacity and health of the crowd with the thoughts of death that torment him and disturb, not only his conscious thoughts, but also his instinctual activities and impulses. Seeing two attractive men, whose body language alludes to desire and sex ("...for a state of ardent life / in which we could all stretch ourselves / and lose our differences..." *CP* 463, ll. 20–22), the poet remains hesitant and disoriented, consumed by the desire to let himself go and the simultaneous, obsessive image of death that lingers in his mind. The hesitation — which recalls the anxiety of the boy in "The Allegory of the Wolf Boy"— is the source of pain: he is incapable of abandoning himself to instinct, and is aware of his defeat because of his inability to reason away his fears. The poem is divided into three stanzas that correspond to phases of a courtship: the friendly gestures of the first stanza, the tortured reactions of the poet in the second ("...am I a fool, / [...] / or are they the fools, ..." *CP* 463, ll. 23, 27), followed by the indifference of the two men who go away in the third stanza. At the beginning of the second stanza, Gunn exposes by interior monologue the flow of his thoughts, in a language that recalls, by reiterating the phrase "know it," the poem "Carnal Knowledge," in *Fighting Terms* ("You know, I know..." *CP* 15), in which the relationship between lovers is reduced to a battle without quarter:

> Their mind is the mind of death.
> They know it, and do not know it,
> and they are like me in that
> (I know it, and do not know it)
> and like the flow of people through this bar.
> [*CP* 463, ll. 14–18]

The sexual liberation so laboriously acquired, the fullness of erotic encounters related to gay life, is disrupted by AIDS, by the horror of a disease irremediably associated with death. Even though the poet never contracted it, even though his body never underwent that physical decay, those atrocious sufferings of friends who did, and for whom most of the elegies of *The Man with Night Sweats* are written, he himself was indirectly the victim of AIDS in that, trapped by fear, he was horrified of running the risk of falling into an abyss from which there was no return.[32]

THE AGING BODY

In addition to AIDS, there is another type of invincible illness, the natural one of aging, which pitilessly devours the body, transforming it into the imprisoning shell of a still free and rebellious spirit. Despite experiences of regeneration and rebirth in the collection *Moly*, despite the sexual freedom laboriously acquired by challenging all cultural and social inhibitions, the poet is conscious of still being prey to the bodily prison that cannot evade the natural process of aging, the exhaustion of passion over time.[33] Especially in the last two collections, this becomes a kind of nostalgia for a loss that cannot be fully accepted (as in the early poems, Gunn was not able to accept completely his homosexuality) — a kind of hunger that cannot be satiated. Whereas in *Moly* the body gradually becomes the means to reach a true identity, free to challenge and question all the inherited cultural models (as in "Rites of Passage"), in the last collections, it is the victim of natural processes that transform it into a prison of a Self that is often condemned to isolation and silence. Thus, the title of the last volume, *Boss Cupid*, changes Cupid ("...devious master of our bodies" *BC* 101, l. 34), who has always been an inspiration for Gunn, into a tyrant — a boss who spreads frustration and suffering rather than joy and love.[34]

This mood is present in many poems where the poet's ironic vein masks a latent tragedy, where old men avidly and desperately observe — with a hopeless desire that seems to devour them from within — strong, muscular, athletic, young bodies, as in "Punch Rubicundus": "The surprises of age are no surprise. I am / like one who lurks at a urinal all afternoon, / with a distant look studying younger males / as if they were problems in chess" (*CP* 398, ll. 6–9), or in "In the Post Office," which starts with the lines, "Saw someone yesterday looked like you did, / Being short with long blond hair, a sturdy kid / Ahead of me in line. I gazed and gazed / At his good back, feeling again, amazed" (*BC* 13, ll. 1–4). "In the Post Office" is a particularly meaningful poem because it compares the discomfort and inhibitions of old age with the suffering of disease. Starting from his envious admiration of a young man who does not even spare him a look while in line at the post office and his realization that he is imprisoned in a body that no longer responds to the needs of the spirit: "If only I could do whatever he did, / With him or as a part of him, if I / Could creep into his armpit like a fly, / [...] / Instead of having to stand back and watch" (*BC* 13–14, ll. 26–28, 30), the poet remembers a similar situation in which the roles were reversed, where he was the object of envy of a dying friend: "I have imaged that he still could taste / That bitterness and anger to the last, / Against the roles he saw me in because / He had to: of victor, as he thought I was" (*BC* 15, ll. 61–64). The relationship between lovers regresses to that battle without quarter that runs through the poems of *Fighting Terms*. Other themes of the early collections re-emerge, such as that of the voyeur whose desire shows narcissistically through his gaze, who observes the staging of passion (as in "The Corridor," for example), who puts on a mask as a daily ritual because of his inability to be himself. Another recurring theme is the isolation of the individual and the impossibility of opening himself to others. While the relationship between the poet and the young man in the post office is one, respectively, of envy and indifference, the same thing happens with his dying friend, whose love has for some time been turned into hate on the part of the sick one ("I had not known he hated me until / He hated me this much, hated me still" *BC* 14, ll. 49–50), and for the speaker, into cold indifference and a total inability to react ("To him I felt, likewise, indifferent. / [...] /... Nothing deflected him, / Nothing I did and nothing I could say. / And so I left. I heard he died next day" *BC* 14–15, ll. 44, 58–60). "In the Post Office" (like "Breaking Ground") reflects a way of writing poetry that Gunn borrows from literary tradition, from Horace's *Odes* and from Baudelaire, which is the combination of two, often utterly different, subjects:

> I suppose most poems are straightforward in that way, but there is another kind of poem, which is even more interesting, and which seems to have been initiated by Horace. He ties together, almost arbitrarily, two completely different subjects. It's almost as though he started two different poems, and the only thing he could think of was to join them together. [...] It does marvellous things to both ideas to have them come into conflict. And Baudelaire does it too, especially in those later poems.[35]

Desire is a planned, calculated game in "American Boy," where the poet, though tragically aware that he is not much different from the old men he hates, abandons himself to the consoling, regenerating touch of a young man, trying to change their encounter into a relationship that is not merely sexual. Yet the last stanza, though it concludes with the lines "...We produce / What warmth we can," clearly reveals the poet's profound discomfort, his awareness that he has now reached a phase of life from which there is no return, in that his desire, though satisfied, no longer produces that mutual exchange and abandon, as it lacks the intensity of passion it once had:

> Affectionate young man,
> Your wisdom feeds
> My dried-up impulses, my needs,
> With energy and juice.
> Expertly you know how to maintain me
> At the exact degree
> Of hunger without starving. We produce
> What warmth we can.
> [*BC* 48, ll. 25–32]

The expression "wisdom feeds" is meaningful because it unites mind and body, intellect and instinct, conferring a tone of profound tragedy to the poem. It is almost as if Gunn — like the beggar in "Sparrow," in desperate search of some change to buy a drop of alcohol — is asking for charity, desperately seeking, like a sick person at the end of his life, that warmth which can give vitality to a body and spirit which are slowly wearing out. Free expression of passion, intensity of desire, which in *The Passages of Joy* (published in 1982, eighteen years before *Boss Cupid*) made any kind of casual encounter sacred — consider "The Miracle" — seem very far away. One could even say that the physical decay linked to aging brought Gunn back into his prison of intellect, to the bodily discomfort (due to the non-expression of his homosexuality during the first years of his artistic career) which characterized the first collections. Whereas in the early poems it was the cultural code that set up the imprisoning barriers, in *Boss Cupid,* the situation is inverted, though the result is the same. Although Gunn overcame the cultural barriers, as *Moly* and the *Passages of Joy* demonstrate, in the later poems it is nature that builds new, oppressive, and insurmountable obstacles. Even art is impotent in the face of these, as the ironic poem, "The Artist as an Old Man" (*Boss Cupid*) shows. As the title suggests, Gunn takes James Joyce's *A Portrait of the Artist as a Young Man,* and turns the Joycean image of the artist upside down. Gunn's attention is turned, not to the mind and its thoughts, but only to the body of the artist, which wears the signs of its age and has exhausted most of its vital energy. The tools of his art, the palette and knife, are reduced to defensive weapons, rendering the old artist not too different from the pathetic heroes in uniform with pretensions of toughness in the early collections:

> The flat palette knife
> in his right hand, and
> the square palette itself
> held low in the other
> like a shield,
> he faces off
> the only appearance
> reality has and makes it
> doubly his. ...
> [*BC* 63, ll. 20–28]

Nostalgia for young passion re-echoes in "Rapallo." Remembering the summer when he and his lover were in their twenties and wished to live together, Gunn becomes sadly aware that, even though they realized this dream, nothing could be done to stem its decline. What was a sacred union, a deep, personal coming together on the beach of Rapallo, was sadly transformed into the separation of quotidian routine. His insistence on an indefinite "something" suggests a desperate attempt to attach himself to a flame that once existed, and that could not disappear entirely, even though it is no longer burning and its warmth is more illusory than real:

> If in four decades matter-of-factly
> Coming to be resigned
> To separate beds was not exactly
> What we then had in mind,
>
> Something of our first impetus,
> Something of what we planned
> Remains of what was given us
> On the Rapallo sand.
> [*BC* 97, ll. 29–36]

Whereas here, as in "The Hug," memory brings past experience alive, and gives new strength to a body and mind that refuse to resign themselves to the dying of passion and youth, in other poems this awareness becomes a sarcastic, anxious, and desperate shout, which could be compared to Edvard Munch's famous painting *The Scream* (1893). This awareness leads the poet to rewrite, in "A GI in 1943," Keats's famous line in "Ode on a Grecian Urn," "'Beauty is truth, truth beauty,'— that is all / Ye know on earth, and all ye need to know"[36] as "...Power / as beauty, beauty / power, that / is all my cock knew or / cared to know, ..." (*BC* 55, ll. 22–26) — and it inspires, as we saw in the previous chapter, the chilling lines written on his fifty-fifth birthday, that paralyze the reader with their cold clarity.

THE DISMEMBERED BODY

The last part of *Boss Cupid* begins with the cycle "Troubadour," whose ferociously ironic title recalls the courtly code of love, which appears the more anachronistic since it refers to the famous serial killer, Jeffrey Dahmer. The poem contains five songs—"Hitch-hiker," "Iron Man," "The Visible Man," "A Borrowed Man," and "Final Song"—in which Dahmer in first person "sings" his experiences and feelings, assuming his own particular role of "troubadour."[37] Gunn's idea was to do "the sort of thing Shakespeare did with Macbeth, another serial murderer."[38] This is the same kind of intertextuality that Gunn tried, in the fifties, when he modeled his poems about motorcyclists on Andrew Marvell's mower poems. Shocking characters, taken from the modern world, had already appeared in Gunn's poetry: Charles Manson is present in Jack Straw's nightmares in the sequence "Jack Straw's Castle."

Jeffrey Dahmer (1960–1994), who killed fifteen people (all of them men) between 1978 and 1991, chose as victims mostly young homosexuals, some black, who he submitted to a series of horrendous tortures before killing them. After his arrest, the bodies of his victims were found preserved in bottles of acid in his apartment, like macabre trophies that included, among other things, heads in the refrigerator and a candle-lit altar made of human rib cages and skulls. The prosecution stressed the fact that Dahmer had practiced acts of necrophilia and cannibalism. He also experimented with the removal of certain parts of the brain, in which he poured chemical mixtures in an attempt (perhaps inspired by the gothic tradition and *Frankenstein* in particular) to give life to automatons that would be responsive to his will and obedient to his sexual desires. Raised by a fundamentalist father who had strictly repressed his homosexuality (and caused him to hate all homosexuals, including himself), Dahmer had a history of abandonment, which caused him to fear any type of loss.[39]

For this cycle of poetry, Gunn found inspiration in Patricia Highsmith's review of two books on the serial killer, "where she very succinctly laid out all the events of Dahmer's life. I couldn't get hold of the books over here, since they were presumably published in England, but eventually I realized that I didn't need them, because I'd got enough facts already, from that review. It was an admirable article."[40]

The first poem in the cycle, "Hitch-hiker," is about Dahmer's first murder of a young man to whom he had given a ride.[41] Written in four stanzas of six lines each, rhyming *abcabc*, and echoing in its language the Elizabethan love poems, "Hitch-hiker" is the desperate song of a man who faces the inevitability of separation and loss (the hitchhiker was about to get out and continue on his journey: "Oh do not leave me now" *BC* 87, l. 1). Dahmer believes that the only alternative is to kill the man, thereby assuring himself of the other's constant presence, albeit a mute one. The word "strain" recurs frequently in the poem; it refers both to song, and to the irresistible impulse that makes Dahmer play the executioner for love:

> Strain of desire, and hope, and worst of all
> The strain of feeling loss, but after these
> Strain of the full possession once again
>   That has a dying fall.
> [*BC* 87–88, ll. 21–24]

The expression "dying fall," like the use of the word "strain," is an intertextual reminder of the *incipit* of Shakespeare's *Twelfth Night*, where the Duke Orsino tells the players that music is "the food of love":

> If music be the food of love, play on;
> Give me excess of it, that, surfeiting,
> The appetite may sicken, and so die.—
> That strain again; it had a dying fall;[42]

The reference to *Twelfth Night* had already been used by T.S. Eliot, in both "Portrait of a Lady" and "The Love Song of J. Alfred Prufrock," in which he created a contrapuntal game of analogies and contrasts between the enthusiastic passions of Orsino, expressed in his insatiable hunger for music, love, and Eros, and the passive satiation, produced by indifference, lethargy, and inner tiredness, of the modern Prufrock:

> I have measured out my life with coffee spoons;
> I know the voices dying with a dying fall
> Beneath the music from a farther room.
>   So how should I presume?[43]

One gets the impression that Gunn had both references in mind—combined in Dahmer, he saw both Orsino's obsessive desire and Prufrock's schizophrenia. Each character is also related to the murderer in the paradigm of food. Dahmer's cannibalism recalls Orsino's insatiable hunger and Prufrock's nauseated satiation, resulting from his inability to establish a loving relationship, which links him to the killer.

From the song "Hitch-hiker" emerges the sense of voiceless desperation of an individual in need of love and unable to manage any type of relationship, except in the form of destructive violence. However, it is an involuntary violence, at the bottom of which are actually tender feelings, as these lines suggest: "Oh do not leave me now" or "and worst of all / The strain of feeling loss." The speaker resorts to the conventional language of love (which in the European tradition began with courtly poetry), among which are lines that insinuate dramatically, with sinister connotations, the expression of a desire realizable only through an act of cannibalism and the dismemberment of the other's body: "...I must hold the ribbed arch of your chest / And taste your boyish glow" (*BC* 87, ll. 5–6). The use of the word "taste" suggests oral as well as sexual gratification.

From the first victim, Gunn moves on to "Iron Man" (the title refers to a body-building magazine as well as the iron man, one of the first superheroes created by Stan Lee in 1963),[44] written in four quatrains rhyming *abab*, to fathom Dahmer's youth, the adolescent period before the first murder, committed when he was eighteen years old. From the poem emerges the image of a seventeen-year-old misfit who experiences his parents' separation in a tortured way ("...I gnawed dissatisfaction" *BC* 89, l. 4) and tries to survive his discomfort by acts of physical stupefaction and sexual self-gratification ("And half-drunk all day, all of the day I mastubated" *BC* 89, l. 6). His stimulation comes from a magazine photo which solicits desire, of both a sexual and a cannibalistic nature, hinting at his need to fill — by completely possessing the other — the emptiness of his life ("Life of my own, life I could own, as cock was my witness" *BC* 89, l. 14). The recurrent internal rhymes as well as the repetition of words ("I played with myself, played with myself, ..." *BC* 89, l. 10) reproduce the mechanicalness of masturbation and reflect the obsessive, delirious character of his thoughts. The last lines ("Later maybe some fräulein might become my wife. / But next day I would buy the latest *Muscle and Fitness*" *BC* 89, ll. 15–16) echo the lacerating dichotomy of "The Allegory of the Wolf Boy," and reveal the inner schism of the adolescent Dahmer (with whom the poet identifies, or at least sympathizes), his conflict between the need imposed by the social code to establish a "normal" relationship, and the irresistible desire for gratifications evoked by the image in the magazine.

In "The Visible Man," composed of two stanzas of six lines rhyming *abcabc*, as in "Hitch-hiker," the poet, continuing to reconstruct the process which leads to the total dissolution of the serial-killer's personality, focuses on the several phases of development of his homicidal rage, representing here the moment in which the defenseless body of the victim is no longer sufficient to fill the emptiness inside of Dahmer, or to satisfy his innermost desires ("Yet nothing lasts, ..." *BC* 90, l. 7). This dissatisfaction, due to a hunger that cannot be satiated, causes the protagonist to bring the body to a secret place in his house, in which he indulges the most prohibited passions. It is there that Dahmer, wanting to penetrate the interior of his victim, will search inside what the "skin hides": "Here, I will help you enter" (*BC* 90, l. 12). The serial killer's inability to communicate, his total isolation from the world, causes his uncontainable desire to possess and annihilate the Other. At the beginning of the first stanza, Dahmer juxtaposes the inert obedience of his victim to the activity of the outside world, from which he is completely alienated: "People are restless and they move too much, / But you no longer have a young man's heart" (*BC* 90, ll. 2–3).

From the description of dismemberment at the end of "The Visible Man," Gunn moves on in the next poem, "A Borrowed Man,"[45] to a review of Dahmer's trophies—each of which contributes something to the "borrowed man" of the title, the ideal partner built piece by piece, according to his wishes: "From one large hands and lazy grin, / From someone reddened genitalia" (*BC* 91, ll. 13–14). Among these body fragments, in total solitude, the character's madness progresses, a desire that alternates between voyeuristic gratification and fantastic projection of his passing emotions. What clearly emerges from this "song," characterized by an obsessive, recurrent refrain ("Iron Man, Only Love," *BC* 91),[46] is the character's anguished solitude. His repressed desire for a type of human contact, which was repressed in turn by the cultural code, forces him to commit frequent acts of self-gratification that seem to happen only in the realm of fantasy, transforming desire into a continuous mental reconstruction of itself (in a way that recalls the "sex in the head" diagnosed by D.H. Lawrence at the beginning of the twentieth century, as one of the greatest ills of our era), rather than a real, physical manifestation of it. This mental reconstruction of desire is also shown by the contrast between the trophies reduced to "cold cuts" and the ardor ("heat") that they should have aroused:

> ... all of my orgasms past,
> Long-dried, or wiped-off, but now massed
> Steeply through memory's survival.
>   (Iron Man, Only Love.)
> They mount, and break, and in recapture
> Flood me with rightness of my rapture.
> [*BC* 92, ll. 37–42]

The final lines, with the words "mount," "break," and "flood," evoke Dahmer's onanistic gratification reached only in the mind. Besides his isolation, Gunn is examining his state of being a victim, whose obscene acts and macabre trophies are none other than devout offerings to a wicked "God" from whom he cannot escape. This God is the "Iron Man" upon whom he released his sexual fantasies during adolescence. With the introduction of a divinity who might be appeased by sacrifices, Dahmer's position changes; he becomes the victim of a power that he cannot control. But it is not only this that forms the poet's view. As the opening lines of "A Borrowed Man" indicate, Dahmer is aware of the horror that his actions produce, aware of his condemnation by the civilized world, but he attributes his actions to the will of a divinity that he must obey, which seems to absolve him in some sense from his guilt: "...I have seen / Such things committed in your name, / Iron Man, Only Love, / As would not be allowed above (*BC* 91, ll. 2–5). The lines, "...I have seen / such things committed in your name," indicate that there is a doubling of his personality such that Dahmer becomes almost a passive audience — not so different from Eliot's Prufrock — who watches a show performed by one part of a self (that which is completely subject to the will of the divinity Iron Man, Only Love), from which he is now broken off and which he can no longer control.

The character's loneliness reaches its peak in "Final Song," a poem composed of unpunctuated stanzas of various lengths — by which technique Gunn drives home the total dissolution of Dahmer's personality. This is a disconnected and desperate monologue of one who savors the emptiness of his own conquests. Beginning with the lines "I fell into myself / nothing could raise me now" (*BC* 93, ll. 1–2), the song evolves into a sad contemplation of the macabre trophies ("a head stood on the shelf / beside lard in a cup" *BC* 93, ll. 3–4) which, with the passing of time become like normal objects for daily use. Dahmer is facing his own failure, aware of the impossibility of constructing the ideal partner, the apparently "perfect" companion, or a number of them, who would be able to constantly obey his wishes, and could never escape or abandon him. Even though the head sits on the table, even though the skin, thanks to chemical experiments, shows no sign of decay, they are nothing but dead matter with which it is not possible to interact. Of the many victims nothing essential remains, and the murderer's initial terror of "feeling lost" (in "Hitch-hiker") ends in a state of total disorientation and the loss of any kind of anchorage; he is, as in his younger years, oppressed and tormented by a wish that is unable to find expression, much less realization:

> only myself remained
> in which I wandered lost
> [...]
>
> burdened by my erection
> [*BC* 93, ll. 16–17, 21]

In a desperate return to the point of departure, so ends the interior monologue of Dahmer, who, like the hero-prisoners of existential angst in the early poetry, reaches a state of absolute solitude, total discomfort, exasperated, in his case, by a sexuality that he now feels like a heavy weight ("burdened by my erection"), like something which does not belong to him any longer. Gunn's identification with, or understanding of, the killer does not lessen once he becomes a complete monster. On the contrary, at this point, he sees Dahmer as more of a victim, and as such, a man deserving his compassion. This is compassion that nobody else, except for the poet, is willing to give him, as the last song suggests. In this poem, the speaker's attention is turned to the head on the shelf and especially to its eyes, eyes which, like many others in Gunn's collections, gaze with cold indifference and even seem to sanction his condemnation.

Thom Gunn Today

As mentioned many times in the course of this study, Gunn's move to the United States (the opposite choice from T.S. Eliot's) put him, in a certain sense, outside both the British and American scenes. The condition of "Anglo-American Poet" who lacked a precise national classification in the literary canon, had a less than positive effect on his critical fortune, insofar as belonging to a well-defined tradition still, paradoxically (in an era of globalization and ethnic pluralism), plays an important role. This is confirmed in an article written by English poet James Fenton on the occasion of Gunn's death:

> Not long ago I took care to ask him casually if he was technically still British. I happened to be serving on a prize-awarding committee, and it is remarkable how often these questions of nationality arise.[1]

The position of "Anglo-American poet," though it certainly offered Gunn that freedom of life and artistic expression that he so avidly sought, especially in his youth, also distanced him from much of British, and even American, criticism.

> To Americans he was indelibly British, while to some British readers his language lacked distinctiveness.[2]

> He [Gunn] was a displaced Englishman, of "decorous, skilful, metrical verse," wrote the young English poet Glyn Maxwell, "who had for his own reasons become absorbed into an alien culture that gave him alien subjects (like sex), alien backdrops (like sunshine) and, most vexing of all, made his forms melt on the page."[3]

> Thom Gunn is least-known among the best living poets. In England he is suspect because he defected to the United States; in America he is suspect as an Englishman. Ridiculously, each country refuses to read the other's poets — and Gunn's readership suffers twice because he is a citizen of both countries and neither.[4]

Nevertheless, after his death some obituaries published in English and American magazines celebrated him as a great poet, even as one of the most important voices in contemporary English poetry[5]:

> I thought he was possibly the best living poet in English. Unlike most poets, he was equally at home in rhyme and non-rhyme, in free verse and patterned

rhythms. He had a quiet, modest, almost impersonal voice as a poet, but every poem he wrote was recognizably his—and his poems about death, particularly about deaths from AIDS, are masterpieces. [...] I will remember him as a dear friend who shaped my life in literature [...] and who made me understand how decent and satisfying and un-careerist the writing life could be.[6]

This relationship—a balance rather than a conflict—between the body's hedonism and the mind's discipline was a central, enduring theme in the work of one of the late 20th century's finest poets.[7]

For those of us who grew up reading Gunn, the news of his death feels like watching a part of the cliff of our own lives fall into the sea. And it deprives every poetry reader, whatever their age, of one of the most forceful, memorable, bracing and tender voices of our time. A voice which stretches across country-barriers as well as generation-barriers.[8]

He [Gunn] brought that wayward gift for being an island maverick and added it to the culture of the West Coast. He made a wonderful, unusual arc between rootedness and experiment, between being the outsider and having insider access. Few poets in our time have been as deeply nourished by tradition and as lovingly open to change.[9]

It was said that his audience was splintered. There were those who loved the formal rigor, those who appreciated the nobility and candor of gay life expressed, those who loved the radical sense of vision and experience from California, and those who wanted more from the best formalist in English, the true successor/extinguisher to T.S. Eliot, whom Thom met when he first published with Faber. All these audiences are now united in being separated from him. Because of their honesty, self-governance, and earned discoveries, because they reach so deeply in poetics, and in the self, his poems will be read and admired long after the works of more popular contemporary poets are forgotten.[10]

Judging from the opinions cited above it seems, as we have often stressed, that the oscillation between two extremes, the belonging to two different worlds, is one of the major elements of Gunn's poetry. Gunn was both the son of "the old country," from which he inherited a great tradition (from Elizabethan poetry to the Metaphysicals, to the Modernists), and an interpreter of the American scene, which was overflowing with new stimuli, poetic forms of which he was formerly unaware, as well as the ideal living environment for him. It is this very double belonging that makes him one of the most representative poets of the second half of the twentieth century.

The element of openness in his poetry makes it impossible to categorize him precisely, to attach him to a school, current or movement (remember his position in regard to the Movement, his ideas about Language Poets and Black Mountain Poets, and his opinion about theory in general),[11] much less to summarily label him a gay poet. He always defended, with extreme rigor and intellectual honesty, his own individuality against any literary, social, or national classification. Individuality is one of the cornerstones of his vision of art and the artist. The defense of diversity, of the individuality of every human being, of his right to live his own life without being classified as necessarily belonging to a group or category, is one of the essential elements in Gunn's work. His insistence on the need to accept the Other should be a warning for future generations in an era like our own, which is marked by racial conflict, insidious ethnic cleansing, and Manichean classifications of good and evil (which bring us back, in the third millennium, to the Dark Ages). In Gunn's poetry — consider especially the misfits and outsiders of *Undesirables* — the characters do not have much in common with each other; they exist as individuals, and that which most interests the poet (they become a source of inspiration and poetic research) is not their position at the margins of society, but how much each one of them, from the old lady in *Positives* to the vagrants of San Francisco, manages to make his or her own life, the unique way in which each one stoically faces the meaninglessness of existence.[12] Not so different is the case of Jeffrey Dahmer, who, through his "songs," comes out, not as a bloodthirsty serial killer, but as a victim of a set of circumstances, as an individual irreparably harmed by loneliness. The same is true for another kind of diseased people, those who have AIDS; despite their common destiny, Gunn's attention is always turned to the singularity of each one, which precludes any type of classification. His defense of individuality and diversity expresses itself also in reference to sexual identity. Gunn constantly and tenaciously defended — as his work testifies — the right of freedom of every individual in the private realm of erotic life, which, since it *is* private, should not be regulated by any code of social behavior. In this regard his poetry is very topical, since we live in a historical moment when there is animated debate about gay marriage. In our multimedia, multiethnic era, there are still those who speak of homosexual relations as a sin.

Gunn's poetry is also the mouthpiece for a great cultural inheritance that he revives in the modern world. Tradition played a central role in his artistic quest; from the first to the last collection, he always established a careful dialogue with the great poets of the past, without ever sinking to an ancillary or imitative position. He always grafted his cultural and literary inheritance onto the contemporary world; like T.S. Eliot, he renewed the tradition, by reviving its themes, myths, and expressive modes in the modern world.

As Clive Wilmer writes:

> It has been said of him that he was the most Elizabethan of modern poets, but his was not an academic matter: in his hands the inherited forms and conventions seemed utterly natural and breathed with his own modernity. His "Street Song," for instance, the monologue of a Californian drug-dealer, recalls the pedlar's songs of Dowland and Campion.[13]

James Fenton states, "Gunn was a true city poet, a modern sensibility, though steeped in a renaissance poetic."[14] Gunn's debt to tradition does not mean that he excludes new forms and models, nor does it preclude further artistic development; his poetic path is marked by experimentation with a variety of new styles, themes and subjects, which never become, as they did for some

Modernists, an end in themselves. Linguistic experimentation (consider the use of free verse and the slang of *Boss Cupid*), as well as the revisiting of traditional forms and models, is an essential ingredient of his poetic quest.

As Gunn wrote in his recent introduction to a selection of Yvor Winters' poems:

> It is not easy to go from free verse to meter after writing free verse poems for a number of years. (It is not easy to go in the opposite direction either.) To redirect one's energies in this way is as difficult as starting over.[15]

In his experimentation with a number of styles, in his alert and constant dialogue with tradition, Gunn is a poet who rarely descends to autobiography ("He disliked the cult of personality, preferring to stand at a distance from his subject-matter").[16] Only in the last collection, *Boss Cupid*, do we note the occasional tendency to speak of himself, as if at this point he wanted to reach an existential and artistic balance (in this collection many of the themes and atmosphere of earlier poems re-emerge). *Boss Cupid* represents a moment of reflection in which Gunn examines his past, trying to discern — without a positive result — a future way of renewing himself. The collection confirms that the poet has nearly reached the end of his poetic vein, as he confesses to Clive Wilmer (see Chapter I) in the course of a London meeting in 2003, on the occasion of receiving the David Cohen British Literature Award:

> He [Gunn] told me then that he had given up writing verse. He had tried to force himself but the poems never flowered. "I have got no juice," he said. That seemed the right expression, if a sad one, for a man whose life had run on a palpable sense of energy.[17]

In most of his work, Gunn appears to be a mouthpiece for his time, for the social, cultural, and historical transformations that have characterized western civilization from World War II until today. Images of the Holocaust and the huge tragedy of the Second World War emerge in some of Gunn's poems about soldiers (like "Innocence," "Claus von Stauffenberg," "Misanthropos," etc.); most of the poems from *Fighting Terms* to *My Sad Captains* witness the existential angst that marks the twentieth century, and provide clear evidence of Sartre's influence. *Positives* (an interesting experiment of interaction between arts) is testimony of a London which the poet, as he said, would have difficulty recognizing some years later. *Moly* and *Jack Straw's Castle* are mirrors for the social and cultural revolutions of the sixties, showing their different faces. The poems range from the liberating effects connected with the use of hallucinogens, to states of disorientation produced by drugs, from euphoric visions to oppressive nightmares that torment the speaker in "Jack Straw's Castle." While in *The Passages of Joy* the poet is the mouthpiece for the life of homosexuals, for sexual liberty finally attained, but also for the search for friendship (one of the recurring themes in all of Gunn's poetry), in *The Man with Night Sweats*, alongside the search for contact and human relations, we find accurate reflections on the tragedy of AIDS, the plague of the century, that not only destroys the lives of its victims, but erodes those of the survivors. Paraphrasing Theodor Adorno (who says that after Auschwitz, one can no longer write poetry), one could say that there is no true sexual liberty after AIDS. In *Boss Cupid*, where we begin to see a certain retreat into the poet's self, an inclination to existential meditation, the poet is still the mouthpiece of a generation, of the malaise linked to aging and the body's physical decline. Nevertheless, his message — again so topical — is never one of resignation, but of resistance and struggle. In his poetry, life wins against death.

APPENDIX

Cole Street, San Francisco: A Conversation with Thom Gunn*

The following interview took place at his home in San Francisco in March 1990. We began by talking about a recent poem, "Old Meg," which was subsequently published in *The Man with Night Sweats*.

TG In "Meg Merrilies" Keats speaks of "Old Meg, she was a gypsy and lived upon the moors." So "Old Meg" is my modern-day version of the Old Meg living on the streets. She's a gypsy, and her house was out of doors, and so on. He got her from Walter Scott's *Guy Mannering*. He never published that during his lifetime. I will read "Old Meg" aloud for you if you like.

SM You have read "Old Meg" and mentioned the line by Keats: was your poem inspired by Keats, or was it an idea you had in mind and then the poem by Keats worked as a stimulus?

TG Oh, no, it came from an old woman, an actual woman who I see in the streets, and who was always sitting on the bus bench when I was there, and indeed, I was once in a supermarket and I had seen her so much. She is not terrible, and I had seen her so much that I smiled at her and nodded at her, and then she said: "Blood on you." Ha-ha. I always called her Old Meg in my mind because I thought that that was what the person in Keats' poem would have looked like, so it came from a bunch of things; it came from certain things I was thinking of in my mind, even before I thought of writing a poem about her. That is what came; I am not sure what caused the poem, mainly all of that.

SM So you get most of your inspiration from everyday life. As in one of my favorite poems, "Three," in *Moly*. Walking down the beach of Southern California, suddenly you bumped into this family, rediscovering nakedness...

TG Yes, right. That came from a real thing, yes. I am glad you liked that poem. I like it too.

*This interview was originally published in QLLSM 8, 1996, pp. 261–88.

SM If you close your eyes, and think of your poetry, without considering chronological order, which poems closely belong to you, which ones do you feel more attached to. Probably all of them?

TG Maybe the thing I was most recently working on would come back to me. I certainly don't think about my own development. I don't think as a literary critic about my poetry. I do not think that would help me.

SM Have you ever had the experience of writing something, then you go back to it and you're surprised at what you have written, in other words you hardly recognize yourself?

TG All the time, yes. The poem seems to belong to me for a few weeks, after that it looks as if it was by somebody else, I mean, with your own poetry, because once you get into a different set of mind, that poem becomes something, yes, you know—"I wrote my name underneath it. I remember I wrote it, I know I wrote it." On the other hand, it does not seem to belong to me any longer. And certainly, after a year or two, it looks as if it were something written by somebody else.

SM It acquires a life of its own, it becomes something independent.

TG *I hope so.*

SM When you write, do you write for yourself without anybody in mind or do you write consciously for a public?

TG Well, obviously I write for other people, otherwise, I would not, I wouldn't try to make my poetry so accessible. Obviously I have some kind of audience in mind, some kind of public in mind. Otherwise, I would be completely obscure, if I were just writing for myself. But it is very difficult, you know, your next question is going to be what public do I write for, and I don't know. Well, I haven't thought of my audience in those terms. Sometimes I do think of myself as writing for a specific person; there was a friend of mine who meant a great deal to me, his name is Tony White, and he was a friend of mine when I was an undergraduate at Cambridge, and he was my best reader for about twenty years or so. He gave me the best advice in criticism that I needed, so, I was, in a certain sense, not writing for him, but I was writing off with him in mind.— What he would think of this or if he thought a part of a poem was no good, in re-writing it I would say to myself—does this make sense there or not— you know, that kind of thing. And sometimes I do find myself as if writing for individuals still, but I don't think of myself as writing for a particular group of people.

SM Did it ever happen before, I mean, at the beginning of your career, when you started writing poetry at Cambridge, that you wrote and you were conscious of your audience?

TG When I was writing at Cambridge, I was hoping to be published in University poetry magazines and so I had in mind what people were at the University, I guess. If you think you are going to be printed somewhere, you do have in mind an audience of the people who read that particular magazine, whatever it is.

Thom Gunn at home, March 1990 (photograph by the author).

SM Don't you think this can affect your poetry? It may turn out to be a kind of limitation to your freedom in writing.

TG It doesn't concern me very much, thinking about the group of people I am writing for, I don't normally, well — I hope I'm writing for everybody, but I don't think about that very specifically — so it really surprises me when I get a letter from somebody in Sweden, you know. I am very happy that somebody has read me in Sweden, but it hadn't crossed my mind, that that could happen, but I *am* delighted, of course.

SM Don't you think that some poets—or artists in general—can develop a kind of arrogance, in the sense of becoming conscious of being a celebrity. Once you are aware of being *officially accepted*, it is possible that you write because you know that somebody is listening to you—since you are popular—and you don't really strive towards perfection.

TG Yes, definitely; you see, I was saved a lot of that, because of the fact that most of my reputation has always been in England, more than in America, and I moved to America right about the time when my first book was published, and my first book, anyway, was about three hundred copies, and not very many people read that, *Fighting Terms,* in its first edition, and so I had the advantage of having quite a considerable reputation in England and not having any reputation at all here. That is certainly fine, because I don't want the embarrassment of being famous, you know. I remember once, Cary Grant, the movie star, when he was famous—that would be twenty years ago I would say—he went to Russia, and when he came back from Russia, er ... somebody, asked him what it was like, and he said: "It was wonderful, nobody recognized me at all." He didn't want to be recognized, poor man. A lot want to be famous, a lot want to be recognized on the street, well, I would say poets on the whole don't get that famous; well, Allen Ginsberg does, Evtushenko does probably. There are a few people, maybe Robert Lowell, but most of us don't get that famous, I wouldn't like to get that famous. I want to live my life, I do not want er ... to be asked to appear in TV and stuff like that. That doesn't interest me at all. I don't want to live the life of a celebrity, and I have never sought to. Also when I was young I didn't want that.

SM Celebrities can become empty, since they perform—most of them put a mask in front of themselves to play a certain role, but some people like being flattered...

TG It's an inconvenience, I mean sometimes. Oh, it must be nice having people fussing about you—for a while, but I think, that the novelty of that probably wears out pretty soon. I'd *hate* to be somebody like Norman Mailer—who everybody knows—but he obviously likes that; some people like that, as you said.

SM When you went to Rome for six months—back in 1954—what drove you there? How do you remember this experience? Did you get in touch with any Italian poets?

TG I didn't know anybody. The only person I knew was the Principessa Caetani, she was American, actually, but she was married to a prince and she edited— quite a famous review at that time—called *Botteghe Oscure,* and she lived in a palace. Well, ... and she was very kind to me; she had been living there many years, and she was very interesting. That literary magazine was published mainly in English, some French, and maybe some Italian and some German contributors, but it was mainly an English and American literary magazine. That literary magazine stopped many years ago, probably with her death. That was about the end of the 1950s. Anyway, I didn't know anybody in Rome, but I had a good time there, I was very poor, I didn't have very much money. I was given a grant, which had been founded in about the year 1910 and which was probably a lot of money in the year 1910, but by the time I was given it, that was very little money, and I couldn't afford to stay in Rome any longer than I did; I was eating those terrible *spaghetti al sugo* from a stall. You know, there is a market somewhere in Rome, where you can get *spaghetti al sugo*, the least expensive, the cheapest plate of spaghetti you can get anywhere. I was getting them and I do not think it was, er ... good nutrition. Yes, that is the right expression. But I was very young then, yes, I was twenty-three or -four.

SM You now have a position at Berkeley. How do you feel about teaching? How much does it affect you as a poet, or in other words, what does it mean for you to be an academic?

TG The Academy can be very narrow; as far as I am concerned, I like part-time teaching. I teach about half and half, literature and creative writing courses, I am teaching a course on Modern American Poetry, Twentieth Century American Poetry, Modernists, Pound and Eliot and William Carlos Williams, and people like that, and Marianne Moore and Robert Duncan — this term — and I also teach a course called The English Lyric, but I only teach in the Spring; I only teach, in fact, for six months of the year — which is ideal — it is just the life I want. I don't get paid very much, but I don't need the money, I can do without that. To be honest, I am a bit lazy. And I don't want the inconvenience. No, I don't want to become an academic. I quite like teaching — when I do teach, I quite like it — probably because I have the rest of the year off, and partly because I'm not good at having life completely at my own disposal; after a time I get out of control of it.

SM Do you choose the courses you teach or do you have a program imposed on you?

TG I choose them. They are very good to me at Berkeley, yes, I have no complaints about them at all. And I get good, bright students.

SM You said you teach creative writing courses as well. How do you actually feel about teaching creative poetry-writing? It sounds very challenging and at the same time rewarding — a poet teaching people how to write poetry — do you think that poetry can be taught to a degree?

TG Oh, I feel I can help people to do something better with what they are doing already. It is like teaching mathematics, if you have a talent for mathematics, you can be taught a bit more in mathematics and — if you have got a talent for writing poetry, you can probably be taught a little bit more about that. I couldn't make a poet from nothing, though. It has to be somebody who has some talent in the first place, and also I don't approve totally of creative writing courses, because I think, really, most good poets, most good writers — it is really done on their own — you know it is. You write alone, you don't write cosily in groups. And then, I don't think I can make poets, but I do think I can help somebody to make a connection between their experience and language, to think about the experience of imagination in relation to language. My aims are very modest. You see, the trouble with the creative writing courses is that they don't make the same kind of demand on you as you would make on yourself, and, the kind of demand that a creative writing course makes on you, a group of people, is never as hard as it can be imagined by themselves, and most people don't realize that.

SM What, for you, is the best approach to interpret a poem? When I was writing my dissertation, discussing it rationally, I had the feeling it was like using violence against it, because, for example, quoting some lines and detaching them from the rest — although part of a critical analysis — seemed to destroy the whole musicality.

TG Why should it destroy it? I don't think it destroys it. People often say that to me, but I don't see that analysis or criticism needs to destroy poetry, if you are intelligent, if you *are perceptive about it.* How could it hurt a poem, to know how it is working, to discuss how it is working. This is what I say in my classes: "If you are a painter, you want to know all kinds of things which go into some painting you admire, all the brush strokes, all the different techniques that go into it — how interesting — but it can't take away from the painting that you are discussing, it can't take away from the total effect of it; then you come back and you look at the painting, and you think, now I know much more about it, I know what went into it." Similarly with a poem. I have never found my own criticism as harming my appreciation of poems. It has only increased it, because my criticism is completely supplementary to my love for a poem and it's an instrument of that love.

SM In other words, it does not destroy the whole emotion.

TG No, of course not. My mind doesn't destroy my emotions, my mind is not opposed to my emotions, and my mind is not opposed to my emotions when I am discussing poetry, either. Actually a poem is doing something both through the mind and through the emotions, because it is through language, and language carries anything you want — it carries both of them at once.

SM When you discuss poems you have written, how does the process work? Do you tend to recollect the inspiration that was behind them, or do you look at them as something external now?

TG I can do it both ways. If it is a poem from a long time ago, I can't remember what went into it, so I have to treat it almost as if I were a reader who did not write it — if I don't remember it — you know, something I wrote in the 1950s. I remember some, I remember what went into some of them, but I don't remember what went into others.

SM If I ask you to analyze one of your poems, supposing I am a new reader, and don't know anything about your poetry. What would your approach be to it?

TG It would embarrass me to do that, because — I figure — I am not that egotistical. I have never taught a poem of mine in class, I wouldn't dream of *teaching myself* in class; I think that would be a dreadfully egotistical thing to do. I teach other people's poetry; I am trying to get people to feel the same love that I feel for other people's poetry ... and ultimately, my reason for teaching is to get people to feel the same enthusiasm I feel for poets they find too difficult, or even don't know about, before-hand. I would never teach myself — it would be such an act of vanity — *I could,* but the reason I wouldn't like to do it would be... — obviously, if I were doing this, I would be doing it with a poem of mine that I like and I would be praising myself, like, "look what I am doing with such and such," "look what I am doing there" — but certainly I could do that, and it would be easy to do, since I know what part it would be easier to talk about.

SM You might run the risk of being far too biased, because it is your own poetry, you can look at it and analyze it, but only from one point of view — from the point of view of the author — and not from a very critical one.

TG Yes, right, but you use criticism as if you mean adverse criticism. I don't write much adverse criticism nowadays; I haven't done so for many years now; I have written a lot of criticism in the last ten years.

SM I see. About your latest collection, *The Passages of Joy*. There are some poems there that I like very much, but I have the impression that — at least in some of them — I find that voice that was speaking long ago from another angle, as if you were recollecting, as if you were re-elaborating what was or could have been once an old poem. I have in mind particularly that poem about Cambridge, "His Rooms in College," where you speak about that professor. It has a kind of climax, or epiphany, at a certain point.

TG It is about, losing yourself in reading, really. I met somebody when I was last in Cambridge — whenever that was. I was staying with a friend of mine, and he introduced me to another man who was living in the house, and he had just broken up with his wife, and I don't think he said anything about it, but I tried to picture, you know, the situation, writing a poem. I don't think he ever knew I wrote a poem about him; he wasn't somebody, in fact, I knew very well; he was just sharing the house when I was in Cambridge. So that struck you as an old poem. That's interesting.

SM Do you think that a poem can be universalized, when you see it as detached from the particular, the specific, or in other words, the personal?

TG Universalized? I don't believe in universalizing. *I hate that word.* I think we write about *the unique*, I don't think we write about *the universal*. This is a quarrel I have with a lot of teachers and a lot of my students who have learned from other teachers to go for the universal, and I say: "No writer writes to the universal," I say: "When Shakespeare writes about Othello, Desdemona and Iago, he writes about a specific bunch of people, they are not universalized." Oh, I will show you a wonderful thing, I was just copying out of it today. It's one of my favorite pieces of prose. It's by Robert Creeley and it's Penguin's *Introduction to Whitman* — he did a selection of Whitman — and he says: "It is paradoxically, the personal which makes the common in so far as it recognizes the existence of the many in the one — in my own joy or despair, I am brought to that which others have also experienced — that is the opposite to the universal, I am saying, the personal which makes the common." So he says he writes about the personal, the individual, the unique, so that other people in their uniqueness may recognize, not what is like them, but what is different from them, you see? I can't think of any good writer, who writes for the universal. That would be the worst way to write well. You only write, you only write about the specific, I think.

SM Yes, but then you make the specific universal.

TG No, no, that's not so easy. It's not so easy to make the specific universal. What I feel, what I experience, is not going to be what everybody experiences. I feel these things in my particular way. I think this is the worst kind of thing that teachers can do, that teachers do, is to suddenly start talking about the universal. If you start talking about Othello as Othello, Desdemona as Desdemona, that is fine, they are not like Romeo and Juliet, that is what would make them universal. They are very distinct, they are in a very distinct situation: he is black and she is white, and he is a Moor from the North of Africa and she is from Venice, and much of their situation comes from this. It is not at all a universal situation. What is so good about a good writer is that he does not write about the universal. Baudelaire is writing about a very *specific* state of mind, a state of mind that I can translate and find an equivalent to in my own, but that is not universalizing it, because my own is alike but different, and what's interesting in reading Baudelaire is to see his difference: he is not feeling something that everybody feels, but it can be translated into what different people feel, but translating is not the same as universalizing. Do you see what kind of distinction I am trying to make?

SM Yes, definitely. You are talking about something unique and individual, that can be interpreted in a particular way and translated into different kinds of emotions, and then in relation to the person who perceives and interprets it, everything becomes a little bit subjective. Let me ask you another question, do you think the experience art in general and poetry specifically convey, do you think that it is more knowledge or pleasure?

TG It is the same. It is not just knowledge, it is a combination of both. The acquiring of knowledge can be pleasure too, and with the poems you like, that is just what it is. You can call it *understanding*, in a large sense, you know. It's true we can speak about knowledge and pleasure as different things but, when we speak about works of art, the two are combined. If it were just acquiring knowledge, that would make it like some subject I was bad at at school, like Latin or Mathematics; if it were just pleasure, that would be like taking drugs or making love or something, or … like eating candies, or something like that. This is what is so wonderful about poetry, that it's both at once; and it's possible to distinguish between them, but I don't think I want to try that.

SM Ezra Pound and T.S. Eliot were two great poets, two tremendous influences, but now, in contemporary American poetry, there are no leading figures…

TG Pound certainly is.

SM He still is, but I was thinking, there are no new leading figures among the contemporaries.

TG Oh you mean, living. Oh no, they are all dead, all dead.

SM T.S. Eliot was a strong leading figure — he did the opposite of what you've done — Eliot decided to move from the United States to England, whereas you have gone the other way round, like W.H. Auden. I think I know what brought you to the United States and the reason why you decided to settle in San Francisco, but I would like to ask you if you have ever reached a moment, when you have regretted it.

TG No, never. I haven't been back for about eleven years.

SM That's a long time. I wonder what Europe means to you now. How do you actually relate to it from here, do you still feel involved in the European scene? The United States seem provincial, most people don't know or don't seem to care about what is happening outside.

TG I live in San Francisco, I live in the North of California, that's the place where I live and where I want to live. The only other place in the United States where I would like to live would be New York, and I find New York very unprovincial indeed, and I don't find San Francisco very provincial, although it is to some extent, but I like its provinciality to that extent. Well, the European scene, I don't even know what the European scene means — I mean, I am so far away from it — and I am certainly not part of the European scene. Certainly as they say, my roots are in Europe and there is nothing I can do about that. You know, your first twenty years, obviously, you learn so much then. To some extent I remain English always, but I like it when somebody calls me an Anglo-American poet; that's what I am, an *Anglo-American poet*. I'm not English, I'm not really an English poet any longer, and I'm not an American poet either. I am somebody between the two, but I have elements of both. But, no, I don't regret living here for a moment; I am much more interested in modern American poetry than I am in modern British poetry. Most of it strikes me as very bad indeed, nowadays, you know; modern American poetry isn't that tremendous since the death of all the older generation, but it is a good deal much more interesting to me than English poetry. English poetry strikes me as *excessively timid*...

SM Are you thinking of anybody in particular?

TG I think, Larkin particularly and his influence. Philip Larkin was a very good poet, but he was very bad for his influence on the younger generation.

SM You were related to him for a while, I mean, some critics put both of you together, but you are very different. I find you much more similar to Ted Hughes than to Philip Larkin — were it only because there is this strong voice speaking in both of you — even if you are different from him as well.

TG Indeed. The idea of putting Larkin and me together, that was nonsense. We haven't even met. But ... there is no daring left in the people who learned from Larkin. It seems like most of the young are trying to write like Larkin. I don't know why anybody young would want to. *I can't even understand that.* It seems to me madness, a very muted kind of madness. It is lack of courage, lack of daring...

SM Can you think of a reason for the present absence of leading figures in poetry?

TG After Pound's generation, the next generation died off rather early, like Robert Lowell and Robert Duncan; they didn't live quite to an advanced age. I compare it in my mind to what happened at the beginning of the 19th century in England, and there you get Wordsworth and Coleridge and Keats and Shelley and that group of people. They are so big and so impressive, that even though many of them died quite early, the rest of the century spent the rest of the time trying to deal with them, and they actually did not get free of them until the beginning of the next century, when we started off with these big people again, another generation, almost exactly a hundred years later, and you know, round about 1910 into the 1920s, and we are still trying to deal with them too. That is what we have been trying to do ever since, and nobody has really been as big as the people of that generation; nobody has been as important for me anyway as, as that generation of Pound and Eliot and of Marianne Moore and Mina Loy and Williams and Stevens and possibly Frost, yes, he was doing something — a nasty old man — but he wrote poetry that was much better than he ever was. Ha — ha. Anyway, what were you saying about the lack of a leading figure?

SM I was saying that the lack of a leading figure after so many years of *tremendous* influence, can help young poets to have less limitation. They may feel less imposed on.

TG It sounds as if you were regarding a leading figure as if it were a father. You said that you have either to obey or oppose that leading figure, but you can just *disregard* a leading figure, you can do that too. That is what my generation was doing: we were disregarding the leading figures. It is not opposing, it is just not taking any notice, and that is what Larkin and I had in common and Ted Hughes too, the three of us, though we were not writing at all similarly; we had that in common, we were trying to disregard the leading figures of our time, because we couldn't see our way towards writing like them, I guess.

SM Yes, and by doing that, you were all trying to give an answer to the next generation, that is actually what all of you had in common when they tried to put all of you together in that group called *The Movement*.

TG Yes, although that was a journalistic invention.

SM That was probably because at that time, you were all coming from the same background and you were approximately the same age...

TG *People like to classify.* I mean the Mannerist painters were never called Mannerist painters till the 19th century or maybe till the 20th century, and the Metaphysical poets were never called Metaphysical poets in their own time. But a lot of people can only think easily about art if they manage to classify; if they manage to put people in groups together, I mean, it is partly journalistic, it is partly what people do in literary history, isn't it? It is not very satisfactory, I think, but they can deal more easily then.

SM Yes, that has been the tendency of the whole of Western culture. It has always tended to classify because it is easier to interpret, discuss or talk about works of art, once they are put in a box. And nowadays, it is even something which is easier to *sell*.

TG You are absolutely right. It's a commercial thing as well; and this involves all the arts. I mean the visual arts, it is a way to make a lot of money. It really is nonsense.

SM Is it difficult for a new poet to achieve a breakthrough nowadays?

TG I would say so, yes. The business is pretty bad. I couldn't live on my poetry. And for a young poet, it is very difficult. It's much more difficult than it was in my time, because nowadays the publishers have got so big, they conglomerate. I don't know what it is like in Italy, but in the United States and in England right now, most of them have become very large companies indeed, and the poets have always been published by small companies, taking a small risk, just bringing out a thousand copies of the book. When I first started writing, a new book of poems by somebody unknown would be in an edition of about a thousand copies or maybe even less—this would be from Faber & Faber, this would be from what was then a big publisher—in England and in America. Nowadays, you get so few independent publishers, you get publishers in New York and in England, that are also part of large companies connected with the petroleum industry and with the movies and stuff like that. They want their best sellers, they want to sell *best-selling* novels. They are not interested in poetry, and they are not interested in new poets, and so it's much more difficult for a young poet to publish a book than it was when I started, in 1954.

SM Is it sometimes the same for an established poet, like you, for instance?

TG It would not be for me, because I think the new book of mine will be about five thousand copies in this country. I don't know how many copies in England, maybe three thousand. That would be enough for them to make a profit, not a large profit, because they are making more money on anthologies, I mean school anthologies. They are all junk, you know. But they probably make me more money, they make publishers more money than the actual books do.

SM Is there actually any contemporary American poet who gets published easily and you don't like, that is to say, you think he does not deserve such popularity?

TG Heaps of them, heaps of them. There are other poets I like though; there are two young poets who are very good, one is just down the street here, called August Kleinzahler, and another is Jim Powell, who had a first book out and I think is very good indeed.

SM What do you think of a poet like Rita Dove? She won the Pulitzer Prize for Poetry in 1987.

TG Well, she's okay. I think she is greatly overpraised, but I think that is partly because they feel comfortable, she's a black woman poet and they feel comfortable with the category; they want to have some black woman poet that they can like a lot. I don't think she is that terrific, though. Do you?

SM Not much. In this connection, I was wondering, the fact that she won the Pulitzer Prize in 1987—the fourteenth woman to win the prize, the second Afro-American and also at the age of 34, one of the youngest poets—don't you think it was also because she was particularly impressive at that time, I mean, extremely convenient, since she was the voice of a minority, and that was exactly what was needed at that particular moment. At Arizona State University, when somebody is called for a poetry reading, most poets belong to a special group, or often to minorities. We had for instance W.S. Merwin from Hawaii. Most teachers in the creative writing program defined him as an impressive minority, for the kind of poetry he writes. He is like a preacher, he wants to be the mouthpiece for his own generation. What do you think of him?

TG Well, he's a very well established poet in the United States—he started publishing about the same time I did, and he lived in England for a while and has published probably more books than I have, and he's very well known—but he's not a racial minority, he's no kind of minority. He has his own political opinions, about the rain forest, that is something else again, it makes him a political poet in a rather limited way.

SM Yes, but who do you speak to being a political poet? Nowadays the poetry public is not very wide, it is itself a minority.

TG In the whole history has it ever been very wide? It was briefly rather wide in the 1960s when there was a kind of convergence, of poetry and rock and roll and politics, but that was only for very few years.

SM Why do you think that has always been like that?

TG Because poetry is difficult; it is not as easy to read as most novels; it is not as easy to deal with as a musical rehearsal, as music or something like that.

SM I see. Anyway, going back to your poetry, I would like to ask you, if you can think of some poems, that worked for you as a turning point of your own development?

TG Well, I think it is there in everything you write, isn't it? You are always redefining yourself, your own direction. Technically I would say the poems I worked in syllabics, in the second half of *My Sad Captains*. I am not sure which came first, maybe the first poem of those.

SM "Waking in a Newly-Built House"?

TG Yes right, I think that was probably the first written of those—although they are not arranged chronologically. That was a turning point in my career, probably.

SM And did it happen that you found yourself writing in a new style, realizing that your old style did not work any more, or was it more that you felt in yourself the need for a change, for coming to terms with something new?

TG I had been thinking about that for quite some time. It was a form that had not been used very much and I was trying to write poems in that form for quite a while before I succeeded. But in anything you write, it is usually a combination of two things, like something extremely conscious and something quite unconscious. They come together and that's how you write the poem. At least that seems the way. There's usually an element of conscious thought beforehand, with me, though this may vary from several years to just a day or so, but a lot of the thought may have to do with the subject matter, you may not realize your thought is really going to end up as a poem, and then of course there's something mysterious that happens and you suddenly find yourself able to write it. But that also might be a gradual process. Sometimes you just carry along a few lines in your head and you just won't be able to go on with it for some time.

SM In the process of writing, do you keep the idea in mind or does your writing develop your idea, I mean, do you have a concept which you put into a poem, like the poem "Three" was about those people you met on the beach. In other words, do you develop the image within yourself, before starting to write, or is it something which develops mostly in the process of writing?

TG We are talking about something which is very difficult for me to know about. I do not know exactly what happens when I am writing. I worked at very short things, which you must have read in *The Occasions of Poetry*, about writing a poem, about writing "Three," that poem, and anything I told you would only be a kind of extension on that, because, you do have a general idea, you do have general concepts, yes, but it is the coming against the instances, the particular instance that makes it ... you want to write about that particular thing, and you don't know what it means, but you want to write about it, almost as you would want to take a photograph, or do a sketch or something, simply to record it, something you're fond of, you are moved by, or you hate, it could be, but something which moves you and ... you want to write about it, and then the concept comes out. "Oh, that's what I was thinking about six months ago, that's what I want to write about. That's what I have been thinking of, after all," that kind of thing. And what happened to me when I was writing "Three," was the kind of thing that happens to me normally in writing a poem: I have certain floating general ideas around, but I cannot write about the floating general ideas, what I can write about are specific instances. The ideas are implicit. They are contained within, they are inferred by the action or by the things, but only implicitly as I say.

SM Because the language of poetry concentrates and filters them...

TG Because the language of poetry tends towards particulars, I think, more than towards generalities.

SM Do you think that language can work as a limitation, can be an oppression for the expression of your ideas?

TG Well, yes, of course it is, language is not the same as what it talks about. It never has been, and so it always has limits, and I suppose, in writing one tries to find ways of getting beyond that limit. If it didn't have those limits, I would write three or four poems a day, or even more. Nothing would stop one from writing on but..., yes, I suppose it is the limits that define it.

SM As far as form is concerned, do you usually decide before if it has to be metre or free verse?

TG Well, this is not always a very deliberate choice, when I write down the notes for a poem, I tend to write them all over the page, so I'm not committing myself to lines, it is not even metrical or free verse, or a formal metre or the length of a free verse line. I try to let it take the form it will take; although, if I have been writing a lot of metrical poems before then, it is quite likely that the next poem may be in metre, or if I have been writing a lot in free verse before that, it is very likely it will be in free verse.... Occasionally, I thought beforehand, yes, I want this to be like a sonnet or I want this to be like a street song, do you remember in *Moly* the "Street Song"? I wanted it to be in a song form, obviously it had to be in metre and rhyme; often it is not a decision very consciously taken beforehand. Again it is very difficult to talk about the actual starting point of writing a poem. That is what everybody is most curious about, what everybody has asked me about. And that is what I know least about, about how you get the first draft of a poem down, I don't know, and in a way I don't want to know too much, otherwise, I would start calculating, I would get recipes, like a recipe for a cake or something, and a poem is not a cake. And so, it can never be the same any two times, but, you see, that is the kind of moment which I can't speak about very coherently, I don't know anybody who can either.

SM Most of *Moly* is written in metre, because as you said, in a way you had to filter this experience, which could not be told when it was happening.

TG Oh yes, I couldn't write when it happened. It wouldn't have been possible, what you feel like, it is an untellable experience, you know.

SM Do you still make use of drugs? Where I am working at the moment, in Arizona, many students make use of drugs...

TG What kind? Cocaine? LSD is coming back, isn't it?

SM Well, acid, LSD, cocaine, it mostly depends on what they get, but it is not like back in the 60s. It is no longer a positive, creative experience, it is more a kind of defeat. When I also think, back in Europe, of the people that make use of drugs, it is mostly a passive reaction, a withdrawing from reality, a self-destruction, it is not a creative process.

TG It was not a very creative process in the 60s, it was not. People did it because it was fashion.

SM I have just a few more questions about some trends in contemporary American poetry. What do you think of the New Formalists? Don't you think that their poetry is — to a certain degree — an involution in the American tradition?

TG They are dreadful. Indeed they are dreadful; I am not interested in movements, and so I am not interested in the New Formalists and I am not interested in the Language Poets on the other hand. Both strike me as a big bore. They don't interest me, I mean, I read them, but I am bored by them.

SM What about the Black Mountain poets?

TG Well, Robert Duncan was my great friend and I have written two essays and an enormous one in *The Times Literary Supplement* about two years ago. I don't like Olson very much, I have got all of Olson's poetry there, and I have not really read through it, but it is not very interesting.

SM One more question about your latest collection, *Undesirables*. I would like to know why the title and what the main topic is.

TG Actually it's a pamphlet. But what is the main topic? I thought it was a good way of bringing together a group of poems I had written in free verse, over a short period of time.

SM Why the title, *Undesirables*. Is there a particular reason for that?

TG The title is not a kind of catalogue title. I thought it was a good title, actually, I loved the photographs, I had never seen the photographs until I saw the book. I didn't choose it; a teenager is undesirable in many people's eyes, as a snake is. That was a publisher's idea, but a very good idea too. Well — a carnivorous plant is undesirable — undesirable, I mean, it is a kind of stuffy word, that you would say provincial people use about people they don't like, it is a fussy old person's word, undesirables, it means people they'd sooner not have around, you get connotations of them, yes; but some of these things are undesirable from my point of view, like in "The Honesty,"[1] he is undesirable, and a gay bar, that is considered an undesirable place.

SM Why?

TG Because that's what people do, I am speaking about the middle-class use of this word, undesirables, and street people are considered undesirable.

SM Could you describe to me your next book? Just a few details about it.

TG It is fifty poems. Many of which you have read probably. A lot of poems in it are about a friend of mine who died of AIDS, about the failure...

SM AIDS — everybody speaks about AIDS, everybody is afraid of AIDS, it is like the plague of our society. What's your experience of it been?

TG Not with happiness, believe me. AIDS is something real, it is a fact, it is a past fact too, and a present fact. Most of my friends have been killed by AIDS, most of my friends.

SM You said most of your friends died of AIDS. Are you obsessively frightened by the idea of getting AIDS yourself?

TG Oh yes, but I don't really think of it. If I had it, well — people have to die of something. Look, I am sixty, I've had a long happy life, really. I don't think of that too much, but well, no, I don't worry about getting AIDS myself, you know, it is like worrying about cancer or something, I have got to die of something.

SM I would like to make an anthology of your poetry and translate it, instead of translating just a collection, because you have been unpublished for long, at least in Italy.

TG There was that selection of mine, that book of poetry published by Mondadori, *I miei tristi capitani and other poems*. Do you think that was good, did you like his translations? I mean, I can't judge.

SM Yes, that was very good, although it is not at all easy to be satisfied with a translation of poems, is it? This is another question I would like to ask you. How do you actually behave towards translations, I mean, how do you feel?

TG I can't judge. I don't know any other language as well as I know English, the only language I would know well enough would be French, and I still wouldn't be able to tell if it is good poetry, I can tell if it is accurate, but not if it is a good poem and certainly I could not do that in Italian.

SM But in a translation of a poem, what do you think is more important, making a good poem or making it accurate?

TG I don't know. You have to work that out. It depends, you see, if I were reading Dante on opposite pages, I would like just plain prose translation, if I am able to refer to the original. If I am not able to refer to the original, then it is better to have good poetry in your own language and rather loose in its literariness. Wouldn't you say?

SM Yes, I think so too. And how do you feel about the idea of your poetry being translated, that I make, for instance, out of your poetry other poetry.

TG Oh I think this is wonderful. I have been stealing something from Flaubert and I have been stealing something from Keats. You know we all take from each other. We feed on each other's imaginations.

Chapter Notes

INTRODUCTION

1. Appendix, pp. 167–68
2. Giorgio Melchiori, *I funamboli. Il manierismo nella letteratura inglese da Joyce ai giovani arrabbiati* (Torino: Einaudi, 1974) [1956]) p. 344.
3. Cf. Giovanni Cianci, *La scuola di Cambridge* (Bari: Adriatica, 1970); and David Perkins, "In and Out of the Movement," in *A History of Modern Poetry* (Cambridge, Mass.: Harvard University Press, 1987) pp. 418–44.
4. Cf. Giorgio Melchiori, *I funamboli*, p. 342; and Renzo S. Crivelli, "La poesia del dopoguerra," in Franco Marenco (ed.), *Storia della civiltà letteraria inglese*, vol. III (Torino: Utet, 1996) pp. 570–73.
5. Most literary histories group the poets of the fifties and sixties into two threads, the Movement and the Group, respectively. See also Renzo S. Crivelli, *Né falchi né colombe: poesia inglese degli anni '50 e '60 dal Movement al Group* (Torino: Tirrenia Stampatori, 1983).
6. The anonymous *Spectator* article was anticipated some months earlier by another published in the same journal, "Poets of the Fifties" by Anthony Hartley; without naming the Movement, it stated that "New names in the reviews, a fresh atmosphere of controversy, a new spirit of criticism — these are signs that some other group of poets is appearing in the horizon ... we are now in the presence of the only considerable movement in English poetry since the thirties." Anthony Hartley, "Poets of the Fifties," *The Spectator*, 27 August 1954, pp. 260–61.
7. William Van O'Connor, *The New University Wits and the End of Modernism* (Carbondale: Southern Illinois University Press, 1963) pp. 3–4.
8. J.D. Scott, "In the Movement," *The Spectator*, 1 October 1954, p. 400.
9. Cf. Renzo S. Crivelli, "La poesia del dopoguerra," p. 570.
10. J.D. Scott, "In the Movement," p. 400.
11. Gunn dedicates the poem to his friend Donald Davie, celebrating "your love of poetry / greater / than your love of consistency" ("To Donald Davie in Heaven," *BC* 59–60, ll. 7–9). See also Patrick McGuiness, "'The Republic of Letters': Thom Gunn and Donald Davie," *Agenda* 37 (2–3), 1999, pp. 114–17.
12. Donald Davie, "Remembering the Movement," in Clive Wilmer (ed.), *With the Grain: Essays on Thomas Hardy and Modern British Poetry* (Manchester: Carcanet Press, 1998) pp. 200–01.
13. Ian Hamilton, *A Poetry Chronicle* (London: Faber, 1973) p. 129.
14. Robert Conquest, "Introduction," *New Lines* (London: Macmillan, 1956) pp. xiv–xv.
15. D.J. Enright, "Introduction," *Poets of the Fifties* (Tokyo: Kenkyusha, 1955) p. 15.
16. *Ibid.*, p. 3.
17. Philip Larkin states that "we are all perfectly convinced that the name at any rate took its origin in a piece of sheer journalism in *The Spectator*. Cf. William Van O'Connor, *The New University Wits and the End of Modernism*, p. 6.
18. Harold Bloom, *The Anxiety of Influence: A Theory of Poetry* (New York: Oxford University Press, 1973).
19. Appendix, p. 168.
20. Hilary Morrish, "Violence and Energy: An Interview," *Poetry Review* 57 (1), 1966, p. 32.
21. Elizabeth Jennings, *Poetry To-Day* (London: Longmans, 1961) p. 9.
22. Elizabeth Jennings (ed.), *An Anthology of Modern Verse 1940–1960* (London: Methuen, 1961) p. 10.
23. Blake Morrison, *The Movement* (Oxford: Oxford University Press, 1980) p. 9.
24. Though the cosmopolitan aspect is largely lacking in some of these poets, for example Philip Larkin (despite some of his poems being set in Ireland), the titles of some works in Conquest's anthology *New Lines*, such as "Afternoon in Florence" and "Piazza San Marco" by

Elizabeth Jennings, "Lerici" by Thom Gunn, "Evening in the Khamsin" and "Baie des Anges, Nice" by D.J. Enright seem to refute this statement.

25. Blake Morrison, *The Movement*, pp. 56–61.

26. A. Alvarez (ed.), *The New Poetry* (Harmondsworth: Penguin, 1966 [1962]) p. 32.

27. *Ibid.*, p. 21.

28. *Ibid.*, pp. 22–23.

29. *Ibid.*, p. 23.

30. *Ibid.*, p. 23.

31. *Ibid.*, p. 23.

32. *Ibid.*, p. 23.

33. The above-mentioned poets are included in the edition revised in 1966. The first edition did not include Sylvia Plath, Anne Sexton, Peter Porter, Jon Silkin, David Wevill, George MacBeth, Ian Hamilton, and Ted Walker.

34. Ian Hamilton, *A Poetry Chronicle*, pp. 129–30.

35. Bernard Bergonzi, "After 'The Movement,'" *Listener*, 24 August 1961, p. 284.

36. Florence Elon, "The Movement Against Itself: British Poetry of the 1950s," *Southern Review* 19 (1), 1983, p. 109.

37. Stephen Regan, "The Movement," in *A Companion to 20th Century Poetry*, ed. Neil Roberts (Oxford: Blackwell, 2001) p. 217.

38. Stephen Regan, "The Movement," pp. 218–19.

39. David Perkins, *A History of Modern Poetry: Modernism and After* (Cambridge, Mass.: The Belkan Press of Harvard University Press, 1987) p. 446.

40. *Ibid.*, p. 419.

41. *Ibid.*, p. 447.

42. Neil Corcoran, *English Poetry since 1940* (London: Longman, 1993) p. 87.

43. See, for instance, *Modernismo/Modernismi* edited by Giovanni Cianci (Milano: Unicopli, 1991), and Peter Nicholls, *Modernisms: A Literary Guide* (Berkeley: University of California Press, 1995) referring to the peak of modernism in the first decades of the twentieth century.

44. *Thom Gunn in Conversation with James Campbell* (London: Between the Lines, 2000) pp. 23–24.

45. Earlier, Anthony Hartley in the article "Poets of the Fifties" had distinguished Thom Gunn from other poets, insisting on an elaboration of a personal style, in which rigorous metrical form was an expression of passion without sensuality and a remarkable presence of intellect.

46. Agostino Lombardo, "Thom Gunn e il Nuovo Movimento," in Thom Gunn, *I miei tristi capitani e altre poesie*, preface by Agostino Lombardo, trans. Camillo Pennati (Milano: Mondadori, 1968) pp. 21–22. See also Lidia De Michelis, *La poesia di Thom Gunn* (Firenze: La Nuova Italia, 1978) pp. 1–20.

47. Giorgio Melchiori, *I funamboli*, p. 341.

48. Alberto Arbasino, "Thom in Frisco," in *Lettere da Londra* (Milano: Adelphi, 1997) p. 306.

49. Appendix, p. 167.

50. Cf. Ian Hamilton, "Four Conversations," *London Magazine* 4 (6), 1964, pp. 64–70.

51. Appendix, p. 167.

52. *Thom Gunn in Conversation with James Campbell*, p. 24.

53. *Ibid.*

Chapter I

1. Consider, for example, the numerous biographies of Joseph Conrad, Virginia Woolf and D.H. Lawrence. In Lawrence's case, the books range from the large, three-volume Cambridge University Press biography (1991, 1996, 1998), to *Living at the Edge* by Michael Squires and Lynn Talbot (2002), whose protagonists are the couple Lawrence and Frieda, to the rewriting of Lawrence's stay in Cornwall during the First World War in Helen Dunmore's novel, *Zennor in Darkness* (1994), to the biographical novel *Out of Sheer Rage* by Geoff Dyer (1997).

2. We should not overestimate the importance of these interviews, since frequently Gunn repeats himself, giving the same answers to similar questions, even over a period of many years. This may be a means of defending himself from total exposure.

3. Gunn's poetic silence regarding his mother's death, which put such a traumatic end to the paradise of his youth ("I had an extraordinarily happy childhood [...]. Until my mother's death," *Thom Gunn in Conversation with James Campbell*, p. 17), can be compared to that of Ted Hughes (harshly targeted by feminist criticism) after his wife Sylvia Plath's suicide — among other things, both women ended their lives by breathing cooking-gas fumes. Hughes' silence was interrupted after thirty-five years with the publication of *Birthday Letters* (1998). Allusion to his mother's death (but not to suicide) occurs as well in Gunn's "Death's Door" (*The Man with Night Sweats*), in which, in the light of all his dear friends decimated by AIDS, his mother's death ("forty years ago") appears "archaic now as Minos" (*CP*, p. 485, l. 3). On "The Gas Poker" see also Langdon Hammer, "Thom Gunn and the Cool Queer Tales of Cupid," *Raritan* 20 (2), 2000, pp. 114–25.

4. Gunn dedicates both "The Gas Poker" and "My Mother's Pride" (*Boss Cupid*) to his mother. The latter is structured "in the same

way as Pound's Canto XIII, which is a slightly random collection of sayings by Confucius." *Thom Gunn in Conversation with James Campbell*, p. 19. The difficult relationship with his father emerges in "From an Asian Tent" (*Poems from the 1960s*), projected mythically onto that between Alexander the Great and Philip: "Yet each year look more like the man I least / Choose to resemble, bully, drunk, and beast. / Are you a warning, Father, or an example?" (*CP* 172, ll. 13–15). Another poem in which Gunn recalls the paternal, or rather the authority figure, and challenges it, is "Rites of Passage" (*Moly*). Cf. Chapter VI.

5. Religious motifs recur in several poems, though the focus is always on the human dimension of the character, as in "Lazarus Not Raised" (*Fighting Terms*), "Jesus and His Mother," "Julian the Apostate," "St Martin and the Beggar" (*The Sense of Movement*), "In Santa Maria del Popolo" (*My Sad Captains*), and "Expression" (*The Passages of Joy*). In some poems of the later collections Gunn confronts, sometimes ironically, the theme of institutionalized religion, as in "The Miracle" (*The Passages of Joy*), in "Secret Heart" (*The Man with Night Sweats*), where the image of a dying friend is compared to Christ on the cross, and in "The Antagonism" (*Boss Cupid*).

6. The choice of a military life, of a uniform, as the product of a troubled youth marked by abandonment and violence, is at the core of "A Los Angeles Childhood," which, after evoking a chilly picture of domestic violence, ends with the lines, "First chance I got, I enlisted, / She's still alive. / I don't go to see her" (*BC* 62, ll. 34–36).

7. Cf. *Thom Gunn in Conversation with James Campbell*, p. 57.

8. *Ibid.*, p. 20.

9. Alan Bold, *Thom Gunn and Ted Hughes* (Edinburgh: Olivery & Boyd, 1976) p. 9.

10. *Thom Gunn in Conversation with James Campbell*, p. 33.

11. Billy Lux, "'It's the instances that hit you': Billy Lux interviews a poet of the century," *The Gay and Lesbian Review Worldwide* 7 (3), 2000, p. 41.

12. Graham Fawcett, "Thom Gunn's Castle," interview of 4 March 1986, BBC Radio 3, p. 4.

13. *Thom Gunn in Conversation with James Campbell*, p. 22.

14. W.I. Scobie, "Gunn in America: A Conversation in San Francisco with Thom Gunn," *London Magazine* 17 (6), 1977, p. 8.

15. Eliotic references resound in many of Gunn's poems. For example, in "The Geyser" (*Jack Straw's Castle*) the line "Like a beginning, also like an end" (*CP* 241, l. 14) recalls one of the motifs of *Four Quartets*. There is also the short poem "Listening to Jefferson Airplane" (*Moly*): "The music comes and goes on the wind," (*CP* 211, l. 1), which echoes the lines "In the room the women come and go / Talking of Michelangelo" in *The Love Song of J. Alfred Prufrock*. Cf. T.S. Eliot, *Selected Poems* (London: Faber, 1954) p. 11, ll. 13–14. Regarding Eliot's influence, Gunn says: "I read *The Waste Land* till I got tired of it.... I wrote a series of really dreadful poems that nobody ever saw, luckily, about old men shuffling through dead leaves. They were very Eliotian in feeling. I don't know why I wrote them. I suppose I was embodying what I thought was some kind of poetic fashion." *Thom Gunn in Conversation with James Campbell*, p. 31.

16. *Ibid.*, p. 54.

17. Appendix, pp. 162–63.

18. *Thom Gunn in Conversation with James Campbell*, p. 30.

19. "He [Yvor Winters] acted as a fertilizing agent, and opened the way to many poets I had known little of — most immediately Williams and Stevens" (*OP* 176).

20. Thom Gunn, "Introduction," Yvor Winters, *Selected Poems* (New York: The Library of America, 2003) p. xxvi.

21. W.I. Scobie, "Gunn in America," p. 9. On Winters' attitude towards certain poets and movements (especially Modernism, whose roots in irrationalism he harshly criticized), Clive Wilmer writes: "There is much in his correspondence to persuade us that Winters was a warm, generous, humorous man, public-spirited, egalitarian and highly principled. But he was also capable of a bluntness that verged on brutality and was not always above plain bullying.... His criticism is therefore most often at fault when he judges in accordance with his own preoccupations. Nothing is less to his credit, for example, than his overestimation of poets he taught himself." Clive Wilmer, Review of R.L. Barth (ed.), *The Selected Letters of Yvor Winters*, *TLS*, 22 June 2001, p. 11–12. By the same author see also "Definition and Flow: A Personal Reading of Thom Gunn," *PN Review* 5 (3), 1978, pp. 53–54. Christopher Ricks states that "Winters' hostility to pseudo-reference in the work of 'the experimental school in American poetry' moved him, mistakenly, to hostility or indifference towards allusion. Because he deplores pseudo-reference, and because the great modern master of pseudo-reference, Eliot, is also a master of allusion (allusion moreover being, for Winters, reference merely), Winters is led to subjugate allusion in the most extreme way, by pretending that it does not exist." Christopher Ricks, "Unacknowledged legislators. How Yvor Winters alluded in his verse to poets he disparaged in his prose," *TLS*, 22 June 2001, p. 15. On Gunn and Winters see also Langdon Hammer, "The American Poetry of Thom Gunn and

Geoffrey Hill," in Steve Clark and Mark Ford (eds), *Something We Have That They Don't: British and American Poetic Relations since 1925* (Iowa City: University of Iowa Press, 2004) pp. 118–36.

22. John Haffenden, *Viewpoints: Poets in Conversation with John Haffenden* (London: Faber, 1981) p. 38.

23. Cf. *Ibid.*, pp. 28–29.

24. *Ibid.*, pp. 29–30.

25. *Ibid.*, p. 28.

26. The verb phrase "to come out" has three meanings here: literally, "come out in the cold," figuratively, "face reality," and "openly declare your homosexuality."

27. W.I. Scobie, "Gunn in America," p. 6.

28. *Thom Gunn Talks to A. Alvarez*, interview of 20 July 1964, BBC Radio 3, p. 1.

29. Clive Wilmer, "Thom Gunn: The Art of Poetry LXXII," *Paris Review* 135, 1995, p. 159. In an interview with Billy Lux Gunn remembers that "he [Winters] was a difficult man, but a very lovable man. It got back to me that a student once asked him: 'Is Thom Gunn a homosexual?' Winters slowly withdrew his pipe and answered: 'Yes, I'm afraid he is.'" Billy Lux, "It's the instances that hit you," p. 42.

30. "A few years ago I came across a reference to myself as an Anglo-American poet and I thought: 'Yes, that's what I am. I'm an Anglo-American poet'" (*SL* 218). In an interview granted to the author, the poet put it this way: "To some extent I remain English always, but I like it when somebody calls me an Anglo-American poet; that's what I am, an *Anglo-American poet*. I'm not English. I'm not really an English poet any longer, and I'm not an American poet either." Appendix, p. 167.

31. *Thom Gunn Talks to A. Alvarez*, p. 4.

32. "Thom Gunn at Sixty," ed. Clive Wilmer, *PN Review* 16 (2), 1989; "Thom Gunn at Seventy," *Agenda* 37 (2–3), 1999.

33. "When Ted Hughes and Philip Larkin died, they made it to the headlines of the quality press and the TV and radio news. Gunn did not. Hughes and Larkin, of course, have many great qualities. One thinks of the sheer animal power of Hughes, especially in his early work, or Larkin's poignancy, wit and immaculate ear. Gunn, too, had his share of such virtues, but with many more in reserve." Clive Wilmer, "Letter from Cambridge: The Tribe of Gunn," *PN Review* 31 (2), 2004, p. 11. In summer 2005, a year after his death, *The Threepenny Review* published "A Symposium on Thom Gunn: W.S. Di Piero, Daisy Fried, Mike Kitay, Wendy Lesser, Philip Levine, Robert Pinsky, Jim Powell, Oliver Sacks, Peter Spagnuolo, and Joshua Weiner."

34. Cf. Tyler B. Hoffman, "Representing AIDS: Thom Gunn and the Modalities of Verse," *South Atlantic Review* 65 (2) 2000, pp. 13–39; Deborah Landau, "'How to Live: What to Do': The Poetics and Politics of AIDS," *American Literature* 68 (1) 1996, pp. 193–221; Steven Saylor, "Thom Gunn in Love in the Time of AIDS," *San Francisco Review of Books* 16 (4), 1992, pp. 14–16.

35. Lidia De Michelis, *La poesia di Thom Gunn*, p. 168, writes: "the nine articles on which he collaborated for the 'Yale Review' are mostly negative, and express the desolation of a poet who looks at a rather dismal panorama with vision embittered by exasperation."

36. Thom Gunn, "Introduction," *Ezra Pound. Poems Selected by Thom Gunn* (London: Faber, 2000) p. xvi.

37. "His politics were abhorrent, but if we forgive Hazlitt for his admiration of Napoleon then we should be prepared to do likewise to Pound for his delusions about Mussolini. And at least he apologized for his anti–Semitism at the last minute, which is more than his genteeler contemporaries did." Thom Gunn, "Introduction," *Ezra Pound. Poems Selected by Thom Gunn*, p. xvi.

38. Clive Wilmer, *Poets Talking: The 'Poet of the Month' Interviews from BBC Radio 3* (Manchester: Carcanet, 1994) pp. 6–7. See also August Kleinzahler, "Diary," *London Review of Books*, 4 November 2004, pp. 46–47.

39. "I don't really see a new movement of concentrated energy, like the Beats in the midfifties, for example. There was a real impulse in Snyder and Ginsberg and Corso and their friends. They really thought they had hold of something." Lee Bartlett, *Talking Poetry. Conversations in the Workshop with Contemporary Poets* (Albuquerque: University of New Mexico Press, 1987) p. 94.

40. Appendix, p. 172.

41. Consider, for instance, *Lyrical Ballads* by Wordsworth and Coleridge, Wilde's Aestheticism, and, in more recent years, the Beat Generation.

42. Most of the criticism of the fifties, sixties, and seventies, especially British, described Thom Gunn as "a poet of violence," associating him with Ted Hughes. Regarding the comparison, Hughes said: "Thom Gunn's is the poetry of tenderness, not violence" (*Thom Gunn in Conversation with James Campbell*, p. 26). "The violence in my poems is of a different sort & the whole basis of my poems is as different from his [Gunn's] as it well could be. He thinks of his poems as concise meditative interpretations of the dilemmas of modern life. I think of mine as the spontaneous self-creation of animals, a creature which is also a god which is a manifestation of the divine force. His poems are thoughtful essays, mine are objects, or incidents in a continuous state of happening." Ted Hughes,

"Letter to Gerald Hughes," 1958, Woddruffe Library, Emory University, Mss 854, ff7.

43. "syllabic verse, a form in which arbitrary structure imposes discipline—felt more by the writer than the reader—upon rhythms as unpredictable as those of free verse." Clive Wilmer, "Definition and Flow," p. 52. The English line is primarily a stressed one; its rhythm is thus determined by the number of accents more than the number of syllables. According to Clive Wilmer, "the number of syllables determines the length of the line but, except in the matter of line-ending, plays no part in the creation of its rhythm. It is a discipline observed by the poet, but it is hardly audible to the reader, though some readers claim to be able to hear it." Clive Wilmer, Letter to Stefania Michelucci, 22 January 2005.

44. *Thom Gunn in Conversation with James Campbell*, pp. 44–45.

45. Clive Wilmer, "Thom Gunn: The Art of Poetry LXXII," p. 165. According to Wilmer, "the poets by whose example his [Gunn's] free verse has developed are, notably H.D., the young Yvor Winters, and, above all, William Carlos Williams. Behind these writers stands Ezra Pound, whom Gunn considers the greatest modern." Clive Wilmer, "Definition and Flow," p. 52.

46. See the critical essays dedicated to the two poets, among them David Holbrook, "The Cult of Hughes and Gunn: The Dangers of Poetical Fashion," *Poetry Review* 54 (2), 1963, pp. 167–83; Lance Lee, "Roots of Violence" [Review of Thom Gunn's *Jack Straw's Castle* and Ted Hughes' *Gaudete*], *Chicago Review* 30, 1978–79, pp. 108–16; and the volume by Alan Bold, *Thom Gunn and Ted Hughes*. See also Paul Giles, "From Myth to History: The Later Poetry of Thom Gunn and Ted Hughes," in James Acheson and Romana Huk (eds), *Contemporary British Poetry: Essays in Theory and Criticism* (Albany: State University of New York Press, 1996) pp. 143–73.

47. *Thom Gunn in Conversation with James Campbell*, p. 26.

48. Cf. Martin Dodsworth, "Thom Gunn: Negatives and Positives," *The Review* 18, 1968, pp. 46–61; William Hunt, "The Poem and the Photograph," *Poetry* 111 (6), 1968, pp. 405–07; and Chapter V in this book.

49. Unlike other collections, *Touch* was not included in *Collected Poems* of 1993, where Gunn distinguishes between "Misanthropos" (1965), originally published in *Touch*, and *Poems of the 1960s*, which contains components taken from *Touch* and from *Positives*. The fact that many poems of the sixties were not included in *Collected Poems* is explained by Clive Wilmer in terms of "'huge uncertainty' about what he [Gunn] was doing as he made the transition into free verse, [...] the poems 'didn't cohere' into a collection, but by the time Gunn wrote *Moly* (1971), 'although it is not in free verse, it evidently benefited from the work he'd been doing.'" Robert Potts, "Thom Gunn: Moving Voice," *The Guardian*, 27 September 2003, p. 23. *Touch* signals a moment of transition in Gunn's artistic career, when he gradually frees himself from his earlier style and slowly proceeds towards new forms. For John Miller, "'Misanthropos' as a whole is a prosodic *tour de force*, utilizing syllabic verse, rhymed couplets, quatrains, and occasional blank verse for its different sections, and thus lacking any metrical continuity or rationale. Each section, in effect, manifests Gunn's willful imposition of a specific rhyme scheme and a recognizable metric pattern upon its material." John Miller, "The Stipulative Imagination of Thom Gunn," *Iowa Review* 4 (1), 1973, p. 71.

50. "There's a lot of Camus behind 'Misanthropos,' the long poem. It's a pervading feeling: I don't know if it comes in specific parts, maybe in the action after the other people turn up, when the man finds that he isn't alone. I was rereading Camus in the early 1960s when I wrote the poem." John Haffenden, *Viewpoints*, p. 44. See also Merle E. Brown, "Inner Community in Thom Gunn's 'Misanthropos'" and "The Authentic Duplicity of Thom Gunn's Recent Poetry," in *Double Lyric: Divisiveness and Communal Creativity in Recent English Poetry* (London and Henley: Routledge & Kegan Paul, 1980) pp. 126–45.

51. W.I. Scobie, "Gunn in America," p. 12.

52. *Ibid*.

53. *Thom Gunn in Conversation with James Campbell*, p. 39.

54. "I was extraordinarily dishonest with myself in my late teens: all my sexual fantasies were about men, but I assumed I was straight. I think it was partly because homosexuality was such a forbidden subject in those days. [...] I didn't want to be effeminate either; I didn't think that was me." *Thom Gunn in Conversation with James Campbell*, p. 19.

55. Stephen Romer, "Thom Gunn: a story of hero-worship and beyond...," *Agenda* 37 (2–3), 1999, p. 35.

56. Two poems of the eighties provide evidence of Gunn's drug-taking, "Smoking Pot on the Bus" and "'1975'" (*Poems from the 1980s*), in which the drug is considered part of a game, an escape from everyday monotony ("I would coast the hotel-corridors / looking for drug-and-wrestling buddies" *CP* 397, ll. 8–9), or as a challenge, somewhat lacking in conviction, to institutions ("what, now, in the eighties! / yet a light vexed whiff / noticeably was travelling up / the bus till the driver / [...] / ... told them / temperately, fairly, / 'Throw away that joint' / so they

did," *CP* 395, ll. 1–4, 7–10). The communal atmosphere and experiences of the seventies are recalled in "Saturday Night" (*Boss Cupid*) but without any nostalgia; on the contrary, the memory becomes a kind of nightmare: "This was the Barracks, this the divine rage / In 1975, that time is gone / [...] / What hopeless hopefulness. I watch, I wait —/ The embraces slip, and nothing seems to stay / [...] / ... Beds crack, capsize, / And spill their occupants on the floor to drown. / Walls darken with the mold, or is it rash? / At length the baths catch fire and then burn down, / And blackened beams dam up the bays of ash" (*BC* 45–46, ll. 17–18, 31–32, 40–44). For Langdon Hammer, "The vision 'Saturday Night' turns out to grant is a vision of the end of visions. Yet Gunn manages not to repudiate, nor really even mourn the passing of, 'our community of the carnal heart.'" Langdon Hammer, "Thom Gunn and the Cool Queer Tales of Cupid," pp. 123–24.

57. Stephen Romer, "Thom Gunn: a story of hero-worship and beyond...," p. 35.

58. Clive Wilmer, *Poets Talking*, p. 2.

59. Clive Wilmer, "Definition and Flow," p. 51.

60. The title *The Passages of Joy* is taken from a work of Samuel Johnson, "The Vanity of Human Wishes" (1749), which Gunn cites in the epigraph to the poem "Transients and Residents": "'*Time hovers o'er, impatient to destroy, / And shuts up all the Passages of Joy*'" (*CP* 374).

61. Cf. Gregory Woods, "Affectionate Gifts," *PN Review* 133, May-June 2000, pp. 67–68.

62. In the course of his artistic career, Gunn received much recognition, such as the *Guggenheim Fellowship* in 1971, the *Forward Prize for Poetry* in 1992, the *Lenore Marshall/Nation Poetry Prize* and the *Mac Arthur Fellowship* in 1993, and the *Lambda Literary Award for Gay Men's Poetry* in 1995.

63. John Ezard, "Poetic Justice for Bainbridge and Gunn," *The Guardian*, 28 March 2003, p. 17. See also Robert Potts, "Thom Gunn: Moving voice," p. 20.

64. Clive Wilmer, "Thom Gunn: Poet of the modern city who exchanged London for San Francisco," *The Independent*, 29 April 2004, p. 34.

Chapter II

1. The collection *Moly* grew out of the experience of "artificial paradise" through taking LSD. It is written in traditional metre. Most of the elegies dedicated to Gunn's friends who died of AIDS (*The Man with Night Sweats*) also use traditional forms.

2. Images of the double and split self are frequent in Gunn's early poems, as we will see later. Consider, for example, "The Wound" ("My own commander was my enemy," *CP* 3, l. 17) and "The Secret Sharer" ("...I saw that some uncertain hand / Had touched the curtains. Mine? I wondered ...," *CP* 13, ll. 14–15).

3. The figure of an actor who is incapable of forming sincere human relationships, whose look ("...like a star, that cannot see") indiscriminately reflects joy and pain, is at the heart of "Looks" (*The Man with Night Sweats*): "And it's a genuine talent he engages / In playing this one character, mean, small, / But driven like Othello by his rages" (*CP* 43–44, ll. 1–3, 30–32).

4. "The self, then, as a performed character, is not an organic thing that has a specific location, whose fundamental fate is to be born, to mature, and to die; it is a dramatic effect arising diffusely from a scene that is presented." Erving Goffman, *The Presentation of Self in Everyday Life* (London: Penguin, 1990) p. 245. In the poem "Death's Door" (*The Man with Night Sweats*), dedicated to friends who died of AIDS, Gunn puts on a true performance, in which the living are actors and the dead are spectators who watch a show on TV ("Sit down in groups and watch TV," *CP* 485, l. 6)—so boring that it becomes irritating ("Their boredom turning to impatience," *CP* 485, l. 24)—of those who remain alive: "Thus they watch friend and relative / And life here as they think it is /— In black and white, repetitive / As situation comedies" (*CP* 485, ll. 17–20).

5. "'At the Barriers': the street fair this commemorates took place in August, 1988, in San Francisco. At least two of Ben Jonson's masques were composed in connection with 'barriers' (which for him meant an exhibition of tilting). I use barriers in a modern sense but retain the associations of a masque" (*CP* 491–92).

6. The idea of the tensions and difficulty of relationships, in which knowledge and mutual discovery rarely occur, and then usually only in reference to past events, remains in later poems. Consider "The Differences" (*The Man with Night Sweats*), and "Rapallo" (*Boss Cupid*), in which the desired union with the lover gives place to a nostalgic memory of embraces long past. In "The Problem" (*Boss Cupid*), the mutual "give-and-take" with a boy ("One of Boss Cupid's red- / haired errand boys," *BC* 23, ll. 16–17), turns out to be illusory since the lover's true passion is far beyond the sexual relationship ("his true / Passion cyphered in chalk beyond my reach" *BC* 24, ll. 40–41). Even in legends of the past—as in "Philemon and Baucis" (*The Man with Night Sweats*), whose characters are a traditional symbol of conjugal love—relationship is seen as conflictual, and is rendered eternal and apparently perfect only by projection onto a myth: "...They put unease behind

them / A long time back, a long time back forgot / How each woke separate through the pale grey night, / A long time back forgot the days when each /— Riding the other's nervous exuberance —/ Knew the slow thrill of learning how to love" (*CP* 416, ll. 13-18).

7. John Mander, "In Search of Commitment: The Poetry of Thom Gunn," in *The Writer and Commitment* (Westport, Conn.: Greenwood Press, 1975) p. 155.

8. "Carnal Knowledge" is the opening poem of the first edition of *Fighting Terms* (1954); "The Wound" opens later editions.

9. The impact of "To his Coy Mistress" on Gunn in noticeable also in the poem "In Trust" (*Boss Cupid*): "We'll hug each other while we can, / Work or stray while we must." (*BC* 99, ll. 34-35), which evokes the lines: "Now let us sport us while we may; / And now, like am'rous birds of prey." Andrew Marvell, *The Poems and Letters of Andrew Marvell*, ed. H.M. Margoliouth, vol. I (Oxford: Clarendon Press, 1927) p. 27, ll. 37-38.

10. For A.E. Dyson, "'Modes of Pleasure' ... is a remarkably frank poem about lust. Of modern poets, only Yeats and Graves have written with entire success on this difficult theme. Eliot's passages in *The Waste Land*, though technically very fine, are too assimilated to a palpable design on us to earn the highest praise. Thom Gunn writes of lust as a fact of mature experience, though inside an accepted promiscuity. The callousness and brevity, the restlessness and the satisfactions, are all evoked, in an economy of style that appears to offer a direct access to emotional truth." A.E. Dyson, "*My Sad Captains* by Thom Gunn," *Critical Quarterly*, 1961, p. 379. The theme of induced sex, reduced to a physical mechanism, projected on a scene of urban degradation, emerges in "Tenderloin" (*The Man with Night Sweats*): "Grease it well / with its own foul / lubricant / / Against the grit / of its own sharp corners / scrape it to orgasm" (*CP* 442, ll. 46-51). In "Nights with the Speed Bros." (*Boss Cupid*) also, the orgiastic experience leaves the speaker unsatisfied: "'...I gave up sleep for this?' / Dead leaves replaced the secret life of gold" (*BC* 34, ll. 15-16).

11. Lidia De Michelis (*La poesia di Thom Gunn*, p. 37) observes that the refrain of the poem "reminds one of a Yeatsian form of *pastiche* and indicates the fundamental distrust upon which this relationship rests."

12. The drying-up of passion through mental processes which erode its essence is at the heart of two short poems in *The Man with Night Sweats*. In the first, "Barren Leaves," whose title is taken from a famous line of Wordsworth's "The Tables Turned": "Close up those barren leaves" (used by Aldous Huxley in the novel *Those Barren Leaves*, 1925), Gunn denounces the castrating effect of intellectual activity upon the expression of passion: "Wet dreams, wet dreams, in libraries congealing" (*CP* 449, l. 2). The second, meaningfully entitled "Jamesian," constitutes, in the space of two very short lines, a criticism of the exasperating intellectualism of the American writer Henry James.

13. In "Aubade" (*Boss Cupid*)— the title and theme, the separation of two lovers at dawn, recall a tradition that was carried over from courtly poetry to metaphysical poetry — the intimacy achieved during the night lessens at sunrise, thus emphasizing the separation between the couple: "Already / you turn away, thoughts / on the future" (*BC* 78, ll. 11-13).

14. A negative image of a woman is also present in "Enough" (*Boss Cupid*), in which Gunn draws, with some irony, a portrait of a divorced middle-aged woman: "Here she lay sour, unneeding and unneeded, / Like a divorcee, like an aging rabbit / On the stale straw, in its hutch. Enough, enough" (*BC* 31, ll. 22-24).

15. In the early poems Gunn uses, like Auden before him, the generic "you" to refer to a male lover ("I referred to the loved one, who was usually Mike, as 'you,'" *Thom Gunn in Conversation with James Campbell*, p. 26). Where there is an explicit reference to a woman, as in "Carnal Knowledge," the poet does not hide the sexual identity of the auditor, addressing himself directly to a female character.

16. Only at the end of the poem, after a relationship of mutual challenge, of union within separation, casting off the protective shell (especially the man) that limits expression of sensation and intimate feelings, do they manage to give themselves to each other:

(He began to sweat.)

And they melted one
into the other
      forthwith
like the way the Saône
joins the Rhône at Lyon [*CP* 281, ll. 49-54].

17. Alan Sinfield, "Thom Gunn in San Francisco: An Interview," *Critical Survey* 2 (2), 1990, p. 224.

18. Cf. Alan Bold, *Thom Gunn and Ted Hughes*, p. 17.

19. *Thom Gunn in Conversation with James Campbell*, p. 24.

20. Cf. Lidia De Michelis, *La poesia di Thom Gunn*, p. 35.

21. The inability to break the chains of isolation reappears in the poem "In the Tank" (*Touch*); the speaker is a condemned man, whose existence is by now deprived of any vital impulse, reduced to a vicious cycle, as suggested by the obsessive repetition of the word "re-enter" in the last verse: "The jail contained a tank, the tank contained / A box, a mere sus-

pension, at the centre, / Where there was nothing left to understand, / And where he must re-enter and re-enter." (*CP* 173, ll. 17–20).

22. *Jack Straw's Castle* is the name of a London pub. Jack Straw is also the hero of the Peasants' Revolt which occurred during Richard II's reign. Gunn uses the term especially in its meaning of a man without substance.

23. "I do recall hearing Gunn say that the castle refers partly to the body at a reading in Cambridge." Clive Wilmer, letter to Stefania Michelucci, 13 December 2004.

24. Charles Manson (1934–), founder of a commune in the sixties, instigated panic in a rich Los Angeles neighbourhood inhabited by VIPs and prominent persons such as Roman Polanski, whose companion Sharon Tate (then eight months pregnant) he killed along with other guests. He was tried in 1971 and given the death penalty. In the following months, California abolished the death penalty. Charles Manson is still serving a life sentence. This is no simple killer: Charles Manson is "the prophet" (he likes to be called Jesus), the guru of a sect whose mission was to kill famous people.

25. "I am the man on the rack. / I am the man who puts the man on the rack. / I am the man who watches the man who puts the man on the rack" (*CP* 274, 7, ll. 1–3).

26. "We should remember too that one of the poets Gunn most values is Thomas Hardy. In a lecture on Hardy he praises him for the 'precision and vividness,' with which he records particulars." Clive Wilmer, "Definition and Flow," p. 51.

27. The poet shows traces of the influence of the French philosopher Albert Camus. Gunn writes in his introduction to Fulke Greville poems, "Camus called life in a temporal world without sanction 'absurd,' but Camus did not discover this fact: he merely put more abruptly what many men have noticed. Interestingly enough, Camus also used the image of Littleease (*le malconfort*), for the state of a man constrained by a sense of guilt in a world where there is no god and thus where there can be no redemption for that guilt.... What is important is not so much the perception of absurdity, which to a certain kind of thinker is inevitable, as how one conducts oneself after making that perception. Camus's great contribution is less in the analysis of the sickness into which we are born than in the determination to live with that sickness, fully acknowledging it and accepting it as the basis for our actions" (*OP* 67).

28. Lidia De Michelis, *La poesia di Thom Gunn*, p. 34.

29. Martin Dodsworth, "Thom Gunn: Poetry as Action and Submission," in Martin Dodsworth (ed.), *The Survival of Poetry* (London: Faber, 1970) p. 209.

30. The vitality as well as the freedom of the world of Nature in contrast to the absence of liberty felt by human beings, oppressed not only by the possibility of choice, but by morals and the cultural codes of social communication, is also the theme of the two poems about the world of animals; for example, "Apartment Cats" (*Moly*) ("She abruptly rises, knowing well / How to stalk off in wise indifference" *CP* 194, ll. 17–18), "Cat Island" (*Boss Cupid*) ("They lack, too, / the prostitute's self-pity, / being beyond pity. / And we lack / what they have" *BC* 33, ll. 36–40), "The Life of the Otter" (*The Man with Night Sweats*), whose metrical structure reflects the surprising vivacity and energy that the otter expresses in its movements:

The small but long brown beast reaches from
    play
Through play
       to play
           play not as relaxation
Or practice or escape but all there is:
Activity   (hunt, procreation, feeding)
Functional but as if gratuitous (*CP* 429, ll. 13–19), and "The Aquarium" (*The Man with Night Sweats*), in which Gunn lets two dolphins speak ("Look at these men ...: / If only they / Would free themselves in play, / As we do even in this confining tank" *CP* 431, ll. 9–12). This poem, along with "The Life of the Otter," echoes certain verses of D.H. Lawrence about the total naturalness and extraordinary life force of animals in contrast to human inhibitions. See, for example, "Lizard": "If men were as much men as lizards are lizards / they'd be worth looking at." D.H. Lawrence, *Pansies* (London: Martin Secker, 1929) p. 116, ll. 5–6.

31. Nomad figures or wanderers appear in many of Gunn's poems. Consider "The Discovery of the Pacific" (*Moly*), where the journey assumes a truly cathartic value, and "Hitching into Frisco" (*Jack Straw's Castle*): "For all I leave behind / There is a new song grown" (*CP* 248, ll. 19–20).

32. In later editions of *Fighting Terms*; the first edition (1954) opens with "Carnal Knowledge."

33. Colin Falck, "Uncertain Violence: Colin Falck on the Poetry of Thom Gunn," *New Review* 3, 1976–77, p. 38.

34. Jay Parini, "Rule and Energy: The Poetry of Thom Gunn," *Massachusetts Review* 23 (1), 1982, p. 135.

35. Clive Wilmer, "'Those Wounds Heal Ill': Thom Gunn in 1954 and 1992," *Agenda* 37 (2–3), 1999, p. 20.

36. *Ibid.*, pp. 18, 21.

37. Anonymous, "Thom Gunn," *The Telegraph*, 29 April 2004, online version.

38. Ian Hamilton, "Four Conversations," p. 69.

39. "I wrote it when I was at Cambridge and I had been reading *Troilus and Cressida*." Ian Hamilton, "Four Conversations," p. 68.
40. John Mander, "In Search of Commitment," pp. 177–78.
41. James Michie, "Fighting Terms by Thom Gunn," *London Magazine*, 1955, p. 99.
42. Clive Wilmer, "Definition and Flow," p. 56.
43. Peter Swaab, "*The Man with Night Sweats* and the Idea of Political Poetry," *Agenda* 37 (2–3), 1999, p. 111.
44. This is a work by several authors (the most famous of whom is Thomas Sackville), *chronicle poems* about figures of British history (especially those of the fifteenth century), in which men killed by catastrophes reflect on their own destinies in poetic monologues from beyond the grave.
45. For John Miller, "The Stipulative Imagination of Thom Gunn," p. 58, "Poets in Elizabethan and early Jacobean England ... could relate to a social and conceptual order, a framework of transcendent beliefs that incorporated, clarified, and superseded the fluctuating violence and egotism of the age. The chief tension and excitement in 'A Mirror for Poets' exist in this dialectic between historical disorder and Platonic transcendence."
46. *The Poet Speaks*, Record 5: Ted Hughes, Peter Porter, Thom Gunn, Sylvia Plath. Ed. Peter Orr (London: Argo Record Company Ltd, 1965, RG 455).

Chapter III

1. For example, the act of killing the bride's father for insulting the family honor of the groom, and nevertheless proceeding to marry the girl. If the hero had not vindicated the insult, he would have lost the respect of his wife, even though his act was monstrous. In the Corneillian world, passion is always subordinated to virtue and honor.
2. "Thom Gunn Writes ...," *Poetry Book Society Bulletin* No. 14, 1957, p. 1.
3. Lawrence R. Ries, "Thom Gunn: The Retreat from Violence," in *Wolf Masks: Violence in Contemporary Poetry* (London: Kennikat Press, 1977) p. 71.
4. John Press, *Rule and Energy: Trends in British Poetry since the Second World War* (London: Oxford University Press, 1963) p. 193.
5. John Mander, "In Search of Commitment," pp. 160–61.
6. Ian Hamilton, "Four Conversations," p. 66.
7. *Thom Gunn in Conversation with James Campbell*, p. 32. Gunn's attraction to strong and vigorous masculine models is clear in all of his work, and expressed in these lines of "Letters from Manhattan" (*Boss Cupid*): "I seek a potent mix / of toughness and tenderness in men. / The paradigm / being the weeping wrestler" (*BC* 72, 4, ll. 1–4).
8. Stephen Spender, *Collected Poems 1928–1953* (London: Faber, 1940) pp. 30, 47.
9. Martin Dodsworth, "Thom Gunn: Poetry as Action and Submission," pp. 197–98.
10. A GI is an American soldier.
11. Awareness of the failure of action as an end in itself reappears in some poems of the later collections, such as "Fever" (*Jack Straw's Castle*), in which Gunn, describing the nocturnal search for a partner, focuses on the defeat of the profligate and uncontrolled desire of the protagonist: "Impatient all the foggy day for night / You plunged into the bar eager to loot. / [...] / ... If you've lost / It doesn't matter tomorrow. Sleep well. Heaven knows / Feverish people need more sleep than most / And need to learn all they can about repose" (*CP* 235, ll. 1–2, 22–25).
12. The idea that animals and angels are not plagued by the uncertainty, due to the schism between intellect and instinct, which troubles human beings, also informs "Wrestling" (*Jack Straw's Castle*): "a messenger / loping, compact / in familiar places / he moves with that / separate grace, that / sureness of foot / you know in / animal and angel" *CP* 261, ll. 34–41), and "To a Friend in Time of Trouble" (*The Man with Night Sweats*), where Gunn compares the disorientation of the friend with the vivacity and naturalness of the gestures, apparently cruel, of beasts of prey: "The certainty, the ease with which it draws / Its arc on blue ... Soon the protesting shriek, / The gorging from the breast, the reddened beak, / The steadying claw withdrawn at last. You know / It is not cruel, it is not human, though / You cringe who would not feel surprised to find / Such lacerations made by mind on mind" (*CP* 408, ll. 18–24).
13. Terry Eagleton, "Myth and History in Recent Poetry," in *British Poetry since 1960*, ed. Michael Schmidt and Grevel Lindop (Oxford: Carcanet Press, 1972) p. 236.
14. Cf. Erich Fromm, *Escape from Freedom* (New York: Owl Books, 1994 [1941]). See also Lidia De Michelis, *La poesia di Thom Gunn*, pp. 51–53.
15. *Thom Gunn in Conversation with James Campbell*, p. 29. From the film *The Wild One* by Laszlo Benedek he takes the poem's epigraph, 'Man, you gotta Go,' which was not included in *Collected Poems*. Cf. *The Sense of Movement* (London: Faber, 1957) p. 11.
16. Alan Bold, *Thom Gunn and Ted Hughes*, p. 28.

17. Thom Gunn, *The Sense of Movement*, p. 36.
18. Alan Bold, *Thom Gunn and Ted Hughes*, p. 31.
19. Edward Lucie-Smith, "The Tortured Yearned as Well: An Enquiry into Themes of Cruelty in Current Verse," *Critical Quarterly* 4 (1), 1962, p. 35.
20. Alan Brownjohn, "The Poetry of Thom Gunn," p. 52.
21. "That's ['The Beaters'] a very unpleasant poem. I was trying to be like Baudelaire, wanting to shock people." *Thom Gunn in Conversation with James Campbell*, p. 33.
22. Thom Gunn, *The Sense of Movement*, p. 36.
23. This is one of the first poems, with "Vox Humana," in which Gunn uses syllabics.
24. The speaker is a male prostitute waiting for a client. The title "Market at Turk" refers to the intersection of two streets in San Francisco frequented by gay men looking for a partner.
25. Neil Powell, "Thom Gunn: A Pierglass for Poets," in *Carpenters of Light: Some Contemporary English Poets* (Manchester: Carcanet New Press, 1979) p. 28.
26. The line "revolt into a style" (for Gunn "[the] only one good line in the poem," *Thom Gunn in Conversation with James Campbell*, p. 29) was used by George Melly for the title of his book *Revolt into Style: The Pop Arts in Britain* (1971).
27. Neil Corcoran, *English Poetry since 1940*, p. 107.
28. Ian Hamilton, "Four Conversations," p. 67.
29. As mentioned earlier, Gunn had in mind "Marvell's mower poems" when writing his poems on motorcyclists.
30. W.B. Yeats, "An Irish Airman Foresees His Death," in *Selected Poetry*, ed. A.N. Jeffares (London: Macmillan, 1966) p. 69, l. 11.
31. The use of a refrain unrelated to the metrical scheme is typical of Yeats. This is also the case in Gunn's "Jesus and his Mother" up to the last two stanzas. A Yeatsian trace appears also in the line "I know you know I know you know I know," which ends, though alternating the initial subject (You know / I know), each stanza of "Carnal Knowledge." A similar refrain ("Not now, not now, not now") is also present in "Memoirs of the World" ("Misanthropos") at the end of each stanza.
32. Martin Dodsworth, "Thom Gunn: Poetry as Action and Submission," p. 195.
33. W.I. Scobie, "Gunn in America," p. 9.
34. The process of disintegration to which every living being is subject, seen with lucid detachment as the same essence of universal life, and certainly no stranger to mankind, is at the heart of "Yellow Pitcher Plant" (*The Man with Night Sweats*), in which, with cold scientific language Gunn reveals the decomposition of a fly inside a flower:
— pool that digests protein —
to become mere
chitinous exoskeleton,
leftovers

of a sated petal

an enzyme's cruelty [*CP* 439–40, ll. 21–26]. The death of the insect irresistibly attracted to the flower, a death trap, is symbol of the destiny of Gunn's friends who died from AIDS.
35. Lawrence R. Ries, "Thom Gunn: The Retreat from Violence," p. 59.
36. *Ibid*.
37. Thom Gunn, *The Sense of Movement*, p. 52.
38. The image of the moon is reversed in "Hide and Seek" (*The Passages of Joy*) where the heavenly body appears as Mother Nature who embraces all creation when dusk falls: "The crescent moon rises / nine-tenths of it still hidden / but imperceptibly moving / below the moving stars / and hugging the earth" (*CP* 334, ll. 32–36).
39. The poem "Sunlight"—"It is as if the sun were infinite" (*CP* 223, l. 12), closes the collection.
40. Neil Powell, "Thom Gunn: A Pierglass for Poets," p. 31.
41. The themes of the interaction between art and life, and the metamorphosis, not only of reality, but also of the artist in poetic creation are at the core of "Words" (*Moly*), where Gunn reflects on ways of rendering lived experience through language: "I was still separate on the shadow's ground / But, charged with growth, was being altered, / Composing uncomposed" (*CP* 197, ll. 10–12).
42. Cf. T.S. Eliot, *Four Quartets* (London: Faber, 1944). The refrain closes, with a small variation ("I end my circle where I had begun" l. 8, "My circle's end is where I have begun" l. 32), the first and last stanzas of "A Plan of Self Subjection."
43. The use of the heroic couplet to which Gunn often has recourse in and after this collection recalls Yvor Winters' lessons. Winters found the rhymed couplet the most flexible of forms. Cf. Yvor Winters, *In Defense of Reason* (London: Routledge, 1960) p. 141.
44. The first is composed of eight lines, the second of sixteen, and the third of ten.
45. Alan Brownjohn, "The Poetry of Thom Gunn," pp. 51–52. In "The Clock" (*Poems from the 1960s*), the clock that impassively marks the passing of time, cruel testimony of existential angst, becomes a monster which makes the speaker its prisoner (in a "room like a cave," l. 1): "I wait upon the dark, I sit / Fearing the mon-

ster that I crave, / Fearing the mercy and the need for it" (*CP* 174, ll. 22–24).

46. The performance of passion becomes the stage for desire by means of the work of art (possession through writing): "I study possibility / Through rigid slats, or ordered verses," ll. 17–18) in "Venetian Blind" (*Poems from the 1980s*), in which the speaker, observing as in "The Corridor" the object of his desire ("...my neighbour's room next door"), creates a doubling of the object itself ("Slightly adjusting them to scan / The self-possession that is you, / Who cannot guess at what I do / Here, light-sliced, with another man" *CP* 392, ll. 2, 21–24).

47. The image of the corridor, this time "wall-less," recurs in "Small Plane in Kansas" (*The Passages of Joy*), in which the poet contemplates the world below until he becomes part of it, emerged within it, freed from his inhibitions, and transcends the dichotomy between intellect and instinct, in the life's flow which animates the surrounding universe: "Mastered by mastering, / I so much belong to the wind / I become of it, a gust / that flows, mindless for ever / along unmarked channel / and wall-less corridor..." (*CP* 330, ll. 20–25).

48. Cf. Erving Goffman, *The Presentation of Self in Everyday's Life*.

49. Cf. Werner Heisenberg, *Physical Principles of the Quantum Theory*, trans. into English by Carl Eckart and Frank C. Hoyt (Chicago: University of Chicago Press, 1930), and *Physics and Philosophy: The Revolution in Modern Science*, intro. by F.S.C. Northrop (New York: Prometheus Books, 1999 [1958]).

50. T.S. Eliot, *Selected Poems* (London: Faber, 1954) p. 13, l. 56.

51. Thom Gunn, *Touch* (London: Faber, 1967) pp. 16–17.

52. The many faces of the city (especially San Francisco in the later collections, which the poet describes in minute detail), its symphony of beauty and degradation, recur in all of Gunn's works; consider "San Francisco Streets" (*The Passages of Joy*), in which he describes the social climbing of a young man from the country who does not succeed in integrating himself completely ("I think I catch / Half-veiled uncertainty / In your expression," *CP* 356, ll. 44–46); "Night Taxi" (*The Passages of Joy*), with its directory of place names; and "An Invitation" (*The Man with Night Sweats*) as examples. The latter's subtitle is "from San Francisco to my brother"; in epistolary form, and colloquial tone, with Ben Jonson's "Inviting a Friend to Supper" as model, Gunn addresses his brother, alluding to the plurality of faces, to the immensity of details that enliven the city ("Or we can take the Ferry across the Bay / Scanning the washed views on our way / [...] / You'll watch the jobless side by side with whores / Setting a home up out of doors" (*CP* 411–12, ll. 19–20, 37–38). August Kleinzahler writes about San Francisco: "For Thom, the city seemed to exist as a complex of erotic sites, assignations, stews. Heterosexual males, in my experience, are without exception tedious and irritating, not to mention unreliable, on this subject. But Thom, on passing a bar or apartment or street corner (in one memorable instance a phone booth in a rather toney part of town) seemed cheerful and nostalgic in equal measure, and almost always had an amusing or interesting anecdote." August Kleinzahler, "Diary," p. 47. See also Peter Swaab, "*The Man with Night Sweats* and the Idea of Political Poetry."

53. Alan Bold, *Thom Gunn and Ted Hughes*, p. 32.

54. John Press, *Rule and Energy*, p. 194.

55. In the eighties and especially in *The Man with Night Sweats*, Gunn's attention is frequently turned to the world of nature, which no longer appears, as in the early poems, dominated by chaos, but animated by a life force unknown to humans. See "Fennel" (*Poems from the 1980s*), "The Life of the Otter," "Three for Children," and "Nasturtium" (*The Man with Night Sweats*).

56. Ian Hamilton, "Four Conversations," p. 66.

57. Clive Wilmer writes about "Iron Landscapes": "It is one of [Gunn's] best poems because ... it shows historical patterns growing from the matrices of feeling the landscape represents. It shows American society as based on the dialectic of permanence and change, the dialectic which determines the creative tensions of Gunn's poetry." Clive Wilmer, "Definition and Flow," p. 57.

58. The title refers to a register of the organ that produces a sound like the human voice.

59. Cf. Gianni Vattimo (ed.), *Heidegger. Saggi e discorsi* (Milano: Mursia, 1976) pp. 125–38.

60. Cf. Waltraud Mitgutsch, "Thom Gunn," *Salzburg Studies in English Literature* 27, 1974, pp. 170–99.

CHAPTER IV

1. William Shakespeare, *Antony and Cleopatra*, III. XIII.

2. John Fuller, "Thom Gunn," in *The Modern Writer: Essays from the Review*, ed. by Ian Hamilton (London: MacDonald, 1968) pp. 17–22.

3. Lawrence R. Ries, "Thom Gunn: The Retreat from Violence," pp. 61–62.

4. On Thom Gunn and Caravaggio see Neil

Powell, "Real Shadow: Gunn and Caravaggio"; Stefania Michelucci, "'The Large Gesture of Solitary Man': Thom Gunn and Caravaggio," in *Agenda* 37 (2–3), pp. 57–62 and 64–69; and Renzo S. Crivelli, "Un abbraccio disperato: Caravaggio e la poesia di Thom Gunn e Edward Lucie-Smith," in *Lo sguardo narrato. Letteratura e arti visive* (Rome: Carocci, 2003) pp. 39–53.

5. On Gunn's use of monosyllabic rhymes see Martin Dodsworth, "Gunn's Rhymes," *PN Review* 16 (2), 1989, pp. 33–34.

6. Gunn's attitude is reminiscent of Philip Larkin's, in a poem published in 1955, a few years before *My Sad Captains*, called "Church Going," in which Larkin reflects on the mysterious force that causes him to drop by a church and rest inside, performing rituals like leaving a small offering, while being fully aware not only of the loss of sacredness of the place, but also the future of decay and death to which it is inevitably subject ("...For, though I've no idea / What this accoutred frowsty barn is worth, / It pleases me to stand in silence here;"). Philip Larkin, "Church Going," in *Collected Poems*, ed. Anthony Thwaite (London: Faber, 1988) p. 98, ll. 52–54.

7. Cf. *Acts of the Apostles*, 9. 10.

8. In a letter to Mr. D.G. Kehl (9 October 1971), Gunn wrote: "The Venus I cannot find, I have a strange feeling I was misremembering the 'Bacchus,' where the model is so effeminate that he could well be a girl."

9. Their communal actions associate them paradoxically with the boys in "On the Move," as if Gunn were preparing the ground for a re-measurement of the heroes in his early work.

10. Alan Bold, *Thom Gunn and Ted Hughes*, pp. 36–37.

11. *Ibid*.

12. P.R. King, "A courier after identity: The poetry of Thom Gunn," in *Nine Contemporary Poets: A Critical Introduction* (London: Methuen, 1979) p. 93.

13. Franco La Cecla, *Perdersi. L'uomo senza ambiente* (Bari: Laterza, 1988) pp. 92–100.

14. Jurij M. Lotman and Boris A. Uspenskij, *Tipologia della cultura*, ed. Remo Faccani and Marzio Marzaduri (Milano: Bompiani, 1987) pp. 145–81.

15. "Black Jackets" is close to "The Byrnies" in both style and theme: both poems use the same metric form, both adopt the motif of the uniforms as models of youth gangs.

16. The figure of today's antihero recurs in all of Gunn's work; consider, for example, the caricatures in the poems "Famous Friends" and "Front Bar of the *Lone Star*" (*Boss Cupid*), and also Falstaff (entertainer like the famous Shakespeare character), who at the end is brutally chased from the stage ("They kicked you out for taking all the space;" *CP* 375, l. 28) and devoured by cancer, and Crystal in the sequence "Transients and Residents" (*The Passages of Joy*). In this category we would also put Tow Head in "Skateboard" (*The Man with Night Sweats*), who, thanks to his sporting gear over which he has perfect control, cultivates the illusion that he is different from his peers ("Hair dyed to show it is dyed," *CP* 433, l. 19) but ends up being an "emblem extraordinary / of the ordinary" (*CP* 433, ll. 23–24).

17. Cf. Erving Goffman, *The Presentation of Self in Everyday Life*.

18. According to Lidia De Michelis, *La poesia di Thom Gunn*, pp. 61–64, the uniform here takes on a quasi-demoniacal dimension.

19. The leather jackets with their letters, "The Knights," act as a kind of armor that links the characters of this poem to the group in "The Byrnies."

20. J.H.J. Westlake, "Thom Gunn's 'Black Jackets': An Interpretation," *Literatur in Wissenschaft und Unterricht* 5, Englishes Seminar der Universität Kiel, 1972, p. 244.

21. *Ibid*.

22. *Ibid*.

23. "I got the incident itself from a book called *Autobiography of an SS Man*, translated by Constantine FitzGibbon, which showed how somebody who began as a humane person could commit an atrocity. I dedicated it to Tony White, one of my best friends, since we had discussed this kind of thing. I was visiting Berlin at the time I wrote it, in about 1960. One had derived a very melodramatic view of Germany from reading newspapers during the war, and one hadn't speculated much on what it might be like for an ordinary German soldier—not a monster—drawn into monstrous situations." John Haffenden, *Viewpoints*, p. 45.

24. Neil Powell, "Thom Gunn: A Pierglass for Poets," p. 36.

25. Ian Hamilton, "Four Conversations," p. 67.

26. Another one not far from death is the soldier in "The Vigil of Corpus Christi" (*Touch*), who, seeking with all his might to maintain that inhuman rigidity required by the code ("'To be steadfast'"), is awakened to new life by the regenerative touch of a dog who, licking him, restores strength and vigor to his body ("...and then, slowly, he grinned / with an unsoldierly joy, at this / soft sweet power awake in his own mass / balanced on his two feet, this fulness" (*CP* 170–71, ll. 21–24).

27. Clean Clothes: a soldier's song," in *Thom Gunn in Conversation with James Campbell*, p. 57, ll. 13, 18, 19–20, 22–24.

28. Count Claus von Stauffenberg is one of the tragic heroes of World War II; in July, 1944 he took part in a plot to assassinate the Führer. Hitler remained unhurt; Claus von Stauffen-

berg was captured, brought to trial and executed.

29. P.R. King, "A courier after identity," p. 90.

30. Francis Hope (ed.), *Poetry Today*, BBC Radio 3, 15 October 1964, p. 11.

31. Cf. Alan Bold, *Thom Gunn and Ted Hughes*, p. 44.

32. In *Collected Poems* the last fragment was replaced with a short poem dedicated to Baudelaire, first published separately in the first part of *My Sad Captains* with the title "Baudelaire among the Heroes." Regarding this choice, Clive Wilmer writes "'Baudelaire among the Heroes' was originally part of 'Readings in French'—in magazine publication. I think he [Gunn] separated it out because its meaning was much weightier than the others." Clive Wilmer, letter to Stefania Michelucci, 16 December 2004.

33. Thom Gunn, "Readings in French," in *My Sad Captains* (London: Faber, 1961) p. 20.

34. Gunn wrote some essays about Marianne Moore, among them, "Three Hard Women: H.D., Marianne Moore, and Mina Loy" (*SL* 33–52).

35. Exposure to the outside world, becoming part of nature's forces, in this case the wind, gives rise to a process of growth, of gradual initiation into a new life, that also implies the discovery of one's sexuality ("...that adolescent / uncertainty of everything, / [...] / I straightened up, facing it, / it seemed a kind of certainty / that I took into me with each breath." *CP* 331, ll. 6–7, 23–25) in "The Exercise: O uncontrollable..." (*The Passages of Joy*): "The wind blew against me till / I tingled with knowledge. / The swiftly changing / played upon the slowly changing" (*CP* 332, ll. 49–52), that recalls Shelley's "Ode to the West Wind." Here nature is not subject to the Hardyesque "Immanent Will," to a chaotic and destructive process alien to humans, as in "The Unsettled Motorcyclist's Vision of His Death," but it is a life force capable of forming all living things ("...without it / the trees would have lacked / a condition of their growth." *CP* 331–32, ll. 27–29), thanks to which the poet brings to light gradually ("The swiftly changing / played upon the slowly changing") his own true self.

36. Ted Hughes, "Wodwo," in *New Selected Poems 1957–1994* (London: Faber, 1995) p. 87, ll. 1, 6.

37. The difference between total immersion in surrounding nature of Hughes poetry and the presence of the protective shell in Gunn is apparent on a formal level as well. Whereas the metrical form of "Wodwo" (a single stanza without punctuation) is close to spoken prose, or interior monologue, Gunn's poem is written in syllabics, five quatrains rhyming *abba*, with strong enjambment, as if each stanza were a further exploration, a successive step approaching the outer world.

38. Philip Larkin, "High Windows," in *Collected Poems*, p. 165, ll. 18–20.

39. Cf. Ingrid Rückert, *The Touch of Sympathy: Philip Larkin and Thom Gunn* (Heidelberg: Carl Winter Universität Verlag, 1982) pp. 159–64.

40. For Gunn, like Lawrence before him, touch is the only form of knowledge truly attainable in our age, wherein the individual has become so cerebral that he or she cannot stand to touch and be touched: "We don't exist unless we are deeply and sensually in touch / with that which can be touched but not known." D.H. Lawrence, "Non Existence," in *Complete Poems*, ed. Vivian de Sola Pinto and Warren Roberts (Harmondsworth: Penguin, 1993) p. 613, ll. 6–7.

41. The hairs convey a sense of fullness completely different from that of the laceration appearing in "The Allegory of the Wolf Boy." The triumph of sunlight, primary source of life and engine that moves the entire universe, contrasted with the "moonlight" of the earlier collections, is at the heart of most of the poems in *Moly*, such as "Flooded Meadows," "The Garden of the Gods," "The Rooftop," "Three," "To Natty Bumppo," "The Discovery of the Pacific" and, of course, "Sunlight."

42. The line is sometimes fragmented and the fragment is also thematically an integral part of the whole: "...bit by bit. / Yet I can not grasp it—/ Bits, not an edifice" (*CP* 203, ll. 10–12).

43. Contemplation of the surrounding from on high, from the privileged point of view offered by an airplane, is the situation also of "Small Plane in Kansas" (*The Passages of Joy*): "...Out there / from the height of self-love / I survey the reduced world" (*CP* 330, ll. 17–19).

44. The participation of all the senses in the beauty of nature until reaching a state of inebriated consciousness finds intense expression in "Fennel" (*Poems from the 1980s*): "And for a second I float free / Of personality, and die / Into my senses, into the unglossed / Unglossable / Sweet and transporting yet attaching smell" (*CP* 391, ll. 20–24).

45. David Holbrook, "The Cult of Hughes and Gunn," p. 183.

46. Neil Powell, "The Abstract Joy: Thom Gunn's Early Poetry," *Critical Quarterly* 13 (3), 1971, p. 44.

47. Emeka Okeke-Ezigbo, "Moore's 'To a Snail' and Gunn's 'Considering the Snail.'" *Explicator* 42 (2), 1984, p. 18.

48. Ted Hughes, "The Thought-Fox," in *New Selected Poems 1957–1994*, p. 3, ll. 17–18.

49. *Ibid.*, ll. 21–24.

50. "Set neat prints in the snow," Ted Hughes, "The Thought Fox," l. 13.

51. For Douglas Chambers, "Between That Disgust and This," *Agenda* 37 (2–3), 1999, p. 105, "Like Donne in 'The Extasie,' Gunn withdraws to reflect upon the fair as 'a concentration, breathing beside our knowledge of the excluded.' This experience is as much a recognition of what is not there (the excluded) as what is."

52. Lebenswelt is the world of life, or "life-world," in which experience precedes the categories of language and intellect, the world of pre-categorical data to which belongs the primordial experience of the body, the environment, and the interaction between internal and external. For Husserl only the horizon of the world of life allows us to transcend the solipsism he considers the oldest and most cunning danger of philosophy. Cf. Edmund Husserl, *The Crisis of European Sciences and Transcendental Phenomenology: An Introduction to Phenomenology* trans. by David Carr (Evanston, IL: Northwestern Univ. Press, 1970 [1954]). Mauro Carbone quotes Merleau-Ponty on "the co-participation of the sentient and the sensible in the same raw sensible being in which the physical dimension — including our body, that of the Other, and things of the world — is not yet constituted as subject and object, and perception consists in the indistinctness of seeing and being perceived, the indifference of activity and passivity, in the reversibility of seeing and being seen." Cf. Mauro Carbone, "Il Cézanne dei filosofi francesi: Da Merlau-Ponty a Deleuze," in *Il Cézanne degli scrittori, dei poeti e dei filosofi*, ed. Giovanni Cianci, Elio Franzini and Antonello Negri (Milano: Bocca, 2001) pp. 254–55.

53. See especially the title poem of the collection.

54. The attempt of "immersion" in non-human beings also characterizes "The Cat and the Wind" (*The Passages of Joy*), composed of two stanzas, one long with very short lines (from two to five words), followed by a final one of three lines. From the objective "thing" (the gust of wind), the poet goes on to describe, trying to imagine or live it from the inside, the cat's reaction, her perception of the wind, which becomes an experience of pleasure, in a symphony of sounds of which, from simply listening, she becomes an integral part: "twigs, leaves, / small pebbles, pause / and start and pause / in their shifting, / their rubbing / against each other" (*CP* 329, ll. 17–22).

55. Cf. Mauro Carbone, "Il Cézanne dei filosofi francesi," pp. 251–70.

56. Andreina Lavagetto, "Rilke: le lettere su Cézanne," in Giovanni Cianci, Elio Franzini and Antonello Negri (eds), *Il Cézanne degli scrittori, dei poeti e dei filosofi*, p. 68.

57. Ian Hamilton, "Four Conversations," p. 65.

58. *Thom Gunn Talks to A. Alvarez*, p. 7.

59. Ian Hamilton, "Four Conversations," p. 65.

60. Thom Gunn, [no title], *Agenda*, 10–11, 1972–73, p. 23.

61. Clive Wilmer, "Definition and Flow," p. 52.

62. Thom Gunn, [no title], *Agenda*, pp. 23–24.

63. One of the harshest attacks on Gunn's use of syllabics is by the American poet Alan Stephens, author of a mischievous poem called "Syllabics for T.G." Cf. Fred Inglis, *Literature and Environment* (London: Chatto & Windus, 1971) p. 83; and Lidia De Michelis, *La poesia di Thom Gunn*, pp. 78–79.

64. Lawrence R. Ries, "Thom Gunn: The Retreat from Violence," p. 80.

65. Clive Wilmer, "Definition and Flow," p. 55.

66. Colin Falck, "Uncertain Violence," p. 39.

67. Neil Powell, "Thom Gunn: A Pierglass for Poets," p. 43.

CHAPTER V

1. See the illustrations for *Kew Gardens and Other Stories* (1919). See also Virginia Woolf, *Immagini*, ed. Flora de Giovanni (Napoli: Liguori, 2002). On the relationship between the two sisters and above all on Virginia Woolf and the visual arts, see D.F. Gillespie, *The Sisters' Arts. The Writing and Painting of Virginia Woolf and Vanessa Bell* (Syracuse, NY: Syracuse University Press, 1988).

2. The invention of photography, as noted, dates from the first experiments of Niépce and Daguerre at the beginning of the nineteenth century, and develops especially in the middle of the century, "in the 1840s and 1850s, photography's glorious first two decades, as in all the succeeding decades, during which technology made possible an ever increasing spread of that mentality which looks at the world as a set of potential photographs." Susan Sontag, *On Photography* (New York: Anchor Books, 1990 [1977]) p. 7.

3. Roberto De Romanis, "Scrivere con la luce. Fotografia e letteratura tra Otto e Novecento," *L'asino d'oro* 9, 1994, p. 3.

4. *Ibid.*, p. 6.

5. Cf. Susan Sontag, *On Photography*; and Roberto De Romanis, "Scrivere con la luce."

6. "The introduction of photography, with its techniques and procedures of an optical and chemical nature, has had profound effects on ways of seeing and of representing reality, on artistic concepts, on the human imagination, on

the linguistic techniques used to think, communicate, and talk about the products of the imagination [...]. Photographic procedures, moreover, have connected in similar ways with the relationship of the subject to reality, perceptibility and subjective perception, reproducibility of reality in images and words. Photography has even touched certain profound anthropological structures, of man, his mental life, his experience of death, his capacity to communicate or influence the interior and exterior lives of others." Remo Ceserani, "L'impatto della tecnica fotografica su alcuni procedimenti dell'immaginario letterario contemporaneo," *L'asino d'oro* 9, 1994, p. 53.

7. Roberto De Romanis, "Scrivere con la luce," p. 28.

8. Cf. Remo Ceserani, "L'impatto della tecnica fotografica su alcuni procedimenti dell'immaginario letterario contemporaneo."

9. Cf. Michel Tournier, *The Golden Droplet*, trans. by Barbara Wright (Garden City: Doubleday, 1987 [1985]).

10. "That most logical of nineteenth-century aesthetes, Mallarmé, said that everything in the world exists in order to end in a book. Today everything exists to end in photograph. [...] the true modern primitivism is not to regard the image as a real thing; photographic images are hardly that real. Instead, reality has come to seem more and more like what we are shown by cameras." Susan Sontag, *On Photography*, pp. 24 and 161. In his essay "Short History of Photography" (1931), Walter Benjamin compares the revolutionary impact of photography to that of the printing press in the fifteenth century: "it has been said that 'not he who is ignorant of writing but ignorant of photography will be the illiterate of the future.'" Walter Benjamin, "Short History of Photography," trans. by Phil Patton, *Artforum* 15 (6), February 1977, p. 51.

11. "The noeme of Photography is simple, banal; no depth: 'that has been.' ... for until this day no representation could assure me of the past of a thing except by intermediaries; but with the Photograph, my certainty is immediate: no one in the world can undeceive me. The Photograph then becomes a bizarre medium, a new form of hallucination: false on the level of perception, true on the level of time: a temporal hallucination, so to speak, a modest shared hallucination (on the one hand, 'it is not there,' on the other 'but it has indeed been'): a mad image, chafed by reality." Roland Barthes, *Camera Lucida: Reflections on Photography*, trans. Richard Howard (New York: Hill and Wang, 1981) p. 115.

12. Roberto De Romanis, "Scrivere con la luce," p. 33.

13. All the photos are next to a poem, except the first which shows a newborn baby in the bath and that which concludes the text, in which the camera lens captures the dark silhouettes of people in a city park that is completely covered in snow; the latter recalls the atmosphere of certain Bruegel paintings.

14. The year spent in London is remembered also in the poem "Talbod Road (where I lived in London 1964-5)" (*The Passages of Joy*) dedicated to his friend Tony White.

15. Cf. Diego Mormorio, "Vittorini e le ombre siciliane," *L'asino d'oro* 9, 1994, pp. 48-52.

16. Susan Sontag writes that "gazing on other people's reality with curiosity, with detachment, with professionalism, the ubiquitous photographer operates as if that activity transcends class interests, as if its perspective is universal. [...]. The photographer is an armed version of the solitary walker reconnoitring, stalking, cruising the urban inferno, the voyeuristic stroller who discovers the city as a landscape of voluptuous extremes." *On Photography*, p. 55.

17. Lidia De Michelis, *La poesia di Thom Gunn*, p. 99. Photography, or more precisely, the activity of the photographer is at the heart of "Song of a Camera" (*The Passages of Joy*), dedicated to the famous photographer of nudes, American Robert Mapplethorpe; here the poet, in short-lined quatrains rhyming *abab*, describes the operation of the camera as a kind of vampirish possession of the object ("I am the eye / that cut the life / you stand you lie / I am the knife," *CP* 348, ll. 37-40), able to produce only a distorted image of reality: "Find what you seek / find what you fear / and be assured / nothing is here" (*CP* 348, ll. 33-36). The metaphor of the photographic image, in reference to poetic creation, is developed in "Interruption" (*The Passages of Joy*), where Gunn, reflecting on the making of his art, its way of relating to reality, asks himself:

...and what makes me think
The group of poems I have entered is
Interconnected by a closer link
Than any snapshot album's?
               I can try
At least to get my snapshots accurate [*CP* 378-79, ll. 18-23].

18. "other experiments, of real photographic production, appear instead as if they pursued a confusion between expressive modes, an overlapping of codes [...]—from Imagism and from Vorticism, from Dadaism to Surrealism and what follows—they joined photographic language with poetic. [...] Robert Doisneau maintained that in poetry, 'the choice of words, the *bouquet* of words without logical construction is similar to that which we find in a photo. Poetry and photography are much closer than photograph and painting." Roberto De Romanis, "Scrivere con la luce," pp. 9-10.

19. For Susan Sontag, "even an entirely accurate caption is only one interpretation, necessarily a limiting one, of the photograph to which it is attached. And the caption-glove slips on and off so easily. It cannot prevent any argument or moral plea which a photograph (or set of photographs) is intended to support from being undermined by the plurality of meanings that every photograph carries." *On Photography*, p. 109.

20. William Hunt, "The Poem and the Photograph," p. 405.

21. Neil Powell, "Thom Gunn: A Pierglass for Poets," p. 45.

22. Martin Dodsworth, "Negatives and Positives," p. 46.

23. Alan Bold, *Thom Gunn and Ted Hughes*, pp. 77–78.

24. *Ibid.*, p. 79.

25. The title refers to Randolph Peter Best or Pete Best, The Beatles's original drummer. Best was drummer for the group from 1960 until August 16, 1962, when the band and their new manager, Brian Epstein, fired him and replaced him with Ringo Starr.

26. "It must be, again, the knowing eye of the photographer which, before the camera, chooses the fragment capable of giving itself as a detail of a story, the impetus and beginning of a reinvented story. Photography is the 'capturing of life,' the 'arresting life in the act in which it is being lived,' as Cartier-Bresson wrote, but it is 'more than anything, the grasping, within the boundaries of a single photograph, of the entire essence of a situation,' which takes place before the eyes of the photographer." Roberto De Romanis, "Scrivere con la luce," pp. 31–32.

27. Syon House is a famous eighteenth-century manor constructed over the original sixteenth-century priory near Isleworth in Middlesex. It is open to the public and easily recognizable in the photograph.

28. "To us, the difference between the photographer as an individual eye and the photographer as an objective recorder seems fundamental, the difference often regarded, mistakenly, as separating photography as art from photography as document. But both are logical extensions of what photography means: note-taking on, potentially, everything in the world, from every possible angle." Susan Sontag, *On Photography*, pp. 175–76. In *Camera Lucida*, p. 98, Roland Barthes asserts that "the age of Photography corresponds precisely to the explosion of the private into the public, or rather into the creation of a new social value, which is the publicity of the private: the private is consumed as such, publicly."

29. Per Lawrence R. Ries "*Positives* ... continues the mellowing of the poet.... As *Positives* traces the diminution of the ripples from the assertion of youth to the accommodation and acceptance of old age, it becomes obvious that the poet is also tracing his own development." Lawrence R. Ries, "Thom Gunn: The Retreat from Violence," pp. 85–87.

30. William Shakespeare, "Sonnet LX," *The Illustrated Stratford Shakespeare* (London: Chancellor Press, 1982) p. 1014, ll. 1–2.

31. In the collection of poetry published in 1989, *Poems 1950–1966: A Selection*, other than "The Conversation of Old Men" and "The Old Woman," Gunn also includes "The Left-handed Irishman," referring to the silhouette of a man raising a pick behind a demolished building, and "Canning Town"; the latter is next to a photo of a young man seated alone at a bar, with a tired, bored look.

32. It is followed by an image of a city park, placed in this instance on the left side of the book. See note 13.

33. It is included in *Collected Poems* with the title "The Old Woman."

34. In *Undesirables* appear figures similar to the old woman in *Positives* (like "Old Meg," the man in "Outside the Diner," who "...licks the different flavours / of greasy paper like a dog / and then unlike a dog / eats the paper too" *CP* 435, ll. 2–5), whose lives—although from the outside they might seem characterized by improvisation, by a minute-to-minute struggle for survival—arise from a series of rituals, as the poet suggests in "Improvisation," portrait of a homeless man: "...his existence / paved with specifics like an Imagist epic, / the only discourse printed on shreds of newspaper, / not one of which carries the word improvisation" (*CP* 437, ll. 21–24).

35. Susan Sontag writes that "it is a nostalgic time right now, and photographs actively promote nostalgia.... Most objects photographed are, just by virtue of being photographed, touched with pathos.... All photographs are *memento mori*. To take a photograph is to participate in another person's (or thing's) mortality, vulnerability, mutability. Precisely by slicing out this moment and freezing it, all photographs testify to time's relentless melt." *On Photography*, p 15.

36. "In terms of image-repertoire, the Photograph (the one I intend) represents that very subtle moment when, to tell the truth, I am neither subject nor object but a subject who feels he is becoming an object: I then experience a micro-version of death (of parenthesis): I am truly becoming a specter." Roland Barthes, *Camera Lucida*, pp. 13–14. On the relation of photography to death, Anne Marie Jaton has also written, with reference to Blaise Cendrars: "Besides showing ... its 'predatory' nature, because it 'takes' or 'retakes' things and possesses them, using on them the same violence as a gun

would, Cendrars also illustrates the changes that the photograph makes to reality: though it doesn't kill like the Winchester that shoots a prairie beast, the photograph immobilizes it, transforming the moment in eternity, and fixing it forever in memory." Anne Marie Jaton, "'Pas un livre qui n'émette un rayon de lumière': fotografia e scrittura in Blaise Cendrars," *L'asino d'oro* 9, 1994, p. 41.

37. The last lines recall Kurtz's final words in Conrad's *Heart of Darkness* ("The horror, the horror"). A similar image of death, with expressions like those given the old woman in *Positives*, appears also in "Elegy" (*The Passages of Joy*), where Gunn reflects on a suicide: "Even the terror / of leaving life like that / better than the terror / of being unable to handle it" (*CP* 311, ll. 10-13). Comparable lines end "Painkillers" (*The Passages of Joy*): "What was the pain / he needed to kill / if not the ultimate pain / / of feeling no pain?" (*CP* 362, ll. 35-38).

38. Burning burning burning burning
 O Lord Thou pluckest me out
 O Lord Thou pluckest

 burning [T.S. Eliot, *Selected Poems*, p. 62, ll. 308-11].

39. After the death of his mother, Gunn, not getting along with his father, was the guest of family friends and spent weekends and school vacations at his aunts' house in Kent. Cf. *Thom Gunn in Conversation with James Campbell*, p. 17.

40. American folksinger born in 1941; she had her debut in 1959 at the Newport Folk Festival. Champion of the doctrine of nonviolence, Baez advocated civil rights and joined the peace movement.

41. In "Let it Be" by the Beatles, Mother Mary (a reference to the mother of Christ, but also to the mother of Paul McCartney, who died when the singer was fourteen) appears to McCartney "whisper[ing] words of wisdom." "Let it be" means "take it easy," "free your mind from worries"; it seems almost that the music, besides evoking the beloved, enters the soul of the poet, helping him to confront the loss of his aunt, to see death in a different light, not as the destruction of the other but as a rebirth in the cosmic flow.

42. Sir Walter Raleigh, *The Poems*, ed. with an introduction by Agnes M.C. Latham (London: Routledge and Kegan Paul, 1951) p. 42, l. 493.

43. There are two photos of motorcyclists in *Positives*. In both cases the lens does not capture the whole image but a part, one side of the bike, the torso and the helmet. The focus on detail, on the part rather than the whole, tends in this case to accentuate the mobility of the figure represented, his being here and almost at the same time elsewhere, the refusal, as in the case of the boys in "On the Move," of *stillness*.

44. "Despite the so-called honesty of the lens, the photographic gaze is deforming because it gives precedence to the fragmentary and mechanical, and does not grasp, due to its own nature, the magnificence of the universal." Régis Durand, "Quale storia (quali storie) della fotografia," *L'asino d'oro* 9, 1994, p. 67.

45. The other poem is "PETE."

46. Attention to music of the fifties and sixties was already present in the poem "Elvis Presley" (*The Sense of Movement*) and in the article, "The New Music," *Listener*, 3 August 1967, pp. 129-30, in which Gunn emphasized the revolutionary and innovative impact of the "New Music" upon stylistics, but even more upon content.

47. Their music was initially ignored, then boycotted because it transgressed boundaries, entering realms that had as yet remained unexplored. Only after 1964, when the Beatles made their world tour, did the public begin to realize the phenomenon.

48. Lidia De Michelis, *La poesia di Thom Gunn*, p. 102.

49. Roland Barthes, *Camera Lucida*, p. 34.

50. "Eliot spoke of his art as being the escape from personality; I like that statement very much. I'm so tired of people imposing their egos on their art. Sure, personality has something to do with art, but it's nice to make the opposite emphasis. I'm so tired of Anne Sexton's troubles, to take an extreme example, and John Berryman's troubles... I want art to be an escape from personality, which is not the same as the self ... surely there's a difference between the idiosyncrasies of the personality, and things that happened to me that might have happened to anyone...." Joseph Shakarchi, "Breaking New Ground: An Interview with Thom Gunn," *Berkeley Poetry Review* 18-19, 1986, p. 266.

51. "Thom Gunn Writes...," *Poetry Book Society Bulletin* 90, 1976, p. 1.

52. About *The Bridge* by Hart Crane Gunn writes "*The Bridge* consisted of fairly substantial poems largely in blank verse, and was intended as an American answer to Eliot's *Waste Land*. It was discursive in intention, Romantic in feeling, and informed by a Whitmanian optimism." Thom Gunn, "Introduction," Yvor Winters, *Selected Poems*, p. xx.

53. Tea is replaced by espresso and "...a tiny slice / of expensive cake" (*Positives* 64, ll. 10-11) in an ironic poem next to a photo of some rich ladies in a café.

54. According to Roberto De Romanis, the photograph "takes upon itself the desire to save 'from oblivion' the forms of a world which is always becoming more 'modern,' in particular those belonging to cities like London, Paris or

Rome [...] photography presents itself from the very beginning as the only tool capable of stopping that dissipation: its registers, collects, cares for in the 'archives of memory' all the 'fallen ruins'—as Baudelaire said—so that we all can possess a bit of history, bring home a miniature of the glorious past." Roberto De Romanis, "Scrivere con la luce," pp. 14–15.

55. Neil Powell, "Thom Gunn: A Pierglass for Poets," p. 45.

56. Alan Bold, *Thom Gunn and Ted Hughes*, pp. 77–79.

CHAPTER VI

1. "The reviewer for the *Economist* [22 February 1992] frankly acknowledged having been unimpressed by the 1982 collection because it 'deals with homosexuality happily,' whereas by the time of the 1992 collection, AIDS 'has given his poetry more life and more raw human vigour than it has ever had before.'" Gregory Woods, *A History of Gay Literature* (New Haven and London: Yale University Press, 1998) p. 370. See also Alan Sinfield, *Cultural Politics—Queer Reading* (London: Routledge, 1994) p. 81; and Gregory Woods, "The Sniff of the Real," *Agenda* 37 (2–3), 1999, pp. 92–97.

2. Gregory Woods writes that in Gunn's early poems "the excessively 'male' male is as scared of himself as are the less aggressive men he threatens. Machismo is a cover for uncertainty." Gregory Woods, "Thom Gunn," in *Articulate Flesh: Male Homo-Eroticism and Modern Poetry* (New Haven and London: Yale University Press, 1987) p. 214. See also Robert K. Martin, *The Homosexual Tradition in American Poetry* (Austin and London: University of Texas Press, 1979) pp. 179–90; and Bruce Woodcock, "'But oh not loose': form and sexuality in Thom Gunn's poetry," *Critical Quarterly* 35 (1), 1993, pp. 60–72.

3. Wendy Lesser writes that "The freedom Gunn gained in 1960s San Francisco was in part the freedom to stop being what he had been brought up to be and become something else, something far less easily defined." Wendy Lesser, "Thom Gunn," *Agenda* 37 (2–3), 1999, pp. 120–21.

4. Cf. Mario Maffi, *La cultura underground* (Bari: Laterza, 1972); Arthur Marwick, *The Sixties* (Oxford: Oxford University Press, 1998); James Campbell, *This Is the Beat Generation* (London: Secker, 1999); P.J. Smith, ed., *The Queer Sixties* (New York and London: Routledge, 1999); Mirella Billi and Nicholas Brownless (eds), *In and Around the Sixties* (Viterbo: Settecittà, 2002).

5. Cf. Martin Dodsworth, "Gunn's Family of Man in 'The Hug,'" *Agenda* 37 (2–3), 1999, pp. 75–80.

6. The desire for tenderness shows in some poems of the early collections such as "Tamer and Hawk" ("I thought I was so tough, / But gentled at your hands," *CP* 29, ll. 1–2), in "For a Birthday" ("The sweet moist wafer of your tongue I taste, / And find right meanings in your silent mouth," *CP* 32, ll. 20–21), and also in "The Beaters" ("Some loose the object of their devastation, / To raise him with an ultimate gentleness, / A candid touch where formerly they hurt." Thom Gunn, *The Sense of Movement*, p. 36, ll. 19–21).

7. On this poem Michael Vince writes that "the act of surfing is literally a balancing act, in which the bodily skill of the surfers shapes and harmonizes their human bodies, so that they take part, as it were, in the powerful event of the wave. They cannot control the wave, only balance on it and blend into it on its own terms." Michael Vince, "Helping us See: A View of 'From the Wave,'" *Agenda* 37 (2–3), 1999, pp. 99–100.

8. Clive Wilmer, Letter to Stefania Michelucci, 3 February 2005.

9. "Duncan" appearing in the collection *Boss Cupid*, was written just after Duncan's death in 1988, and was published also in *The Threepenny Review* (1989) and in an edition of *PN Review* dedicated to the sixtieth birthday of the poet (1989). "Wrestling" (*Jack Straw's Castle*) and "At the Barriers" (*Poems from the 1980s*) are also dedicated to Robert Duncan. The subtitle to "At the Barriers" reads: "(Dore Alley Fair) in memory Robert Duncan." "Beside Winters he [Duncan] is probably the poet who meant most to me in my life." *Thom Gunn in Conversation with James Campbell*, p. 37.

10. Cf. Nicholas de Jongh, "Nicholas de Jongh Meets the Emigré Poet Thom Gunn on the Circuit Again: The Changing Face of the Brando Bard," *The Guardian*, 14 November 1979, p. 9. The theme of adolescent disorientation is at the core of "Slow Waker" (*The Passages of Joy*), where the protagonist, like the boy in "The Allegory of the Wolf Boy" is required to perform rituals from which he wants to escape: "He wants to withdraw into / a small space, like / the cupboard under the stairs / where the vacuum cleaner is kept, / so he can wait, and doze, / and get in nobody's way" (*CP* 364, ll. 39–44), and of "Autobiography" (*Jack Straw's Castle*): "life seemed all / loss, and what was more / I'd lost whatever it was / before I'd even had it" (*CP* 285, ll. 16–19). On "Autobiography" Gunn writes: "It's this kind of desolate feeling you have as an adolescent that you're never going to be any good as an adult and nothing's going to come out right. Everybody has that." *Thom Gunn in Conversation with James Campbell*, p. 18.

11. Cf. Gregory Woods, "Thom Gunn," pp. 222–23; and Robert K. Martin, *The Homosexual Tradition in American Poetry*, p. 187.

12. "When I was near the house of Circe, I met Hermes in the likeness of a young man, the down just showing on his face. He came up to me and took my hand, saying: 'Where are you going, alone, and ignorant of the way? Your men are shut up in Circe's sties, like wild boars in their lairs. But take heart, I will protect you and help you. Here is a herb, one of great virtue: keep it about you when you go to Circe's house.' As he spoke he pulled the herb out of the ground and showed it to me. The root was black, the flower was as white as milk; the gods call it Moly." (*CP* 183). A pastoral, almost Arcadian vein runs through *Moly*, a collection in which the poet seems to remember the suggestions of Ovid's *Metamorphoses*.

13. The theme of metamorphosis is also at the heart of some poems in *Boss Cupid* where Gunn proposes the rewriting of certain classical myths, as in "Arethusa Saved," "Arethusa Raped," and "Arachne."

14. On the sexual connotations of the word "horny" see William L. Leap, *Word's Out: Gay Men's English* (Minneapolis: University of Minnesota Press, 1996) p. 153.

15. In the composition, moreover, we find an Englishman's realization of the possibilities of the American experience, of liberty, mobility, and rootlessness.

16. For Stephen Burt ("Kinaesthetic Aesthetics: On Thom Gunn's Poems," *Southwest Review* 84 (3), 1999, p. 400) "The Miracle" evokes "The Relic" by John Donne, "the blasphemous, worshipful, erotic, anti–Catholic precedent Gunn has in mind."

17. "'—There at the counter?'—'No, that's public stuff:' / [...] / '—'Snail-track?'—'Yes, there.'—'That was six months ago. / How can it still be there?' ..." (*CP* 357, ll. 5, 16–17). Bruce Woodcock ("'But oh not loose': form and sexuality in Thom Gunn's poetry," p. 66) writes that "the effect of the questions, with their tone of incredulity or disbelief, is precisely to distance the main speaker's innocent celebration of his love affair."

18. Cf. Alan Sinfield, "Thom Gunn in San Francisco," p. 225. The importance of the uniqueness of every individual, of diversity within equality, is confirmed by several poems, such as "The Differences" (*The Man with Night Sweats*): "When casually distinct we shared the most" (*CP* 414, l. 34), "Coffee Shop" (*Boss Cupid*) which ends with the lines: "'We are the same in different ways, / We are different in the same way'" (*BC* 95, ll. 23–24), and "Epitaph" (*Boss Cupid*), whose subtitle is "carved in the AIDS Memorial Grove, Golden Gate Park." The epitaph invites the survivors to reflect on the uniqueness of every human being: "Although they all died of one cause, / Remember how their lives were dense / With fine, compacted difference" (*BC* 44, ll. 2–4).

19. Alan Sinfield, "Thom Gunn in San Francisco," p. 225. After the death of the poet an anonymous obituary came out on an Italian gay website, called: "Gay poet Thom Gunn is dead," which labels him in a way that he always rejected.

20. Bruce Woodcock, "Future Selves. Thom Gunn and Michel Foucault," *Bête Noire* 14–15, 1996, p. 309.

21. The well-known Gustav Klimt painting *Die Umarmung* is translated in English with the word "embrace."

22. The image of two bodies stretched out on a bed, intermingled like the statues of classical tradition, is also at the heart of "The Bed" (*Jack Straw's Castle*): "Loose-twined across the bed / Like wrestling statues; ..." (*CP* 229, ll. 6–7).

23. The image of shoulder blades in a sexual relationship also occurs in "The Menace" (*The Passages of Joy*): "And we sleep at the end / as a couple. I cup / the fine warm back, / broad fleshed shoulder blades" (*CP* 342, 8, ll. 13–16).

24. The desire for a family, for a microcosm brimming with affection, is at the heart of "A Blank," which not coincidentally closes the volume *The Man with Night Sweats*. Here the poet reflects on the choice of a friend who, with great courage ("...without a friend or wife" *CP* 487, l. 16), decided to adopt a baby, giving it all of his energy: "The expectations he took out at dark / —Of Eros playing, features undisclosed —/ Into another pitch, where he might work / With the same melody, and opted so / To educate, permit, guide, feed, keep warm, / And love a child to be adopted, though / The child was still a blank then on a form" (*CP* 487–88, ll. 22–28). For Lawrence Norfolk, "A Blank" "is a tribute to the interlocking mesh of images which gives Gunn's vision its conviction in these poems that what strikes us about the moment (and about the relationship between man and boy) is an equivalent of the various erotic and companionable embraces fleshed out within the book as a whole." Lawrence Norfolk, "Between playground and graveyard," *TLS*, 10 March 2000, p. 23.

CHAPTER VII

1. "why can't I leave my castle / [...] / sometimes I find myself wondering / if the castle is castle at all / a place apart, or merely / the castle that every snail / must carry around till his death" (*CP* 270, ll. 4, 7–11).

2. There is a vast literature on werewolves; stories include "Dream of the Wolf" by Scott Bradfield; "The Wolfman" by Ramsey Campbell (written as Carl Dreadstone); "The Werewolf and the Vampire" by Ronald Chetwynd-Hayes; *Werewolf* by Richard Corben; "A Witch's Curse" by Arlton Eadie; *Lycanthropy* by Daniel Ellis; *Half Human, Half Animal: Tales of Werewolves and Related Creatures* by Jamie Hall; and "Azuna" by Gianni Pilo. The film industry has also shown an interest in the subject; consider *The Howling* (1981), *An American Werewolf in London* (1981), and *Wolf* (1994).

3. This is what happens, for example, to the protagonist of the poem "Dolly" (*Jack Straw's Castle*) and is also the seed that will contribute to the formation of Jeffrey Dahmer's monstrous nature.

4. See "An Invitation," "Well Dennis O'-Grady," "Outside the Diner," "Improvisation," "Tenderloin," "Nasturtium," "'All Do Not All Things Well.'" Figures of vagabonds and homeless recur in all of the poet's work; consider "Looking Glass" (*Fighting Terms*), "Hitching into Frisco" and "Sparrow" (*Jack Straw's Castle*).

5. Cf. Appendix, p. 159; The poem "Keats at Highgate" (*The Passages of Joy*) is dedicated to Keats.

6. Cf. Alan Sinfield, "Thom Gunn in San Francisco," p. 225.

7. In his youth the poet sometimes signed his poems "Tom" or "Tommy." "Thom" for "Thomson" soon became the most frequent, a sign of his adult identity and personality. "Incidentally he [Gunn] once told me he identified as a child with Tom Kitten in Beatrix Potter's tales, *The Tale of Tom Kitten* and *The Tale of Samuel Whiskers*. Clive Wilmer, Letter to Stefania Michelucci, 13 February 2005.

8. Regression to a prenatal state occurs as well in "Thomas Bewick" (*Jack Straw's Castle*), where the protagonist "...reverts / to an earlier self, not yet / separate from what it sees," (*CP* 259, ll. 30–32). Thomas Bewick (1753–1828) is known for his wood engravings, used to illustrate certain literary works, such as *The Traveller* (1764) and *The Deserted Village* (1770) by Oliver Goldsmith, and Aesop's fables. The work to which Bewick owes his fame, cited at the end of Gunn's poem, is the *History of British Birds* (1797–1804).

9. The theme of the discovery of origins, of unity with the surrounding universe, as well as the recovery of memory, also informs "Bringing to Light" (*Jack Straw's Castle*), in which the poet reflects on the origins and meaning of words, on language as a tool of communication and rendering of experience: "fewer and fewer / joining each other in their origins / separate words return to their roots / lover and mother melt into / one figure that covers its face / nameless and inescapable" (*CP* 256–57, ll. 44–49). The motif of language is at the center of "Wrestling," whose title, with its strong physical connotation, suggests the constant struggle of the artist with his medium, with words:

language of
    tides and season
luminous discourse
    telling about
    beginnings [*CP* 262, ll. 52–56].

Gunn described this poem as "an attempt to deal with the way we acquire knowledge intuitively (as, for example, an animal does)." Cf. Clive Wilmer, "Definition and Flow," p. 54.

10. The reversed image of birth, seen not as a moment of joy but as a wound, even as torture, characterizes the poem "A Kill" by Ted Hughes in the collection *Crow* (1970).

11. The way in which the speaker compares the discoveries made during his aimless journey to the rhythms of new songs emphasizes the profound influence of sixties music, which is a "lifestyle," an element that leads to artistic creation. The image of the hitchhiker recurs in other poems such as "Selves" (*The Passages of Joy*), dedicated to his friend, painter Bill Schuessler: "You got used to the feel / like a hitchhiker / shifting his knapsack / as he improvises his route / along roads already adjusted / to their terrain. ..." (*CP* 323, ll. 40–45). Bill Schuessler illustrated some of Gunn's texts, such as *Songbook* (New York: Albondocani Press, 1973), and *Lament* (Champaign, IL: Doe Press, 1985); for a while he even lived in Gunn's house in San Francisco.

12. Jack Kerouac, *Scattered Poems* (San Francisco: City Lights Books, 1971) p. 61. Kerouac writes in "The Origins of Joy in Poetry," "The new America poetry as typified by the SF Renaissance ... is a kind of new-old Zen Lunacy poetry, writing whatever comes into your head as it comes, poetry returned to its origin, in the bardic child, truly ORAL as Ferling [Ferlinghetti] said, instead of gray faced Academic quibbling" (*Scattered Poems*, p. iii).

13. In "Hitching into Frisco" Gunn distinguishes himself from poets of the Beat Generation in his form, too, opting for traditional meter.

14. Jack Kerouac, *Scattered Poems*, p. 61, ll. 2–5.

15. In reference to the relationship with his mother, "Hitching into Frisco" recalls the poem "Don't Let That Horse..." by Lawrence Ferlinghetti, about Chagall's mother, in which the poet focuses on the anguished freedom of the artist, gained by a gradual, conflictual separation from the maternal figure.

16. The line "And everywhere to go" evokes the end of "On the Move": "one is always nearer by not keeping still." (*CP* 40, l. 40).

17. The theme of the need to recover the nat-

uralness of one's nudity, the only tool for getting close to and communicating with fellow humans, throwing off all the inhibitions imposed by the cultural and social code, informs "Saturnalia" (*Jack Straw's Castle*): "finding our likeness in / being bare, we / have thrown off / the variegated stuffs that / distinguished us one from / one" (*CP* 265, ll. 15–20).

18. The metaphor of the tree tied to human relationships reappears, other than in "Back to Life" (*Touch*), in "The Differences" (*The Man with Night Sweats*), where the union of two lovers assumes the aspect of "...two trees, bough grazing bough, / The twigs being the toes of fingertips." (*CP* 414, ll. 30–31).

19. The words "From this fat dungeon I could rise to skin" recall the first line of "A Dialogue between the Soul and the Body" by Marvell: "O who shall, from this Dungeon, raise." Andrew Marvell, *The Poems and Letters of Andrew Marvell*, p. 20, l. 1.

20. Andrew Marvell, *The Poems and Letters of Andrew Marvell*, pp. 20–21, ll. 1–3, 11–12.

21. *Ibid.*, p. 21, ll. 41–44.

22. Cf. Susan Sontag, *Illness as Metaphor and AIDS and Its Metaphors* (London: Penguin, 1991) pp. 110–11.

23. The description of physical sensations from the inside, the pain and wounds produced by the disease, in this case the cancer, is also present in the tenth poem of "Misanthropos": "...But now my mind loses hold / / and, servant to an unhinged body, / becoming of it, sinks rapidly / / beneath the stitched furs I'm swaddled in, / beneath the stink of my trembling skin, / / till it enters the heart of fever, / as its captive, unable to stir" (*CP* 141–42, ll. 8–14).

24. "Charlie, to whom 'The J Car' is addressed, wrote poetry, and even wrote a novel. The novel wasn't up to much, but the poetry was really quite good. He was new to it, of course; he was very young; he died at the age of thirty." *Thom Gunn in Conversation with James Campbell*, p. 50.

25. Susan Sontag writes that "Thomas Mann, whose fiction is a storehouse of early-twentieth-century disease myths, makes his notion of syphilis as muse central to his Doctor Faustus, with its protagonist a great composer whose voluntarily contracted syphilis ... confers on him twenty-four years of incandescent creativity.... But with AIDS — though dementia is also a common, late symptom — no compensatory mythology has arisen, or seems likely to arise. AIDS, like cancer, does not allow romanticizing or sentimentalizing, perhaps because its association with death is too powerful." *Illness as Metaphor and AIDS and Its Metaphors*, pp. 108–09.

26. On this poem see Clive Wilmer, "'Those Wounds Heal Ill.'"

27. "In 'The Man with Night Sweats,' Gunn's rhyming cunningly evokes the decay of the speaker's self-defenses and physical integrity, a crisis imaged as his failing effort to 'hug' his own body to him and hold himself together." Langdon Hammer, "The American Poetry of Thom Gunn and Geoffrey Hill," p. 125.

28. Clive Wilmer writes, "Gunn's formal command, his intellectual toughness and the plainstyle rhetoric he learned from Jonson and Shakespeare gave him the strength to find words for tragic loss, when tragic loss was the last thing he would have sought." Clive Wilmer, "Letter from Cambridge," p. 11.

29. Deborah Landau, "'How to Live. What to Do': The Poetics and Politics of AIDS," *American Literature* 68 (1), 1996, pp. 198–99.

30. Gunn described his home (the house in San Francisco that he shared with Mike Kitay and other friends) as "the family."

31. Tyler B. Hoffman, "Representing AIDS: Thom Gunn and the Modalities of Verse," *South Atlantic Review* 65 (2), 2000, p. 27

32. "I am not much of a risk-taker but I've always found the taking of risks rather admirable in a wonderful and showy kind of way. And that's exactly one of the things one can't do any longer in one's sexual behaviour because taking risks can have mortal consequences now." Clive Wilmer, "The Art of Poetry LXXII," pp. 185–86. See also Clive Wilmer, "'Those Wounds Heal Ill,'" pp. 13–21.

33. This is what happens, for example, to the protagonist of "Selves" (*The Passages of Joy*), who seeks, like Oscar Wilde's Dorian Gray, by constant physical exercise to keep the youth of the painting intact: "Day after day you / went to the gym / where you lifted toward nothing / and your body kept pace / with the body in the self-portrait / you were painting. ..." (*CP* 322–23, ll. 29–34).

34. Classical allusions echo through all of the collection, as the titles of several poems suggest: "Arethusa Saved," "Arethusa Raped," "Arachne," the sequence "Dancing David," "Bathsheba" and "Abishag."

35. *Thom Gunn in Conversation with James Campbell*, p. 34.

36. John Keats, "Ode on a Grecian Urn," *The Norton Anthology of English Literature*, 7th ed. vol. 2, edited by M.H. Abrams and Stephen Greenblatt (New York: W.W. Norton & Company, 2000) p. 851.

37. "Well, the troubadours sang for love without getting much in the way of recompense for their romantic feelings." *Thom Gunn in Conversation with James Campbell*, p. 55. "I know he [Gunn] was also thinking of Ezra Pound's poems about and based on Troubadour love poetry." Clive Wilmer, Letter to Stefania Michelucci, 13 February 2005.

38. *Thom Gunn in Conversation with James Campbell*, p. 54.

39. On Jeffrey Dahmer see Edward Baumann, *Step into my Parlor: the Chilling Story of Serial Killer Jeffrey Dahmer* (Chicago: Bonus Books, 1991); Stéphane Bourgoin, *Le cannibale de Milwaukee* (Paris: Méréal, 1999); Robert J. Dvorchak and Lisa Holewa, *Milwaukee Massacre: Jeffrey Dahmer and the Milwaukee Murders* (New York: Dell, 1991); Lionel Dahmer, *A Father's Story* (New York: W. Morrow & Co., 1994); Richard Tithecott, *Of Men and Monsters: Jeffrey Dahmer and the Construction of the Serial Killer* (Madison: University of Wisconsin Press, 1997).

40. *Thom Gunn in Conversation with James Campbell*, p. 54.

41. "He [Dahmer] was out driving, and picked up a hitchhiker, a guy called Steve, I think, who was on his way to see his girlfriend. Steve had long blond hair going down his back, and a bare chest, and for Jeffrey Dahmer the chest was the best feature in the human male. He never carried it out, but later on he even conceived the idea of constructing an altar out of the skeleton of a human chest, putting candles at different corners of it. So, Dahmer, who was staying by himself in his parent's house, asked the guy to come back for a beer and a joint. Steve came back for the beer but refused the joint, and was about to go when Dahmer was suddenly struck by the horrified realization that he'd fallen deeply in love with somebody — it had been love at first sight — and he was never going to see him again. So he did the obvious thing, came up behind him, pressed a dumbbell against Steve's throat and choked him to death." *Thom Gunn in Conversation with James Campbell*, p. 55.

42. William Shakespeare, *Twelfth Night*, I. I. 4.

43. T.S. Eliot, *Selected Poems*, p. 13, ll. 51–54.

44. It is the story of the industrialist and mechanical engineer Anthony Stark, who, during a visit to one of his many factories in Vietnam, was struck in the heart by shrapnel from a mine. To avoid death, Stark built a machine that allowed his heart to beat, reducing him, however, to life enclosed in a thick iron armor endowed with certain powers (flying, emitting repulsing rays from his hands, and so on). Without the armor he would be dead; the armor, his superpower, thus became the source of all of his super-problems, making him a prisoner. He could remove his helmet, the leg pieces and the gloves, but not the breast plate under which was kept the machine that kept him alive. Having become a man of iron, Stark decided to call himself Iron Man.

45. The title is taken from "The Borrowed Lady" by Provençal poet Bertrand de Born (c. 1140–c. 1215).

46. The refrain is present in the last stanza within parentheses, almost as if to indicate the tormented and disjointed flow of the protagonist's thoughts.

Thom Gunn Today

1. James. Fenton, "The Tough and the Tender," *The Guardian*, 8 May 2004, p. 24.

2. Clive Wilmer, "Thom Gunn: Poet of the modern city who exchanged London for San Francisco," p. 34.

3. Edward Guthmann, "Thom Gunn — poet of the odd man out," *San Francisco Chronicle*, 28 April 2004, p. 87.

4. Donald Hall, "Thom Gunn," *PN Review* 16 (2), 1989, p. 29.

5. In the brief anonymous obituary appearing in Italy's newspaper *La Stampa* Gunn was described as "one of the most representative English poets after Dylan Thomas," *La Stampa*, 29 April 2004, p. 27.

6. Wendy Lesser cited in Edward Guthmann, "Thom Gunn — poet of the odd man out," p. 87.

7. Neil Powell, "Thom Gunn: Gifted poet who explored the balance of life's contradictions," *The Guardian*, 28 April 2004, p. 25.

8. Andrew Motion, "A memorable, bracing and tender voice," *The Observer*, 2 May 2004, online edition.

9. Eavan Boland, "Remembering Thom Gunn," *Crossroads: The Journal of the Poetry Society of America* 62, 2004, p. 4.

10. David Gewanter, "Remembering Thom Gunn," *Crossroads: The Journal of the Poetry Society of America* 62, 2004, p. 6.

11. Cf. Appendix, p. 172. Of his teacher Yvor Winters' criticism, Gunn especially admired the fact that "both his criticism and his teaching were derived from his practice as a poet, which was all-important." Thom Gunn, "Introduction," Yvor Winters, *Selected Poems*, p. xvii.

12. "'There was a special quality that had to do with the underside of life,' said poet Philip Levine. 'The characters who walked through Thom's poems — they were everybody. He had such an affinity for the odd man out, the nonbelonger, the despised, the downtrodden. He had his sympathy and insight, and he really humanized these people and made them lovable in his poems.'" Edward Guthmann, "Thom Gunn — poet of the odd man out," p. 87.

13. Clive Wilmer, "Thom Gunn: Poet of the modern city who exchanged London for San Francisco," p. 34. By the same author see also "Thom Gunn, Shakespeare and Elizabethan Poetry, *PN Review* 182, 34 (6), 2008, pp. 54–62.

14. James Fenton, "The Tough and the Tender," p. 24.

15. Thom Gunn, "Introduction," Yvor Winters, *Selected Poems*, p. xxiii.
16. Clive Wilmer, "Thom Gunn: Poet of the modern city who exchanged London for San Francisco," p. 34.
17. *Ibid.*

Appendix

1. The poem was not included in *Collected Poems*.

Bibliography

The major works of the poet are as follows: collections of poetry, critical essays, works edited by Gunn, and interviews, as well as the critical works consulted and cited. For further reading, see the last section of *Thom Gunn in Conversation with James Campbell* (2000) and the following sources: Jack W.C. Hagstrom and George Bixby, *Thom Gunn: A Bibliography, 1940–1978* (London: Bertram Rota, 1979); Jack W.C. Hagstrom and Joshua Odell, "Emendations to *Thom Gunn: A Bibliography, 1940–1978*" (Part I), *Bulletin of Bibliography* 49 (3), 1992, pp. 171–77; (Part II), *Bulletin of Bibliography* 49 (4), 1992, pp. 263–68; (Part III), *Bulletin of Bibliography* 50 (2), 1993, pp. 129–37; (Part IV), *Bulletin of Bibliography* 50 (4), 1993, pp. 309–15; (Part V), *Bulletin of Bibliography* 51 (1), 1994, pp. 75–106. I cite the American and English first editions. Only in the case of *Fighting Terms* do I include the three editions.

Works by Thom Gunn

Poetry (in order of publication)

Fighting Terms. Oxon: Fantasy Press, 1954; New York: Hawk's Well Press, 1958; London: Faber, 1962.
The Sense of Movement. London: Faber, 1957; Chicago: University of Chicago Press, 1959.
My Sad Captains and Other Poems. London: Faber, 1961; Chicago: University of Chicago Press, 1961.
Selected Poems by Thom Gunn and Ted Hughes. London: Faber, 1962.
Positives (verses by Thom Gunn, photographs by Ander Gunn). London: Faber, 1966; Chicago: University of Chicago Press, 1967.
Touch. London: Faber, 1967; Chicago: University of Chicago Press, 1968.
Poems 1950–1966: A Selection. London: Faber, 1969.
Moly. London: Faber, 1971.
Moly and My Sad Captains. New York: Farrar, Straus and Giroux, 1973.
Jack Straw's Castle and Other Poems. London: Faber, 1976; New York: Farrar, Straus and Giroux, 1976.
Selected Poems 1950–1975. London: Faber, 1979; New York: Farrar, Straus and Giroux, 1979.
The Passages of Joy. London: Faber, 1982; New York: Farrar, Straus and Giroux, 1979.
The Man with Night Sweats. London: Faber, 1992; New York: Farrar, Straus and Giroux, 1992.
Collected Poems. London: Faber, 1993; New York: Farrar, Straus and Giroux, 1994.
Boss Cupid. London: Faber, 2000; New York: Farrar, Straus and Giroux, 2001.

Essays

The Occasions of Poetry. Edited by Clive Wilmer. London: Faber, 1982.
The Occasions of Poetry: Essays in Criticism and Autobiography, an expanded edition. Edited by Clive Wilmer. San Francisco: North Point Press, 1985.

Shelf Life: Essays, Memoirs and an Interview. Ann Arbor: University of Michigan Press, 1993; London: Faber, 1994.

Editions

Ben Jonson. Harmondsworth: Penguin Books, 1974.
Ezra Pound. Poems Selected by Thom Gunn. London: Faber, 2000.
Five American Poets: Edgar Bowers, Howard Nemerov, Hyam Plutzik, Louis Simpson, William Stafford. Edited by Thom Gunn and Ted Hughes. London: Faber, 1963.
Poems by Charlie Hinkle. Edited by Thom Gunn and William McPherson. San Francisco: N.p, 1988.
Poetry from Cambridge, 1951–52. London: The Fortune Press, 1952.
Selected Poems of Fulke Greville. Edited and with an Introduction by Thom Gunn. London: Faber, 1968; Chicago: University of Chicago Press, 1969.
Yvor Winters. Selected Poems. New York: The Library of America, 2003.

Interviews

Abbott, Steve. "Writing One's Own Mythology: An Interview with Thom Gunn." *Contact II,* 5 (26), 1982, pp. 20–24.
Bartlett, Lee. *Talking Poetry: Conversations in the Workshop with Contemporary Poets.* Albuquerque: University of New Mexico Press, 1987, pp. 88–101.
Campbell, James. *Thom Gunn in Conversation with James Campbell.* London: Between the Lines, 2000.
Fawcett, Graham. "Thom Gunn's Castle." Interview dated March 4, 1986, BBC Radio 3.
Gewanter, David. "An Interview with Thom Gunn." *Agni* 36, 1992, pp. 289–99.
Haffenden, John. *Viewpoints: Poets in Conversation with John Haffenden.* London: Faber, 1981, pp. 35–56.
Hamilton, Ian. "Four Conversations." *London Magazine* 4 (6), 1964, pp. 64–70.
Jenkins, Alan. "In Time of Plague" (an interview and a review of *The Man with Night Sweats*). *Independent on Sunday,* 1 February 1992, pp. 24–25.
de Jongh, Nicholas. "Nicholas de Jongh Meets the Emigré Poet Thom Gunn on the Circuit Again: The Changing Face of the Brando Bard." *The Guardian,* 14 November 1979, p. 9.
Kleinzahler, August, and John Tranter. "An Interview with Thom Gunn." *Scripsi* 5 (3), 1989, pp. 173–94.
Lux, Billy. "'It's the instances that hit you': Billy Lux interviews a poet of the century." *The Gay and Lesbian Review Worldwide* 7 (3), 2000, pp. 41–44.
Michelucci, Stefania. "Cole Street, San Francisco: A Conversation with Thom Gunn." *Quaderni del Dipartimento di Lingue e Letterature Straniere Moderne* 8, 1996, pp. 261–88.
Morrish, Hilary. "Violence and Energy: An Interview." *Poetry Review* 57 (1) 1966, pp. 32–35.
Nuwer, Hank. "Thom Gunn: Britain's Expatriate Poet." *Rendezvous* 21 (1), 1985, pp. 68–78.
Powell, Jim. "An Interview with Thom Gunn." *PN Review* 16 (2), 1989, pp. 52–56, reprinted in *Shelf Life* as "An Anglo-American Poet, Interview with Jim Powell."
Scobie, W.I. "Gunn in America: A Conversation in San Francisco." *London Magazine* 17 (6), 1977, pp. 5–15.
Shakarchi, Joseph. "Breaking New Ground: An Interview with Thom Gunn." *Berkeley Poetry Review* 18–19, 1986, pp. 258–71.
Sinfield, Alan. "Thom Gunn in San Francisco." *Critical Survey* 2 (2), 1990, pp. 223–30.
"Thom Gunn Talks to A. Alvarez." Interview dated July 20, 1964, BBC Radio 3.
Wilmer, Clive. *Poets Talking: The "Poet of the Month" Interviews from BBC Radio 3.* Manchester: Carcanet, 1994, pp. 1–7.
_____. "Thom Gunn: The Art of Poetry LXXII." *Paris Review* 135, 1995, pp. 142–89.

Criticism on Thom Gunn

Monographs

Bold, Alan. *Thom Gunn and Ted Hughes.* Edinburgh: Olivery & Boyd, 1976.
De Michelis, Lidia. *La poesia di Thom Gunn.* Firenze: La Nuova Italia, 1978.
Rückert, Ingrid. *The Touch of Sympathy: Philip Larkin and Thom Gunn: Zwei Bei-*

träge zur Englischen Gegenwartsdichtung. Heidelberg: Carl Winter Universitäts-Verlag, 1982.

Essays, Articles, Reviews

Arbasino, Alberto. "Thom Gunn." *Sessanta Posizioni*. Milano: Feltrinelli, 1974, pp. 232–36.

———. "Thom in Frisco." *Lettere da Londra*. Milano: Adelphi, 1997, pp. 305–15.

Bayley, John. "Castle and Communes." *TLS*, 24 September 1976, p. 1194.

Boland, Eavan. "Remembering Thom Gunn." *Crossroads: The Journal of the Poetry Society of America* 62, 2004, pp. 4–5.

Brown, Merle E. "Inner Community in Thom Gunn's 'Misanthropos'" e "The Authentic Duplicity of Thom Gunn's Recent Poetry." *Double Lyric: Divisiveness and Communal Creativity in Recent English Poetry*. London and Henley: Routledge & Kegan Paul, 1980, pp. 126–45 and 178–200.

Brownjohn, Alan. "The Poetry of Thom Gunn." *London Magazine* 2 (12), 1963, pp. 45–52.

Burt, Stephen. "Kinaesthetic Aesthetics: On Thom Gunn's Poems." *Southwest Review* 84 (3), 1999, pp. 386–403.

Campbell, James. "Thom Gunn, Anglo-American Poet." *Agenda* 37 (2–3), 1999, pp. 70–74.

Carpenter, Peter. "Thom Gunn's Bodies and the Poetry of Apprehension." *Agenda* 37 (2–3), 1999, pp. 81–86.

Cassidy, Turner. "Palo Alto and the Pampa." *Parnassus Poetry in Review*, Spring-Summer 1977, pp. 243–55.

Chambers, Douglas. "Thom Gunn: The Poetic Implications of the Sensory Life." *PN Review* 16 (2), 1989, pp. 31–32.

———. "Between That Disgust and This." *Agenda* 37 (2–3), 1999, pp. 102–06.

Conquest, Robert. "On Syllabics: Honest Doubt." *The Abomination of Moab*. London: Temple Smith, 1979, pp. 261–63.

Cookson, William, ed. "Thom Gunn at Seventy." *Agenda* 37 (2–3), 1999.

Crivelli, Renzo S. "Un abbraccio disperato: Caravaggio e la poesia di Thom Gunn e Edward Lucie-Smith." *Lo sguardo narrato. Letteratura e arti visive*. Roma: Carocci, 2003, pp. 39–53.

D'Agostino, Nemi. "Introduzione" to Thom Gunn. *Tatto*. Translated by Luciano Erba. Milano: Guanda, 1979, pp. 7–11.

Davie, Donald. "Thom Gunn." *PN Review* 16 (2), 1989, p. 38.

Dodsworth, Martin. "Taking Pleasure." *Listener*, 19 October 1967, pp. 506–07.

———. "Negatives and Positives." *The Review* 18, 1968, pp. 46–61.

———. "Thom Gunn: Poetry as Action and Submission." *The Survival of Poetry: A Contemporary Survey*. Edited by Martin Dodsworth. London: Faber, 1970, pp. 193–215.

———. "Gunn's Rhymes." *PN Review* 16 (2), 1989, pp. 33–34.

———. "Gunn's Family of Man in 'The Hug.'" *Agenda* 37 (2–3), 1999, pp. 75–80.

Dyson, A.E., "*My Sad Captains* by Thom Gunn." *Critical Quarterly* 3 (4), 1961, pp. 377–80.

———, ed. "Thom Gunn." *Three Contemporary Poets: Thom Gunn, Ted Hughes and R.S. Thomas*. London: Macmillan, 1990, pp. 15–98.

Eagleton, Terry. "New Poetry [Review of *Jack Straw's Castle*]." *Stand* 18 (3), 1977, pp. 75–78.

———. "Recent Poetry [Review of Thom Gunn, *Selected Poems 1950–1975*]," *Stand* 21 (3), 1980, pp. 336–40.

———. "New Poetry [Review of *The Passages of Joy*]." *Stand* 24 (3), 1983, pp. 77–80.

Esch, Arno. *Zur Situation der Zeitgenössischen Englischen Lyrik*. Opladen: Westdeutcher Verlag, 1980, pp. 17–24.

Ezard, John. "Poetic Justice for Bainbridge and Gunn." *The Guardian*, 28 March 2003, p. 17.

Falck, Colin. "Uncertain Violence: Colin Falck on the Poetry of Thom Gunn." *New Review* 3, 1976–77, pp. 37–41.

Faulkner, Peter. "Matter and Spirit." *Agenda* 37 (2–3), 1999, pp. 87–91.

Fellner, Steve. "On Love, Sex, and Thom Gunn." *Another Chicago Magazine* 38, 2001, pp. 73–88.

Fenton, James. "The Tough and the Tender." *The Guardian*, 8 May 2004, p. 24.

Fraser, G.S. "The Poetry of Thom Gunn." *Critical Quarterly* 3 (4), 1961, pp. 359–67.

Fuller, John. "Thom Gunn." *The Modern Writer: Essays from the Review*. Edited by Ian Hamilton. London: MacDonald, 1968, pp. 17–22.

Gewanter, David. "Remembering Thom Gunn." *Crossroads: The Journal of the Poetry Society of America* 62, 2004, pp. 5–6.

Giles, Paul. "Landscapes of Repetition: The Self-Parodic Nature of Thom Gunn's Later Poetry." *Critical Quarterly* 29 (2), 1987, pp. 85–99.

———. "From Myth to History: The Later Poetry of Thom Gunn and Ted Hughes." *Contemporary British Poetry: Essays in Theory and Criticism.* Edited by James Acheson and Romana Huk. Albany: State University of New York Press, 1996, pp. 143–73.

Glazier, Lyle. "Thom Gunn." *Credences* 3 (2), 1985, pp. 155–62.

Guthmann, Edward. "Thom Gunn — poet of the odd man out." *San Francisco Chronicle*, 28 April 2004, p. 87.

Hall, Daniel. "Form and Freedom: Thom Gunn in America." *Newsletter of the Friends of the Amherst College Library* 27, 2000–01, pp. 20–21.

Hall, Donald. "Thom Gunn." *PN Review* 16 (2), 1989, pp. 29–30.

———. "In Memoriam: Thom Gunn." *Poetry* 184 (4), 2004, pp. 329–31.

Hammer, Langdon. "Thom Gunn and the Cool Queer Tales of Cupid." *Raritan: A Quarterly Review* 20 (2), 2000, pp. 114–25.

———. "The American Poetry of Thom Gunn and Geoffrey Hill." *Something We Say That They Don't: British and American Poetic Relations Since 1925.* Edited by Steve Clark and Mark Ford. Iowa City: University of Iowa Press, 2004, pp. 118–36.

Hirsch, Edward. "The Existential Imagination of Thom Gunn." *Southern Review* 17 (3), 1981, pp. 648–53.

Hoffman, Tyler B. "Representing AIDS: Thom Gunn and the Modalities of Verse." *South Atlantic Review* 65 (2), 2000, pp. 13–39.

Holbrook, David. "The Cult of Hughes and Gunn: The Dangers of Poetical Fashion." *Poetry Review* 54 (2), 1963, pp. 167–83.

Holloway, John. "*The Sense of Movement* by Thom Gunn." *London Magazine* 4 (9), 1957, pp. 69–73.

Hope, Francis, ed. *Poetry Today*, BBC Radio 3, 15 October 1964.

Hulse, Michael, "The Repossession of Innocence: The Poetry of Thom Gunn." *Quadrant* 27 (4), 1983, pp. 65–69.

Hunt, William. "The Poem and the Photograph." *Poetry* 111 (6), 1968, pp. 405–07.

Jones, Brian. "*Touch* by Thom Gunn." *London Magazine* 7 (9), 1967, pp. 89–91.

King, P.R. "A courier after identity: The poetry of Thom Gunn." *Nine Contemporary Poets: A Critical Introduction.* London: Methuen, 1979, pp. 77–106.

Klawitter, George. "Piety and the Agnostic Gay Poet: Thom Gunn's Biblical Homoerotics." *Journal of Homosexuality* 33 (3–4), 1997, pp. 207–32.

Kleinzahler, August. "The Plain Style and the City." *Agenda* 37 (2–3), 1999, pp. 36–48.

———. "Diary." *The London Review of Books*, 4 November 2004, pp. 46–47.

———. "Introduction" to *Thom Gunn: Poems Selected by August Kleinzahler.* London: Faber, 2007. pp. ix–xx.

———. "Introduction" to *The Man with Night Sweats.* New York: Farrar, Straus and Giroux, 2007.

Landau, Deborah. "'How to Live: What to Do': The Poetics and Politics of AIDS." *American Literature* 68 (1), 1996, pp. 193–225.

Lee, Lance. "Roots of Violence [Review of Thom Gunn's *Jack Straw's Castle* and Ted Hughes's *Gaudete*]." *Chicago Review* 30, 1978–79, pp. 108–16.

Lesser, Wendy. "Thom Gunn." *Agenda* 37 (2–3), 1999, pp. 118–22.

———, Philip Levine, Oliver Sacks, et al. "A Symposium on Thom Gunn." *The Threepenny Review* 102, Summer 2005, pp. 6–13.

Lombardo, Agostino. "Thom Gunn e il Nuovo Movimento." In Thom Gunn, *I miei tristi capitani e altre poesie.* Translated by Camillo Pennati. Milano: Mondadori, 1968, pp. 7–25.

Lucie-Smith, Edward. "The Tortured Yearned as Well: An Enquiry into Themes of Cruelty in Current Verse." *Critical Quarterly* 4 (1), 1962, pp. 38–43.

Mander, John. "In Search of Commitment: The Poetry of Thom Gunn." *The Writer and Commitment.* London: Secker and Warburg, 1961, pp. 153–78.

Marchetti, Paola. "Re-reading 'On the Move.'" *L'analisi linguistica e letteraria* 1–2, 2002, pp. 315–23.

McGuiness, Patrick. "'The Republic of Letters': Thom Gunn and Donald Davie." *Agenda* 37 (2–3), 1999, pp. 114–17.

Michelucci, Stefania. "The Large Gesture of Solitary Man: Thom Gunn and Caravaggio." *Agenda* 37 (2–3), 1999, pp. 64–69.

———. "Celare ostentando: la messa in scena della passione in *Fighting Terms*." *Le passioni tra ostensione e riserbo*. Edited by Romana Rutelli and Luisa Villa. Pisa: ETS, 2000, pp. 199–207.

———. "Passion and Performance in *Fighting Terms*." *English* 50, 2001, pp. 39–46.

———. "Wrestling with the 'rappel à l'ordre': Thom Gunn and the New Modernism of the Sixties." *In and Around the Sixties*. Edited by Mirella Billi and Nicholas Brownless. Viterbo: Settecittà, 2002, pp. 119–30.

———. "Metamorphoses of the Body in Thom Gunn's Poetry." *Annales Du Monde Anglophone* 17, 2003, pp. 107–17.

Michie, James. "*Fighting Terms* by Thom Gunn." *London Magazine* 2 (1), 1955, pp. 96, 99–100.

Miglior, Giorgio. "La poesia di Thom Gunn." Claudio Gorlier, ed. *Studi e Ricerche di Letteratura Inglese e Americana*. Vol. II, Milano: Cisalpino-Goliardica, 1969, pp. 21–51.

Miller, John. "The Stipulative Imagination of Thom Gunn." *Iowa Review* 4 (1), 1973, pp. 54–72.

Mitgutsch, Waltraud. "Thom Gunn." *Salzburg Studies in English Literature* 27, 1974, pp. 170–99.

Motion, Andrew. "A memorable, bracing and tender voice." *The Observer*, 2 May 2004, online edition.

Nardi, Paola A. "Linearità e circolarità in 'The Discovery of the Pacific' di Thom Gunn." *Strumenti critici* XIV (3), 1999, pp. 445–62.

Noel-Tod, Jeremy. "Out of the Eater [Review of *Boss Cupid*]." *The London Review of Books* 2 July 2000, pp. 31–32.

Norfolk, Lawrence. "Between playground and graveyard." *TLS*, 10 March 2000, p. 23.

Okeke-Ezigbo, Emeka. "Moore's 'To a Snail' and Gunn's 'Considering the Snail.'" *Explicator* 42 (2), 1984, pp. 17–18.

Parini, Jay. "Rule and Energy: The Poetry of Thom Gunn." *Massachusetts Review* 23 (1), 1982, pp. 134–51.

Peck, John. "On Two Stanzas by Thom Gunn." *PN Review* 16 (2), 1989, pp. 35–36.

Perloff, Marjorie G. "Roots and Blossoms [Review of *Moly* and *My Sad Captains*]." *Washington Post Book World* 16, 1973, pp. 6–7.

Pinsky, Robert. "Thom Gunn." *PN Review* 16 (2), 1989, pp. 42–43.

———. "The Lenore Marshall / Nation Poetry Prize—1993." *The Nation*, 6 December 1993, pp. 701–03.

Potts, Robert. "Thom Gunn: Moving Voice." *The Guardian*, 27 September 2003, p. 20.

Powell, Neil. "The Abstract Joy: Thom Gunn's Early Poetry." *Critical Quarterly* 13 (3), 1971, pp. 219–27.

———. "Thom Gunn: A Pierglass for Poets." *Carpenters of Light: Some Contemporary English Poets*. Manchester: Carcanet New Press Ltd, 1979, pp. 19–59.

———. "Loud Music, Bars and Boisterous Men." *PN Review* 16 (2), 1989, pp. 39–41.

———. "Real Shadow: Gunn and Caravaggio." *Agenda* 37 (2–3), 1999, pp. 57–62.

———. "Thom Gunn: Gifted poet who explored the balance of life's contradictions." *The Guardian*, 28 April 2004, p. 25.

———. "A Love of Chance." *PN Review* 31 (1), 2004, pp. 5–6.

Pritchard, William H. "Weighing the Verse." *Poetry* 138 (2), 1981, pp.107–16.

Ries, Lawrence R. "Thom Gunn: The Retreat from Violence." *Wolf Masks: Violence in Contemporary Poetry*. New York: Kennikat Press, 1977, pp. 59–91.

Romer, Stephen. "Thom Gunn: a story of hero-worship and beyond..." *Agenda* 37 (2–3), 1999, pp. 31–35.

Saylor, Steven. "Thom Gunn in Love in the Time of AIDS." *San Francisco Review of Books* 16 (4), 1992, pp. 14–16.

Stimpson, Catharine R. "Thom Gunn: The Redefinition of Place." *Contemporary Literature* 18 (3), 1977, pp. 391–404.

Swaab, Peter. "*The Man with Night Sweats* and the Idea of Political Poetry." *Agenda* 37 (2–3), 1999, pp. 107–13.

Swinden, Patrick. "Thom Gunn's Castle." *Critical Quarterly* 19 (3), 1977, pp. 43–61.

Thirlby, Peter. "Thom Gunn—Violence and Toughness." *Delta* 8, 1956, pp. 16–21.

Vince, Michael. "Helping us See: A View of 'From the Wave.'" *Agenda* 37 (2–3), 1999, pp. 99–100.

Westlake, J.H.J. "Thom Gunn's 'Black Jackets': An Interpretation." *Literatur in Wissenschaft und Unterricht* 5, Englishes Seminar der Universität Kiel, 1972, pp. 240–45.

Williams, Hugo. "Rough Types." *London Magazine* 22 (12), 1983, pp. 94–100.

Wilmer, Clive. "Clive Wilmer on New Poetry." *The Spectator*, 29 May 1971, pp. 742–44.

———. "Definition and Flow: A Personal Reading of Thom Gunn." *PN Review* 5 (3), 1978, pp. 51–57.

———, ed. "Thom Gunn at Sixty." *PN Review* 16 (2), 1989, pp. 7–8.

———. "'Those Wounds Heal Ill': Thom Gunn in 1954 and 1992." *Agenda* 37 (2–3), 1999, pp. 13–21.

———. "Thom Gunn: Poet of the modern city who exchanged London for San Francisco." *Independent*, 29 April 2004, p. 34.

———. "Thom Gunn." *PN Review* 30 (6), 2004, pp. 11–13.

———. "Letter from Cambridge: The Tribe of Gunn." *PN Review* 31 (2), 2004, pp. 10–11.

———. "The Self You Choose. What's in a name? For Thom Gunn, Everything Was." *Times Literary Supplement*, 15 April 2008, pp. 13–15.

———. "Tom Gunn, Shakespeare and Elizabethan Poetry." *PN Review* 182, 34 (6), 2008, pp. 54–62.

———. "In and Out of the Movement: Donald Davie and Thom Gunn." *The Movement Revisited*. Edited by Zachary Leader. Oxford: Oxford University Press, forthcoming.

Witemeyer, H. "Thom Gunn's *The Man with Night Sweats*." *Agenda* 31 (3), 1993, pp. 90–93.

Woodcock, Bruce. "'But oh not loose': form and sexuality in Thom Gunn's poetry." *Critical Quarterly* 35 (1), 1993, pp. 60–72.

———. "Future Selves: Thom Gunn and Michel Foucault." *Bête Noire* 14–15, 1996, pp. 309–18.

Woods, Gregory, "Thom Gunn." *Articulate Flesh: Male Homo-Eroticism and Modern Poetry*. New Haven, CT: Yale University Press, 1987, pp. 212–31.

———. "The Sniff of the Real." *Agenda* 37 (2–3), 1999, pp. 92–97.

———. "Affectionate Gifts." *PN Review* 133, May–June 2000, pp. 67–68.

GENERAL REFERENCES
(to English and American Poetry from World War II)

Alvarez, A. *The Shaping Spirit: Studies in Modern English and American Poetry*. London: Chatto & Windus, 1958.

———. "English Poetry Today." *Commentary* 32 (3), 1961, pp. 217–23.

———, ed. *The New Poetry* (1962). Harmondsworth: Penguin, 1966.

Amoruso, Vito, *La letteratura Beat Americana*, Bari: Laterza, 1975.

Bartlett, Lee, ed. *The Beats: Essays in Criticism*, Jefferson, NC: McFarland, 1981.

Bergonzi, Bernard. "After 'The Movement.'" *The Listener*, 24 August 1961, pp. 284–85.

Billi, Mirella, and Nicholas Brownless, eds. *In and Around the Sixties*. Viterbo: Settecittà, 2002.

Bloom, Harold. *The Anxiety of Influence: A Theory of Poetry*. New York: Oxford University Press, 1973.

Bradbury, Malcolm. *The Social Context of Modern English Literature*. Oxford: Basil Blackwell, 1971.

Campbell, James, *This is the Beat Generation*. London: Secker, 1999.

Conquest, Robert, ed. *New Lines*. London: Macmillan, 1956.

———, ed. *New Lines II*. London: Macmillan, 1963.

Cook, Bruce. *The Beat Generation*. New York: Charles Scribner's Sons, 1971.

Corcoran, Neil. *English Poetry Since 1940*. London: Longman, 1993.

Cox, C.B., and A.E. Dyson. *Modern Poetry: Studies in Practical Criticism*. London: Edward Arnold, 1963.

———, and ———. Dyson. *The Practical Criticism of Poetry: A Text Book*. London: Edward Arnold, 1965.

Crivelli, Renzo S. *Né falchi né colombe: poesia inglese degli anni '50 e '60 dal Movement al Group*. Torino: Tirrenia Stampatori, 1983.

———. "La poesia del dopoguerra." *Storia della civiltà letteraria inglese*, vol. III.

Edited by Franco Marenco. Torino: Utet, 1996, pp. 570–73.
Davie, Donald. *Purity of Diction in English Verse*. London: Chatto & Windus, 1952.
———. *Articulate Energy*. London: Routledge, 1955.
———. "Remembering the Movement." With *the Grain: Essays on Thomas Hardy and Modern British Poetry*. Edited by Clive Wilmer. Manchester: Carcanet Press, 1998, pp. 199–203.
Day, Gary and Brian Docherty, eds. *British Poetry from the 1950s to the 1990s*. London: Macmillan, 1997.
Dodsworth, Martin. "The Climate of Pain in Recent Poetry." *London Magazine*, November 1964, pp. 86–95.
Elon, Florence. "The Movement Against Itself: British Poetry of the 1950s." *Southern Review* 19 (1), 1983, pp. 88–110.
Enright, Dennis J., ed. *Poets of the Fifties*. Tokyo: Kenkyusha, 1955.
Fraser, G.S. *The Modern Writer and His World* (1953). Harmondsworth: Penguin, 1970.
———, ed. *Poetry Now*. London: Faber, 1956.
———. *Vision and Rhetoric: Studies in Modern Poetry*. London: Faber, 1959.
———. *Metre, Rhyme and Free Verse*. London: Methuen, 1970.
———. *Essays on Twentieth-Century Poets*. Leicester: Leicester University Press, 1977.
Gioia, Dana. "Poetry and the Fine Presses." *Hudson Review* 35 (3), 1982, pp. 483–98.
———. *Barrier of a Common Language: An American Looks at Contemporary British Poetry*. Ann Arbor: University of Michigan Press, 2003.
Grubb, Frederick. *A Vision of Reality: A Study of Literature in Twentieth Century Verse*. London: Chatto and Windus, 1965.
Hall, Donald, Robert Pack, and Luis Simpson, eds. *New Poets of England and America*. New York: Meridian Books, 1957.
Hamilton, Ian. *A Poetry Chronicle*. London: Faber, 1973.
Hartley, Anthony, "Poets of the Fifties." *The Spectator*, 27 August 1954, pp. 260–61.
Hobsbaum, Philip, and Edward Lucie-Smith, eds. *A Group Anthology*. London: Oxford University Press, 1963.
Inglis, Fred. *Literature and Environment*. London: Chatto & Windus, 1971.
Jennings, Elizabeth, ed. *An Anthology of Modern Verse 1940–1960*. London: Methuen, 1961.
———. *Poetry To-Day*. London: Longmans, 1961.
Jones, Peter, and Michael Schmidt, eds. *British Poetry Since 1970: A Critical Survey*. Manchester: Carcanet Press, 1980.
Lattimore, Richmond. "Poetry Chronicle." *Hudson Review* 36 (1), 1983, pp. 205–16.
Lucie-Smith, Edward, ed. *British Poetry Since 1945*. Harmondsworth: Penguin, 1970.
Maffi, Mario. *La cultura underground*. Bari: Laterza, 1972.
Martin, Robert K. *The Homosexual Tradition in American Poetry*. Austin and London: University of Texas Press, 1979.
———, ed. *The Continuing Presence of Walt Whitman*. Iowa City: University of Iowa Press, 1992.
Marwick, Arthur. *The Sixties*. Oxford: Oxford University Press, 1998.
Melchiori, Giorgio. *I funamboli. Il manierismo nella letteratura inglese da Joyce ai giovani arrabbiati* (1956). Torino: Einaudi, 1974.
Moore, Geoffrey. *Poetry To-Day*. London: Longmans, 1958.
———, ed. *The Penguin Book of American Verse*. Harmondsworth: Penguin, 1977.
Morrison, Blake. "In Defence of Minimalism." *Critical Quarterly* 18 (2), 1976, pp. 43–51.
———. *The Movement*. Oxford: Oxford University Press, 1980.
Perkins, David. *A History of Modern Poetry: Modernism and After*. Cambridge, MA: The Belkan Press of Harvard University Press, 1987.
Press, John. *Rule and Energy: Trends in British Poetry Since the Second World War*. London: Oxford University Press, 1963.
———. *A Map of Modern English Verse*. London: Oxford University Press, 1969.
Roberts, Neil, ed. *A Companion to 20th Century Poetry*. Oxford: Blackwell, 2001.
Rosenthal, M.L. *The New Poets: American and British Poetry Since World War II*. New York: Oxford University Press, 1967.
———. "Modern British and American Poetic Sequences." *Contemporary Literature* 28 (3), 1977, pp. 416–21.
Sanesi, Roberto, ed. *Poesia inglese del dopoguerra*. Milano: Schwarz, 1958.
———. *Poeti inglesi del '900*, 2 volumes. Milano: Bompiani, 1978.
Schmidt, Michael, and Grevel Lindop, eds.

British Poetry Since 1960: A Critical Survey. Oxford: Carcanet, 1972.

Scott, J.D. "In the Movement." *The Spectator*, 1 October 1954, pp. 399–400.

Silkin, Jon. *The Life of Metrical and Free Verse in Twentieth-Century Poetry.* London: Macmillan, 1997.

Sinfield, Alan, *Literature, Culture and Politics in Postwar Britain.* Oxford: Basil Blackwell, 1989.

———. *Cultural Politics — Queer Reading.* London: Routledge, 1994.

Smith, P.J. ed. *The Queer Sixties.* New York and London: Routledge, 1999.

Smith, Stan. *Inviolable Voice: History and Twentieth Century Poetry.* Dublin: Gill and Macmillan, 1982.

Splendore, Paola. "Il secondo Novecento." *Storia della letteratura inglese*, vol. 2. Edited by Paolo Bertinetti. Torino: Einaudi, 2000, pp. 245–316.

Swinden, Patrick, "Old Lines, New Lines: The Movement Ten Years After." *Critical Quarterly*, Winter 1967, pp. 347–59.

Thwaite, Anthony. *Contemporary English Poetry.* London: Heinemann, 1959.

———. *Twentieth-Century English Poetry.* London: Heinemann, 1978.

———. *Poetry Today: A Critical Guide to British Poetry 1960–1995.* London: Longman, 1996.

Tomlinson, Charles. "The Middlebrow Muse." *Essays in Criticism*, April 1957, pp. 208–17.

Van O'Connor, William. *The New University Wits and the End of Modernism.* Carbondale: Southern Illinois University Press, 1963.

Wain, John. "English Poetry: The Immediate Situation." *Sewanee Review* 3, 1957, pp. 353–74.

Wallat, Reiner. "Die Englische Lyric nach dem Zweiten Weltkrieg." *Zeitschrift für Anglistik und Amerikanistik* 33 (1), 1985, pp. 17–32.

Williams, John. *Twentieth Century British Poetry.* London: Edward Arnold, 1987.

Wood, Michael. "We All Hate Home: English Poetry Since World War II." *Contemporary Literature* 18 (3), 1977, pp. 305–18.

Woods, Gregory. *A History of Gay Literature.* New Haven and London: Yale University Press, 1998.

Index

Abbott, Steve 200
Abrams, M.H. 195
Acheson, James 179, 202
Adorno, Theodor W. 57, 157
Aesop 194
Africa 166, 169
Alexander the Great 72, 177
Alvarez, A. 1, 18–19, 23, 176, 178, 188, 200, 204
Amis, Kingsley 14, 19, 22
Amoruso, Vito 204
Arbasino, Alberto 22–23, 176, 201
Arizona 5, 169, 172
Arnett, Chuck 76
Asia 177
Atlantic Ocean 6
Auden, Wystan Hugh 11–12, 14, 18, 28, 35, 57, 166, 181
Auschwitz 57, 157
Avedon, Richard 121

Bacon, Francis 133
Baez, Joan 116, 191
Bainbridge, Beryl 42, 180, 201
Bakhtin, Mikhail 67
Balzac, Honoré de 97
Banville, John 109
Barth, Robert L. 177
Barthes, Roland 110, 121, 189–191
Bartlett, Lee 178, 200, 204
Baudelaire, Charles 27, 100, 145, 166, 184, 187, 192
Baumann, Edward 196
Bayley, John 201
Beatles 39, 115–116, 118, 190–191
Bell, Martin 23
Bell, Vanessa 109, 188
Benedek, Laszlo 33, 133, 183
Benjamin, Walter 189
Bergonzi, Bernard 19, 176, 204
Bergson, Henri 44, 68
Berkeley 5, 33, 163
Berlin 33–34
Berryman, John 19, 191

Bertinetti, Paolo 21, 205
Best, Randolph Peter 190
Bewick, Thomas 194
Billi, Mirella 124, 192, 203–204
Bixby, George 199
Blake, William 49, 83, 109, 139
Bloom, Harold 15, 94, 175, 204
Boland, Eavan 196, 201
Bold, Alan 63–64, 77, 85–86, 112, 123, 177, 179, 181, 183–187, 190, 192, 200
Bourgoin, Stéphane 196
Bowers, Edgar 38, 200
Boyars, Arthur 19
Bradbury, Malcolm 204
Bradfield, Scott 194
Brando, Marlon 33, 61, 66, 133
Brontë, sisters 17
Brooke, Rupert 95
Brooklyn 121
Brown, Merle E. 179, 201
Brownjohn, Alan 14, 23, 64, 74, 184, 201
Brownless, Nicholas 124, 192, 203–204
Bruegel, Pieter the Elder 189
Brutus, Marcus Junius 93
Buchan, John 57
Burt, Stephen 193, 201
Byatt, Antonia Susan 109
Byron, George Gordon 55

Caetani, Princess 162
Caffee, Mike 136
California 5, 18, 30, 33–34, 70, 94, 100, 116, 129–130, 135, 139, 154–155, 159, 167, 182
Cambridge 4, 12, 19, 28, 30–31, 57, 60, 124, 127, 160, 165, 175, 178, 182, 195, 200, 204
Campbell, James 25, 63, 176–179, 181, 183–184, 186, 191–192, 195–196, 199, 200–201, 204
Campbell, Ramsey 194
Campion, Thomas 155
Camus, Albert 30, 57, 179, 182
Canada 19, 110
Capuana, Luigi 109

Caravaggio 82–85, 97, 115, 185–186, 201–203
Carbone, Mauro 188
Carpenter, Peter 201
Carr, David 188
Carroll, Lewis 54
Cartier-Bresson, Henri 110, 190
Casanova, Giacomo Girolamo 91
Casby, William 121
Cassidy, Turner 201
Cendrars, Blaise 190–191
Ceserani, Remo 189
Cézanne, Paul 105, 188
Chagall, Marc 194
Chambers, Douglas 188, 201
Chaucer, Geoffrey 28
Chetwynd-Hayes, Ronald 194
Cianci, Giovanni 175–176, 188
Clark, Steve 178, 202
Cleopatra 81, 185
Cohen, David 42, 156
Coleman, John 30
Coleridge, Samuel Taylor 11, 167, 178
Confucius 177
Conquest, Robert 14–16, 18, 22–24, 175, 201, 204
Conrad, Joseph 53, 176, 191
Cook, Bruce 204
Cookson, William 201
Cooper, Catherine 23
Cooper, Julian 23
Corben, Richard 194
Corcoran, Neil 21, 66, 176, 184, 204
Coriolanus, Gaius Marcius 72
Corneille, Pierre 59, 183
Cornwall 176
Corso, Gregory 178
Cox, C.B. 204
Crane, Hart 121, 191
Creeley, Robert 2, 36, 165
Crichton Smith, Ian 19
Crivelli, Renzo S. 21, 175, 186, 201, 204

D'Agostino, Nemi 201
Daguerre, Louis 188
Dahmer, Jeffrey 29, 147–151, 155, 194, 196
Dahmer, Lionel 196
Dante 51, 174
Davie, Donald 12–14, 19, 20–24, 175, 201–202, 204
Day, Gary 204
Day Lewis, Cecil 14
Dean, James 61, 66
de Born, Bertrand 196
de Giovanni, Flora 188
de Jongh, Nicholas 192, 200
Deleuze, Gilles 188
De Michelis, Lidia 53, 111, 119, 176, 178, 181–183, 186, 188, 191, 200
De Romanis, Roberto 109–110, 188–189, 190–192
Descartes, René 68

de Sola Pinto, Vivian 187
Di Piero, W.S. 178
Docherty, Brian 204
Dodsworth, Martin 53, 61, 67, 111, 179, 182–184, 186, 190, 192, 201, 204
Doisneau, Robert 189
Donne, John 3, 28–29, 32, 66, 73, 83, 125, 188, 193
Dove, Rita 169
Dowland, John 155
Duncan, Robert 11, 36, 41, 127, 131, 163, 167, 172, 192
Dunmore, Helen 176
Durand, Régis 191
Dvorchak, Robert J. 196
Dyer, Geoff 176
Dylan, Bob 39
Dyson, A.E. 181, 201, 204

Eadie, Arlton 194
Eagleton, Terry 62, 183, 201
Eckart, Carl 185
Eliot, Thomas Stearns 11, 15, 29, 39, 42, 51, 57–58, 60, 70, 72, 93, 106, 115, 120–121, 127, 135, 148, 151, 153–155, 163, 166, 168, 177, 184–185, 191, 196
Elizabeth I 116
Ellis, Daniel 194
Elon, Florence 20, 176, 204
Empson, William 12, 13, 19, 60
England 1, 3–5, 7, 11–21, 23–25, 28, 30–35, 37, 41, 43, 65–66, 105, 122–126, 153–154, 162, 166–167, 169–170, 173, 175–176, 178–179, 183, 185, 193, 195, 199, 200–201, 204–206
Enright, Dennis J. 14–16, 19–20, 22–23, 175–176, 204
Epstein, Brian 190
Erba, Luciano 201
Esch, Arno 201
Europe 5–6, 21, 23, 39, 60, 167, 172
Evtushenko, Evgenij A. 162
Ezard, John 180, 201

Faccani, Remo 186
Falck, Colin 55, 108, 182, 188, 201
Far East 15
Faulkner, Peter 201
Fawcett, Graham 177, 200
Fellner, Steve 201
Fenton, James 153, 155, 196, 201
Ferlinghetti, Lawrence 194
Finland 66
Fitzgerald, F. Scott 82, 95
FitzGibbon, Constantine 186
Flaubert, Gustave 174
Florence 175
Ford, Mark 178, 202
Formby, George 72
Foucault, Michel 193, 204
France 27, 59, 66, 94, 162, 173, 182
Franks, Jill 7

Franzini, Elio 188
Fraser, G.S. 201, 204
Fried, Daisy 178
Fromm, Eric 63, 183
Frost, Robert 168
Fuller, John 19, 81, 185, 201
Fuller, Roy 21

Germany 27, 90, 162, 186
Gewanter, David 196, 200, 202
Gibbon, Edward 26
Giles, Paul 179, 202
Gillespie, D.F. 188
Ginsberg, Allen 40, 162, 178
Gioia, Dana 205
Glazier, Lyle 202
Goffman, Erving 44, 180, 185–186
Goldsmith, Oliver 194
Gorlier, Claudio 203
Grant, Cary 162
Graves, Robert 11, 13, 18, 181
Gray, Thomas 71, 142–143
Great Britain 2, 5–6, 11, 19–20, 35–36, 38, 42, 60, 153, 167, 176, 178–179, 183, 194, 200, 202, 204–206
Greece 42
Greenblatt, Stephen 195
Greville, Fulke 36, 182, 200
Grubb, Frederick 205
Gunn, Ander 6, 9, 38, 110–113, 115, 117–119, 120–122
Gunn, Herbert Smith 25
Guthmann, Edward 196, 202

Haffenden, John 178–179, 186, 200
Hagstrom, Jack W.C. 199
Hall, Daniel 202
Hall, Donald 196, 202, 205
Hall, Jamie 194
Hamburger, Michael 19
Hamilton, Ian 19, 23, 175–176, 182–186, 188, 200–201, 205
Hammer, Langdon 176–177, 180, 195, 202
Hampstead 26
Hardie, Keir 26
Hardy, Thomas 12, 18, 52, 68, 175, 182, 187, 204
Hartley, Anthony 175–176, 205
Hawaii 169
Hazlitt, William 178
H.D. 127, 179, 187
Heidegger, Martin 79, 80, 185
Heisenberg, Werner 75, 185
Herbert, George 132
Highgate 194
Highsmith, Patricia 147
Hill, Geoffrey 19, 21, 177–178, 195, 202
Hinkle, Charlie 36, 200
Hirsch, Edward 202
Hitler, Adolf 92, 186
Hobsbaum, Philip 23, 205
Hockey, David 110

Hoffman, Tyler B. 142, 178, 195, 202
Holbrook, David 19, 101, 179, 187, 202
Holewa, Lisa 196
Holloway, John 14, 22, 202
Homer 128
Hope, Francis 93, 187, 202
Hopkins, Gerald Manley 31
Horace 145
Hörderlin, Friedrich 79
Howard, Richard 189
Hoyt, Frank C. 185
Hughes, Gerald 179
Hughes, Ted 1, 15–17, 19, 21–24, 38, 57, 95–96, 101, 127, 167–168, 176–179, 181, 183–187, 190, 192, 194, 200, 202
Hugo, Victor 109
Huk, Romana 179, 202
Hulme, Thomas Ernest 29
Hulse, Michael 202
Hunt, William 111, 179, 190, 202
Husserl, Edmund 102, 188
Huxley, Aldous 181

Inglis, Fred 188, 205
Ireland 175
Isherwood, Christopher 33–35
Isle of Wight 125
Isleworth 190
Italy 4–5, 7, 21–22, 162, 169, 173, 193

James, Henry 25, 181
Japan 110
Jaton, Anne Marie 190–191
Jeffares, A. Norman 184
Jefferson Airplane 177
Jenkins, Alan 200
Jennings, Elizabeth 14, 16, 19, 22, 175–176, 205
Johnson, Samuel 180
Jones, Brian 202
Jones, Peter 205
Jonson, Ben 2, 28, 36, 180, 185, 195, 200
Joyce, James 146, 175, 205

Kafka, Frank 69, 128, 134, 142
Kansas 130, 185, 187
Keats, John 11, 26, 55, 134–135, 147, 159, 167, 174, 194–195
Kehl, D.G. 186
Kent 116, 191
Kerouac, Jack 125, 138, 194
Khamsin 176
Kierkegaard, Sören 53
King, P.R. 86, 92, 186–187, 202
Kitay, Mike 30, 33, 178, 181, 195
Klawitter, George 202
Kleinzahler, August 36, 169, 178, 185, 200, 202
Klimt, Gustav 193

La Cecla, Franco 89, 186
Landau, Deborah 142, 178, 195, 202

Larkin, Philip 14–17, 19–22, 24, 38, 69, 96, 167–168, 175, 178, 186–187
Latham, Agnes M.C. 191
Lattimore, Richmond 205
Lavagetto, Andreina 188
Lawrence, David Herbert 7, 24, 32, 37, 74, 106–107, 115, 130, 139, 150, 176, 182, 187
Lawrence, Frieda 176
Leap, William L. 193
Leavis, Frank Raymond 5, 12–13, 28, 30–31, 43, 124
Lee, Lance 179, 202
Lee, Stan 149
Lerici 23, 176
Lesser, Wendy 178, 192, 196, 202
Levine, Philip 178, 196, 202
Lewis, Wyndham 61
Lindop, Grevel 183, 205
Liverpool 118
Lombardo, Agostino 22, 176, 202
London 6, 12, 18, 26, 29–30, 38–39, 42, 58, 111, 113, 121–122, 127, 156, 176, 180, 182, 189, 191, 194, 196–197, 201, 204
Los Angeles 33, 177, 182
Lotman, Jurij M. 89, 186
Lowell, Robert 11, 19, 162, 167
Loy, Mina 168, 187
Lucie-Smith, Edward 23, 64, 184, 186, 201–202, 205
Lux, Billy 177–178, 200

MacBeth, George 19, 23, 176
MacCaig, Norman 19
Maffi, Mario 192, 205
Magritte, René 51
Mailer, Norman 162
Mallarmé, Stéphane 96, 189
Mander, John 57, 60, 181, 183, 202
Manhattan 183
Mann, Thomas 195
Manson, Charles 51, 147, 182
Mapplethorpe, Robert 189
Marchetti, Paola 202
Marenco, Franco 21, 175
Margoliouth, H.M. 181
Mark Antony 72, 81, 185
Marlowe, Christopher 26
Martin, Robert K 192–193, 205
Marvell, Andrew 46, 60, 66, 140, 147, 181, 184, 195
Marwick, Arthur 192, 205
Marzaduri, Marzio 186
Matisse, Henri 109
Maxwell, Glyn 153
McCartney, Paul 191
McGuiness, Patrick 175, 202
McPherson, William 36, 200
Mediterranean 17, 100
Melchiori, Giorgio 22, 175–176, 205
Melly, George 184
Meredith, George 26

Merleau-Ponty, Maurice 102, 188
Mersey 118
Merwin, William Stanley 169
Michelangelo 177
Michelucci, Stefania 3–4, 179, 182, 186–187, 192, 194–195, 200, 202
Michie, James 57, 183, 203
Middlesex 190
Middleton, Christopher 19
Miglior, Giorgio 203
Miller, John 179, 183, 203
Miller, Karl 30
Milton, John 26
Mitgutsch, Waltraud 80, 185, 203
Monteith, Charles 38
Monterey 116
Moore, Geoffrey 205
Moore, Marianne 95, 163, 168, 187, 203
Mormorio, Diego 189
Morrish, Hilary 175, 200
Morrison, Blake 16–17, 19–20, 175–176, 205
Motion, Andrew 196, 203
Muir, Edwin 11
Munch, Edvard 147
Mussolini, Benito 178

Napoleon I 178
Nardi, Paola A. 203
Negri, Antonello 188
Nemerov, Howard 38, 200
New York 18, 29, 41, 121, 167, 169
Nicholls, Peter 176
Niépce, Joseph Nicéphore 188
Nietzsche, Friedrich 37, 59, 85
Noel-Tod, Jeremy 203
Norfolk, Lawrence 193, 203
Northrop, F.S.C. 185
Nuwer, Hank 200

Odell, Joshua 199
Okeke-Ezigbo, Emeka 101, 187, 203
Olson, Charles 172
Orr, Peter 183
Orwell, George 13
Ovid 193
Oxbridge 17
Oxford 12, 14, 19, 29, 127

Pacific Ocean 129, 187, 203
Pack, Robert 205
Parini, Jay 56, 182, 203
Paris 27, 191
Patton, Phil 189
Peck, John 203
Pennati, Camillo 176, 202
Perkins, David 20–21, 175–176, 205
Perloff, Marjorie G. 203
Philip II of Macedon 177
Piazza San Marco 175
Pilo, Gianni 194
Pinsky, Robert 178, 203

Index

Pisa 5
Plath, Sylvia 19, 38, 176, 183
Plato, vi 79, 134, 183
Plutzik, Hyam 38, 200
Polanski, Roman 182
Pope, Alexander 12, 16
Porter, Peter 19, 23, 38, 176, 183
Potter, Beatrix 194
Potts, Robert 179, 180, 203
Pound, Ezra 11, 29, 36, 60, 163, 166–168, 177–179, 200
Powell, Jim 36, 169, 178, 200
Powell, Neil 65, 71, 91, 101, 108, 111, 122, 184–188, 190, 192, 196, 203
Presley, Elvis 65–66, 191
Press, John 60, 77, 183, 185, 205
Pritchard, William H. 203
Proust, Marcel 27–28, 94, 109

Raleigh, Walter 116, 191
Rapallo 146, 180
Redgrove, Peter 19, 23
Regan, Stephen 20, 176
Richard II 182
Ricks, Christopher 177
Ries, Lawrence R. 60, 68–69, 81, 108, 183–185, 188, 190, 203
Rilke, Reiner Maria 96, 105, 188
Roberts, Neil 176, 205
Roberts, Warren 187
Rochester, John Wilmot 86
Rodin, Auguste 132
Rolling Stones 39
Rome 30, 82–83, 162–163, 192
Romer, Stephen 179, 180, 203
Rosenthal, M.L. 205
Rückert, Ingrid 187, 200
Ruskin, John 109
Russia 90, 162
Rutelli, Romana 43, 202–203

Sacks, Oliver 178, 202
Sackville, Thomas 183
San Antonio 33
Sanesi, Roberto 205
San Francisco 5–6, 18, 22–23, 34–35, 39, 41, 58, 102, 125, 127–128, 138–139, 159, 166–167, 176–177, 180–181, 184–185, 192–197, 200, 204
Sartre, Jean-Paul 6, 30, 32, 37, 54, 59, 63, 66, 86, 156
Saylor, Steven 178, 203
Schenkel, Elmar 7
Schmidt, Michael 183, 205
Schuessler, Bill 194
Scobie, W.I. 177–179, 184, 200
Scotland 19, 26
Scott, J.D. 13, 175, 205
Scott, Walter 159
Sexton, Anne 19, 176, 191
Shakarchi, Joseph 191, 200
Shakespeare, William 1, 28–29, 32–33, 46, 56, 72, 81–82, 87, 113, 147–148, 165, 185–186, 190, 195–196
Shelley, Percy Bysshe 11, 55, 167, 187
Silkin, Jon 19, 176, 205
Simpson, Louis 38, 200, 205
Sinfield, Alan 131, 181, 192–194, 200, 205
Sisson, Charles Hubert 21
Smith, P.J. 192, 205
Smith, Stan 205
Snyder, Gary 178
Sontag, Susan 141, 188–190, 195
Spagnuolo, Peter 178
Spain 57
Spender, Stephen 14, 61, 183
Splendore, Paola 205
Squires, Michael 176
Stafford, William 38, 200
Stanford 30, 33
Stark, Anthony 196
Starr, Ringo 190
Stendhal 29, 32
Stephens, Alan 188
Stevens, Wallace 31, 43, 106, 168, 177
Stieglitz, Alfred 110
Stimpson, Catharine R. 203
Swaab, Peter 57, 183, 185, 203
Sweden 161
Swinden, Patrick 203, 205

Talbot, Lynn 176
Tate, Sharon 182
Tennyson, Alfred 26
Texas 33
Thames 113
Thirlby, Peter 203
Thomas, Dylan 11–12, 15, 18, 50, 196
Thomas, Ronald Stuart 21
Thomson, Ann Charlotte 25
Thwaite, Anthony 14, 186, 205
Tithecott, Richard 196
Tomlinson, Charles 19, 21, 206
Tournier, Michel 109–110, 189
Tranter, John 200
Travolta, John 66, 112

United States 1–7, 11, 18–19, 21, 23–25, 28–37, 39, 41, 60, 66, 105, 119, 121, 125, 127, 129, 135, 141, 145, 153–154, 162, 166–167, 169–170, 172, 177–179, 181, 185, 188–189, 191, 193–195, 199–202, 204–205
Uspenskij, Boris A. 186

Van O'Connor, William 13, 175, 206
Vattimo, Gianni 79, 185
Venice 166
Verga, Giovanni 89, 109
Villa, Luisa 43, 202
Vince, Michael 192, 203
Vittorini, Elio 110, 189
von Stauffenberg, Claus 92–93, 156, 186
Vuillard, Edouard 39

Wain, John 19, 22, 206
Walker, Ted 19, 176
Wallat, Reiner 206
Warhol, Andy 110
Weiner, Joshua 178
Westlake, J.H.J. 90, 186, 203
Wevill, David 19, 176
White, Minor 110
White, Tony 30, 160, 186, 189
Whitman, Walt 41, 43, 77, 100, 119, 121, 165, 191, 205
Wilde, Oscar 178, 195
Williams, Carlos William 2, 31, 41, 43, 102, 106–107, 119, 123, 163, 168, 177, 179
Williams, Hugo 203
Williams, John 206
Wilmer, Clive 1, 4, 7, 9, 36, 41–42, 56, 106, 108, 126, 155–156, 175, 177–180, 182–183, 185, 187–188, 192, 194–197, 199, 200, 203–204

Winters, Yvor 1, 23, 30–33, 35, 71, 91, 101, 125, 156, 177–179, 184, 191, 196–197, 200
Witemeyer, H. 204
Wood, Michael 206
Woodcock, Bruce 131, 192–193, 204
Woods, Gregory 7, 42, 124, 180, 192–193, 204, 206
Woodstock 125
Woolf, Virginia 42, 95–96, 103, 109, 176, 188
Wordsworth, William 11, 167, 178, 181
Wright, Barbara 189

Yeats, William Butler 11, 28–29, 31–32, 42, 66–67, 181, 184
Yorkshire 17

Zola, Émile 109